Flexner on FINISHING

Finally. Answers to Your Wood Finishing Fears and Frustrations

by Bob Flexner

Popular Woodworking Books
Cincinnati, Ohio
www.popularwoodworking.com

Distributed in Canada by Fraser Direct
100 Armstrong Avenue
Georgetown, Ontario L7G 5S4
Canada

Distributed in the U.K. and Europe by David & Charles
Brunel House
Newton Abbot
Devon TQ12 4PU
England
Tel: (+44) 1626 323200
Fax: (+44) 1626 323319
E-mail: postmaster@davidandcharles.co.uk

Distributed in Australia by Capricorn Link
P.O. Box 704
Windsor, NSW 2756
Australia

Visit our Web site at www.popularwoodworking.com for information on more resources for woodworkers.

Other fine F+W Media woodworking books are available from your local bookstore, or direct from the publisher at www.WoodworkersBookShop.com.

14   13   12   11   10   5   4   3   2   1

Library of Congress Cataloging-in-Publication Data

Flexner, Bob.
  Flexner on finishing, finally : answers to your wood finishing fears and frustrations / by Bob Flexner. -- 1st ed.
     p. cm.
  Includes bibliographical references and index.
  ISBN-13: 978-1-4403-0887-1 (alk. paper)
  ISBN-10: 1-4403-0887-X (alk. paper)
  1. Wood finishing--Amateurs' manuals. 2. Stains and staining--Amateurs' manuals. I. Title.
  TT325.F53 2010
  684'.084--dc22
                    2010022508

media
www.fwmedia.com

Publisher: Steve Shanesy
Editor: Megan Fitzpatrick
Designer: Linda Watts
Illustrator: Hayes Shanesy
Photographers: Bob Flexner, Al Parrish and Christopher Schwarz
Production Coordinator: Mark Griffin

TABLE OF CONTENTS

INTRODUCTION

I love this book – maybe because it's not really a book. It's a collection of articles, all but two of which were first published in my long-running column in *Popular Woodworking Magazine*.

I hadn't thought of it before, but a column is very different from a stand-alone book, especially a textbook type of book. A textbook is organized information – beginning at the beginning, proceeding logically through all the topics, covering everything that the title implies.

A column is also information, of course, but in addition it's opinion and philosophy. Reading over my columns, getting them ready for publication, made me realize just how much of me, as well as what I think, is included. In many cases I was addressing specific issues brought to my attention by woodworkers, or issues dealing with the misinformation published in magazines or spread by manufacturers in their marketing.

In other cases I was taking on some of the most pervasive myths that have hobbled the woodworking community for decades: For example, that finishes sold as "Tung Oil" are really tung oil, or that some finishes aren't safe to eat off of, or that wood should be finished on both sides to prevent warping.

Books are forever. Authors tend to hold back a little on their opinions when writing a book. But a column usually lasts only until the next issue of the magazine appears. Columns are therefore looser and freer; they are meant to be opinionated, to stir things up a little, to say it like it is and to point fingers now and then. I was pleased in reading over my columns that I had done this where appropriate.

There's also a bit of repetition in a column that you don't find in a book. In some cases I removed the repetition, but in others I left it in. Sometimes it helps the learning process to be told the same thing several times from different angles. For example: the first coat of any finish is the sealer coat; shellac is not necessarily the best sealer; sanding sealer speeds production but weakens the total finish; a washcoat is a thin sealer; and so on, all in different columns addressing different issues. You can make the connections easily through the index if you want, or you can go to my "textbook," *Understanding Wood Finishing*.

I've also added four columns addressing major wood-repair issues. I was fortunate to be able to do this. The book's designer, Linda Watts, was so efficient in laying out the pages that there was room at the end for more columns. I chose the ones on regluing and veneer repair because these are skills most woodworkers are fully capable of doing but are rarely taught how to do properly. (You can see me do these and other repairs on a DVD from Taunton Press: "Repairing Furniture with Bob Flexner.")

Because all the topics in this book were written originally as standalone articles, there's no reason you need to read straight through from beginning to end. You can jump in wherever you want. In fact, the first five topics under the heading "Overview" are placed there because they didn't fit well elsewhere. They are broad looks at issues I hope you find interesting.

I didn't want to start at the beginning (sanding and wood preparation) anyway. This isn't a textbook.

1

Overview

A History of Wood Finishing

A poorly explored subject gets some coverage.

About 15 years ago I was in Boston and spent an afternoon looking at the fine collection of antique furniture housed at the Museum of Fine Arts. I stopped at each piece, checked it out and read the blurb, usually pinned to the wall nearby. Information was provided on the furniture style, when and where the piece was made, the maker and the primary and secondary woods used.

But there was not a word about what I was interested in: the original finish, whether the piece had been refinished, and if so, what finish had then been used.

Providing this information would not have been difficult. Just as woods can be associated with different period styles and just as woods can be tested to learn what they are, so can finishes be associated with period styles and tested to learn what they are. In other words, if you know when the furniture was made, usually by its style, you can almost always know what finish was used. And if you have access to the furniture, you can test the finish with solvents or more sophisticated means to confirm what the style is telling you.

Though shellac is the most durable of the alcohol-soluble resins, the variety craftsmen had available until the 1820s was very dark. So they often blended the shellac with lighter colored resins to get a lighter result. Clockwise from the dark shellac on the right are damar, sandarac and benzoin.

Nevertheless, I've never seen this information provided by any museum. As a result, we learn much less about the history of finishes than we do about furniture styles and woods.

So, using my 30 years experience restoring antique furniture and the knowledge I've acquired about what finishes were available at different times, I've put together the following history.

Eighteenth-century Finishes

The earliest finishes were whatever the maker had at hand: usually beeswax or linseed oil. If the maker lived near a port,

To confirm that a finish is shellac, dab some denatured alcohol onto an inconspicuous area and see if the finish gets sticky or dissolves entirely. This very deteriorated finish on a mid-19th-century Empire chest-of-drawers is clearly shellac. It is also a very dark variety of shellac.

he might have access to some alcohol- or oil-soluble resins. But the best studies done on surviving pieces of furniture to determine original 18th-century finishes usually report wax or oil at the bottom of what is now a build of finish film.

This runs counter to the popular belief that shellac was widely used on better quality 18th-century furniture. In fact, shellac by itself seems rarely to have been used. The shellac that was available at the time was too dark for the tastes of many. So when alcohol-soluble resins were available, shellac was usually mixed with lighter-colored resins such as sandarac, benzoin and damar to produce a lighter result.

The reason shellac gets associated with 18th-century furniture is that the furniture was usually coated over with shellac sometime in the 19th century. To determine what was used originally, a chip of finish has to be removed and tested to see what is at the bottom. This requires special testing equipment, and many of the larger museums possess this equipment.

Nineteenth-century Finishes

Shellac didn't come into its own as a finish until the early 19th century. French polishing was introduced into England – probably from Holland – very early in the century, and

In the 18th century and earlier, craftsmen used whatever finish they had available, usually beeswax or linseed oil (though they didn't have the convenient packaging we have now).

into the United States in the teens. Methods of lightening the color were figured out in the 1820s.

Lightening the color of the shellac, which is the most durable of the alcohol-soluble resins, was the key that made this finish widely acceptable, though the darker varieties were still used. Improved transportation also made shellac available inland.

So, from the 1820s to the 1920s, almost all furniture made in the United States (and also in Europe) was finished with shellac. In the United States this includes the following styles: late Federal, American Empire, Shaker, many varieties of Victorian and Arts & Crafts or Mission. If you come across any of these styles and the original finish is still intact, you can bet that finish is shellac.

If you want to confirm this, simply use your finger to dab a little denatured alcohol on an inconspicuous area such as the backside of a leg. If the finish is shellac, it will become tacky within a few seconds and be completely removed if you keep it wet a little longer.

Until the 1920s shellac was often referred to as "spirit varnish" to distinguish it from oil varnish, which was similar to our modern varnish and made by cooking linseed oil with a hard natural, fossilized pine-tree resin. When you hear someone say, "the old varnish has cracked," or refer in some other way to varnish on 19th- or early 20th-century furniture, it's most likely the finish referred to is actually shellac in our modern terminology.

Nineteen Twenties

The 1920s saw two major changes in finishes and finishing. Nitrocellulose lacquer replaced shellac as the finish used on production furniture, and spray guns replaced brushes.

The changeover occurred slowly (just as industry today changes slowly from one finish to another), so no precise date can be given. But by the early 1930s, virtually all factory-made furniture was being finished with sprayed lacquer. (There was no large amateur or small-shop professional woodworking community as there is today.)

If you see a piece of furniture made after the 1920s and with its original finish intact, you can assume the finish is lacquer – at least until the last three or four decades when catalyzed finishes were introduced and became popular for use on office and institutional (not household) furniture.

Lacquer replaced shellac for two principal reasons.

First, lacquer uses lacquer thinner as a solvent. This thinner is a combination of a number of individual solvents, which can be varied to control the evaporation rate in different weather conditions – cold, hot, humid or dry.

The alcohol used to dissolve and thin shellac is much less versatile. Its evaporation rate can't be varied.

This mid-18th century walnut chest has a top that folds open to make a writing desk. Though it is English rather than American, the assumption concerning its original finish is still the same: probably wax or oil unless the maker had access to some alcohol- or oil-soluble resins. In fact, the original finish was wax, which, in the typical English fashion, has been kept up with additional waxing rather than coated over with shellac as is so common with early American furniture.

Eastlake Victorian furniture, of which this chest is a typical example, was popular from the 1870s to the 1890s. Based on that date of construction, you could confidently say that the original finish applied to this chest was shellac. And in fact, the dabbing test confirms this to be so.

Second, lacquer is a synthetically made finish, so the greater the demand the cheaper the product. Shellac, by contrast, is a natural resin, which increases in price as demand goes up. Lacquer was coming down in price while shellac was going up.

Two additional factors that encouraged the changeover specifically in the 1920s were the large stockpiles of gun cotton, used to make nitrocellulose in addition to explosives, left over from World War I, and the adoption of lacquer over slow-drying varnish as the finish of choice in the burgeoning automobile industry.

Though lacquer replaced shellac in the furniture industry, house painters and amateurs continued to use shellac until the 1950s and 1960s. The amber coloring so common to trim and paneling in buildings constructed before the mid-20th century is almost always created by the use of orange shellac. (I consider it a real shame that so much of this finish is being stripped and replaced with lacquer or polyurethane – not that I have a problem with stripping the deteriorated finish but that the warm coloring is lost with these modern finishes.)

Spray gun technology had existed from the turn of the 20th century, but very few factories adopted spray guns for applying shellac. Spray guns seemed to become popular together with the adoption of lacquer as the finish. As with shellac, brushes continued to be used by house painters until the 1950s and 1960s and are still in wide use, of course, by amateurs.

Lacquer made glazing easier and spray guns made toning possible, so furniture made since the 1920s is often glazed or toned for decorative effect. These techniques were rarely used before the 1920s.

The test for lacquer is the same as for shellac, just with lacquer thinner instead of alcohol.

Evaporative Finishes & Repair

Notice that up to this point, which means up to the present for the majority of furniture still being finished with lacquer, the principal finishes used were of the evaporative type. That is, the finishes dry entirely by the evaporation of their solvent and redissolve in contact with their solvent: shellac in alcohol and lacquer in lacquer thinner. Evaporative finishes also melt in contact with heat. Dissolving and melting are very significant for repair because it means that invisible repairs can be accomplished.

Manufacturers are most concerned with the ability to make invisible repairs because it's rare that furniture can survive all the transport, loading, unloading and moving around factory or store floors without sustaining some damage to the finish. Being able to make invisible repairs at any point between the finish room and the ultimate customer virtually eliminates the need to return the furniture to the factory to be refinished.

Invisible repairs are considerably more difficult on catalyzed, polyester, UV-cured and water-based finishes that have been introduced since the 1960s. (The same is true for varnish and polyurethane.) The procedure usually involves disguising the visible boundary between the repair and the existing finish using coloring tricks and requires considerably more skill.

Staining

Before getting to the modern changes in finishes, I want to bring stains up to date. The woods used in the 18th and 19th centuries were of very high quality and few makers wanted to change their color. The darker woods such as mahogany, walnut and cherry aged to become more beautiful, and linseed oil (which darkens as it ages) and orange shellac added a warm amber coloring to lighter woods such as oak, maple and birch. So stains were rarely used.

It wasn't until the late 19th century, after the Centennial of the American Revolution, that staining became desirable. What changed was the new-found wish of many Americans to possess new furniture (not the originals) in the style of the furniture the Founders had possessed. The problem was that the new wood didn't have the aged coloring of the old wood, so stains were used to create this coloring.

Stains in the late 19th and early 20th centuries were dyes, not pigment. Pigmented colorants were called paint.

The store-bought stains we are familiar with today that contain a binder (oil, varnish or water-based finish) and usually some pigment, didn't come into wide use until sometime between the 1920s and 1940s. They probably started as toners, pigmented colorants that were added to the lacquer finish and sprayed on top of a sealer coat. A lot of furniture made after the introduction of spray guns was toned to even the coloring of lesser-quality woods. Eventually, these "toners" were sold separately as stains to be applied directly to the wood.

To get back to the late 19th century, ani-

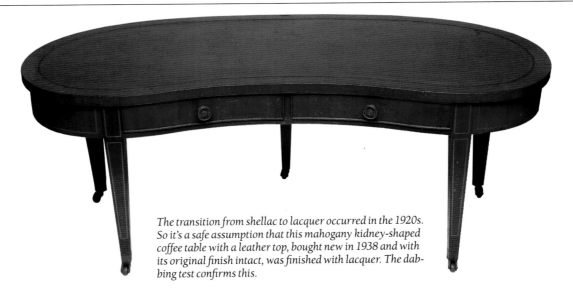

The transition from shellac to lacquer occurred in the 1920s. So it's a safe assumption that this mahogany kidney-shaped coffee table with a leather top, bought new in 1938 and with its original finish intact, was finished with lacquer. The dabbing test confirms this.

line dyes saw a rapid development for use in the textile industry following their discovery in the late 1850s. When a market developed for stained furniture, it didn't take long for the dyes to be adopted by the furniture industry. Dyes are much more effective than pigment for adding color to wood.

It's fortunate that one of the companies that provided dyes to the furniture industry in the late 19th century has survived because it allows us to see precisely what colors were being used at the time. This company is W.D. Lockwood (www.wdlockwood.com). Furniture makers who wanted to imitate the color of aged woods hired Lockwood (or other companies in existence at the time) to blend the dye colors available to create the effect they wanted. You can get an idea of the result just by the names of the dye blends, which are still offered by Lockwood: Phyfe Red, Antique Cherry, Sheraton Mahogany, Flemish Brown etc.

As coloring wood became more popular, some manufacturers of oak furniture in the Arts & Crafts style introduced ammonia fuming to darken the oak. Fuming has the advantage over dye and pigment of coloring the very dense rays ("tiger stripes") in quartersawn oak to blend better with the rest of the wood.

With the continuing deterioration in the quality of the woods used in the manufacture of furniture, designers and finishers have become ever more creative with their finishes to produce an even and interesting coloring. For the last four or five decades manufacturers have added most, and often all, of the coloring within the finish (rather than in the wood) by using glazes, toners, fly specking (small dark dots), cowtailing (short curved linear marks), and so on, sometimes with a dozen or more coloring steps.

In contrast, most one-off furniture makers, both amateur and professional, have gone back to choosing high-quality woods and relying on them to create all the coloring effects without the use of stains. Some have adopted the late 19th-century practice of dying their woods to imitate the colors associated with antique furniture.

Nineteen Sixties
Finishes and finishing techniques remained fairly constant from the 1920s until the 1960s when a number of changes began occurring.

First, there was a desire among consumers for more durable finishes, comparable in hardness to plastic laminates (Formica),

Typical of so much of the furniture made in the last 30 or 40 years by individual woodworkers, this reproduction Gustav Stickley "Poppy Table," built by Robert W. Lang, is finished with an oil/varnish blend.

which were coming into wide use. This led to the introduction of one-part polyurethane for amateurs, and catalyzed finishes and eventually polyester, two-part polyurethane and UV-cured finishes in factories.

Second, air pollution was becoming a growing problem, so a push began to reduce solvent emissions into the atmosphere. Laws were passed in the 1960s and '70s that led to the introduction of water-based finishes and High-Volume Low-Pressure (HVLP) spray guns in the 1980s. Water-based finishes contain less solvent, and HVLP spray guns produce a softer spray with less "bounce-back" so more of the finish stays on the object.

Third, increasing competition led to automation, beginning with hand-held electrostatic spray guns and leading eventually to machinery that largely removes human contact from the finishing process. (If you haven't already, you should treat yourself by attending either IWF in Atlanta or AWFS in Las Vegas to see the extent furniture manufacturing has been automated. Both shows are in late summer, with IWF in even-numbered years and AWFS in odd-numbered years).

Fourth, increasing concern for the health of workers using finishes led to the establishment of OSHA in 1971. OSHA has authority over working conditions for all employees but has no authority over amateurs or self-employed people with no employees.

Fifth, the do-it-yourself market began to experience rapid growth. This led to the introduction of less expensive (and lower quality) tools, and a great deal of incorrect information about finishes disseminated by manufacturers and published in amateur woodworking magazines and books.

Sixth, the Internet, introduced in the 1990s, is having a profound effect on the spread of information. Though inaccurate information persists, there's hope that it will be culled by the rapid exchange made possible by this medium.

Finishing in the early 21st century is going through its greatest changes ever.

Woodworking Renaissance
Up to this point, my emphasis has been on finishes used by professionals, including small shops in the 18th and early 19th centuries, and factories since then. Beginning in the 1960s and 1970s, however, a renaissance of sorts has taken place in the woodworking community with thousands and even hundreds of thousands of individuals making cabinets and one-of-a-kind pieces of furniture, sometimes for sale and sometimes not.

Few of these woodworkers, as we are now called (rather than the old term "cabinetmakers," which has come to refer just to those making kitchen cabinets), have the facilities to spray shellac, lacquer or one of the newer high-performance finishes. Instead, most use some form of oil or varnish, which are easy to wipe or brush on the wood.

Shellac can also be wiped (French polishing) or brushed, but few woodworkers use this finish except on reproduction furniture. And not many use water-based finishes either.

So, in keeping with the themes I've been emphasizing—that furniture made from the 1820s to the 1920s is most likely finished with shellac, and furniture made since the 1920s is most likely finished with lacquer (except for office and institutional furniture made since the 1960s) – I will make the further assumption that most one-off furniture made after the 1960s is finished with oil or varnish.

Though there are, of course, many individual exceptions to this organization, I think knowing this history helps in making sense of finishing.

Reprinted from Woodwork, *June 2008.*

Some Basic Finishing Rules

They explain so much.

It's often possible to sum up a lot of situations with a rule or principle that applies in almost all cases. When I teach seminars on finishing, I often find myself citing a rule I've created to explain a procedure or to answer a question. These rules can be very helpful for understanding finishing.

Here are my five favorites, the ones I repeat most often.

Rule #1
Choose a grit of sandpaper that removes the problem efficiently without creating larger than necessary scratches that then have to be sanded out.

This rule answers the question, "What grit sandpaper should I use?" It varies for different situations.

For example, you would choose a coarser-grit sandpaper (#80 or #100) to remove severe washboarding caused by a jointer or planer but a finer grit (#120 or #150) on pre-sanded, veneered plywood or MDF. And you would begin sanding with an even finer grit (#180 or #220) if you were just checking to make sure your stripper had removed all the old finish from a refinishing project.

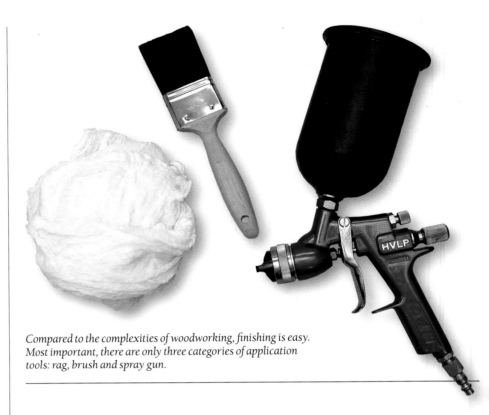

Compared to the complexities of woodworking, finishing is easy. Most important, there are only three categories of application tools: rag, brush and spray gun.

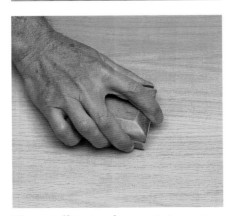

The most efficient sandpaper grits to use vary with the situation. It's inefficient, for example, to begin sanding with #80 or #100 grit on this pre-sanded veneered plywood. The #120-grit sandpaper I'm using here is coarse enough to be efficient and doesn't create more work.

Likewise, you would choose a coarser-grit sandpaper (#220 or #320) to sand out brush marks in a finish but a finer-grit (#400 or #600) to remove fine dust or orange peel.

It's most efficient if the grit you begin with isn't any coarser than necessary so you don't have to sand out the deeper scratches.

How do you determine which grit is appropriate? Experience is the best teacher. In the meantime begin with a grit you think is about right, or even a little finer than necessary, then "cut back" to coarser grits until you find the one that removes the problems efficiently. Woodworkers will disagree here because everyone sands differently. But keeping this principle in mind will help you reduce the amount of work.

In all cases remove coarser-grit scratches with finer grits until you reach the grit you want to end with. Skipping a grit will require you to sand more to remove previous grit scratches than progressing through each successive grit, but either way is legitimate.

Rule #2
There are only three common tools used to apply finishes: a rag, a brush and a spray gun (including aerosols).

Finish application is therefore far less complicated than woodworking, with its dozens of tools. Each of the three finish tools transfers liquid – finish, paint, stain, whatever – from a can to the wood and is simple to use. Even a spray gun is no more difficult than a router.

On large surfaces, fast-drying finishes are harder to apply with a rag or brush because you can't move fast enough to keep a "wet edge." But there's less problem if the surface is small – for example, a turning. All finishes, no matter how fast or slow they dry, are easy to spray onto any surface.

The real differences in the tools are cost, speed and the degree to which they produce a level film.

Rags are cheap and efficient for applying any stain or finish you intend to wipe off, but they leave pronounced ridges in finishes when you're trying to build a film.

Brushes are also inexpensive and are the least wasteful of finish material, but they're very inefficient because they transfer the liquid so slowly, and they leave ridges (brush marks) in the film.

Spray guns transfer the liquid very rapidly and leave the most level film. But they, and the added compressors or turbines needed for operation, are expensive. And because of the finish that misses or bounces off the surface, spray guns are wasteful of finish material and require an exhaust system, which further increases the expense.

Rule #3

The only thing you can do in finishing that can't be fixed fairly easily is to blotch the wood with a stain.

The purpose of this rule is to encourage you to relax about finishing; you can't "ruin" your project unless you're staining a blotchy wood, such as pine, cherry or birch. All problems other than blotching can be fixed, with the worst case being you have to strip off the finish and begin again. Professional finishers know from sad experience that having to strip and start over is not that uncommon. It's equivalent to the woodworker's distress over having to make a new part because of cutting a board too short.

To fix blotching, you have to sand, scrape or plane the wood to below the depth the stain has penetrated.

To avoid blotching, the stain has to be kept from penetrating. Do this using a gel stain or by partially sealing the wood with a thinned finish called a "washcoat." An example is wood conditioner, which is varnish thinned with two parts mineral spirits. Be sure to let whichever washcoat you use dry thoroughly (six or eight hours for wood conditioner) or it won't eliminate the blotching.

Rule #4

The first coat of any finish seals the wood; all additional coats are topcoats.

This rule is important for understanding that products labeled or promoted as "sealers" don't seal the wood any better than the finish itself. They are used to solve a problem.

Sanding sealers contain a soap-like lubricant that reduces sandpaper clogging, making the sanding of varnishes and lacquers easier and faster. Sanding sealers are great for production situations but offer little advantage for most home or small-shop projects, especially when you can get similar easy sanding by thinning the first coat half with the appropriate thinner. In fact, sanding sealers weaken water resistance (because of the soap) and the bonding of the topcoat, so it's better not to use them unless you have a big project.

Shellac is effective as a barrier against silicone and odors (refinishing problems), and

pine resin and the oily resin in oily woods such as teak and rosewood. These substances can interfere with the flow and drying of finishes. But there's no reason to use shellac as the first coat if the wood you're finishing doesn't have one of these problems.

Of course, shellac is an excellent finish in its own right and can be used effectively for all the coats.

Rule #5

Apply a wet coat of stain and wipe off the excess before it dries.

This is the basic instruction for applying all stains. As long as the wood is not naturally blotchy, and as long as it has been prepared well (all the milling marks and other flaws are

sanded out), this method of stain application will produce an even coloring.

Confusion has been introduced by marketing, which often shows brushing thick coats of stain and not wiping off the excess. This procedure cannot produce an even coloring.

To get a darker coloring, you can leave a stain on the wood for a while to allow some of the thinner to evaporate, essentially increasing the colorant-to-binder ratio. Then wipe off the excess. You can also leave a little of the excess, called a "dirty wipe," or apply a second coat of stain after the first has dried.

But in all cases, unless you're spraying the stain, you have to wipe off most or all the excess to get an even coloring.

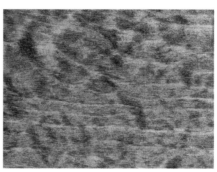

Some woods, such as the pine shown here, blotch when stained. Blotching is the only situation in finishing that can't be fixed fairly easily, with stripping and starting over being the worst-case scenario.

Sanding sealers contain a soap-like lubricant that causes the finish to powder so it doesn't clog the sandpaper. But sanding sealers don't seal the wood any better than the finish itself and, in fact, weaken water resistance and the bond of the finish.

As long as you wipe off excess stain, the coloring will always be even unless the wood is naturally blotchy or, as with this oak, the grain is highlighted.

The Thick & Thin of Wood Finishing

A penetrating look at protection.

Combining the terms "thick" and "thin" is a clever method I'm using here to emphasize two very important but unrelated facts about wood finishing.

The first is: The thicker the finish film after all coats have dried, the better the protection for the wood against water penetration and moisture-vapor exchange.

The second is: The more you thin a finish the better it lays out flat. That is, the thinner the finish you are applying (which is not the same as the thinner you apply it to the wood), the more reduced the brush marks, orange peel and rag tracks.

Protecting Against Moisture

A finish has two functions. The obvious one is to improve the appearance of the wood. The more important one is to protect the wood from water absorption and moisture-vapor exchange.

Water absorption causes black staining and delamination of veneer. It can also cause warping and splitting if the wetting and drying out continues long enough. Look at what happens to deck boards after a few years of wet/dry cycles.

Excessive moisture-vapor exchange leads to joints breaking down sooner because of

Oil finishes are always thin on the wood because the excess has to be wiped off after each application to keep the oil from drying gummy. As a result, watermarks like this one are common.

The thicker a finish film, the better it protects the wood against moisture penetration and moisture-vapor exchange. This photo is of the end of a Gabon ebony board with a thick coat of wax applied to reduce the chances of splitting caused by damp/dry cycles in humidity.

increased shrinkage and swelling in the cross-grain construction.

No finish totally stops the passage of moisture in vapor form (humidity). Finishes merely slow the passage. Consider wood windows and doors with many coats of paint and how they still swell so tight in the summer that they stick, and they become loose and leak air in the winter when the air is drier.

Reactive finishes (varnish and "catalyzed" finishes) are better at slowing water penetration and moisture-vapor exchange than evaporative finishes (shellac and lacquer) and coalescing finishes (water-based finish). Far more important than the finish, however, is the thickness of the film that is applied. The thicker the finish film, no matter which finish used, the better it is at keeping liquids and vapors from penetrating.

Take wax as an example. Wax is used to seal the ends of lumber. The wax is brushed on these ends and left thick. Wax is also used as a finish on small objects and as a polish over another finish.

In the first case, the wax is very effective at reducing moisture penetration because it is thick. In the latter two cases, wax is almost totally ineffective because it is so thin that moisture can find a way through with little problem.

The same is the case for oil and oil/varnish blend finishes. Even though these finishes cure by molecular crosslinking and are therefore of the reactive type, all the excess finish has to be wiped off after each coat to prevent it from drying gummy on the wood. These finishes are therefore too thin to be very effective. Water penetrates through within seconds or minutes. (The claim of some suppliers that their oil/varnish blend finish protects from inside the wood is nonsense.)

In contrast to wax and oil finishes, consider epoxy-resin finishes often applied to bar tops and restaurant tables. These finishes are poured on, sometimes as thick as a quarter-inch. They are so effective at reducing moisture-vapor exchange that boards can be assembled in butt and miter configurations without fear of the boards breaking apart due to cross-grain swelling and shrinking.

One important caveat when it comes to thickness is that catalyzed finishes tend to crack if applied too thick. Three or four coats is the upper limit with these finishes.

Creating a Level Finish

Achieving a level finish should always be your goal because the more level it is the better it looks and feels. Of course, you can always make a finish level by sanding it after all the coats have been applied, but the work required can be reduced and even eliminated if you apply the finish level to begin with. In every case, except when wiping off the excess, you will improve the leveling of your finish by thinning it.

Let's take each application method – wiping, brushing, spraying and French polishing – in turn.

In most cases the reason you apply a finish by wiping is because you intend to wipe off the excess. If you do this, you will always achieve perfect levelness as long as you have prepared the wood well and you get the finish wiped off before it sets up too hard. There's no need to thin the finish except to increase the amount of time you have to wipe off.

The common wiping finishes are oil, oil/ varnish blend, wiping varnish, gel varnish and wax. (Wiping varnish is any oil-based varnish that has been thinned enough so that it levels well.)

When you intend to build a thicker finish film, you usually brush or spray the finish. Brushing can leave brush marks and spraying can leave orange peel. With any hard-curing finish, including regular or polyurethane varnish, water-based finish, shellac, lacquer and catalyzed lacquer, you can reduce these flaws by thinning the finish with the appropriate thinner.

Use mineral spirits (paint thinner) with any type of varnish, denatured alcohol with shellac, and lacquer thinner with lacquer and catalyzed lacquer.

Thinning water-based finish is more complicated. You can add a little water, but this seldom corrects the problem because water has a high surface tension. It's better to use the manufacturer's "flow out" additive. Unfortunately, only a few manufacturers commercially supply one.

It's easy to picture how thinning can be used to achieve total flatness. Imagine brushing or spraying just one of the thinners onto wood. The thinner will level out perfectly of course. It's only logical, therefore, that a finish can be made to level perfectly somewhere between full strength and no strength – that is, just the thinner.

The downside of thinning is that you reduce the build of each coat. To get a good build quickly and still achieve a level end result, apply several full-strength coats, sand the surface level, then apply one or two thinned coats.

French polishing is a method of applying shellac with a cloth to achieve a perfectly flat, high-gloss finish. The cloth is made into a pad and the shellac wiped on, often in circles or figure eights and usually with the aid of mineral oil to lubricate the rubbing.

Similar to the brush marks left by brushing, the pad will leave rag tracks if the shellac is too thick. The way to achieve a perfectly flat French-polished surface, therefore, is to begin thinning the shellac as you proceed through the final applications.

The most efficient way to do the thinning is right on the pad. After you have built the thickness you want, begin adding alcohol to the pad along with the shellac. Use two dispensers and add more alcohol and less shellac each time you refill the pad until you are adding only alcohol.

In summary, thicker finish films are most effective for protecting wood from water penetration and moisture-vapor exchange. Thinned finishes flow out and level better than unthinned finishes.

One of the thickest and most protective of all finishes is an epoxy-resin finish which is applied very thick and commonly used on bar tops and restaurant tabletops such as this one.

The thicker a finish during application, the less it flattens out and the more brush marks and orange peel show. On the left side of each of these panels, I applied the finish right out of the can – brushing varnish on the top panel and spraying lacquer on the bottom panel. On the right side of the panels I brushed and sprayed the same finishes thinned significantly with the appropriate thinner.

Home Center Finishing

You can achieve a great finish from commonly available products.

We all love home centers for the good stuff they carry and for their low prices. But home centers cater to the lowest common denominator consumer – that is, they carry only the stuff that has a big market.

The result is that many of the finishing products used on furniture and cabinets, products you read about in woodworking magazines or hear about in woodworking classes, are rarely found in these stores. Examples include very fine-grit sandpapers, dyes, glazes, grain fillers, spray lacquers and high-performance finishes such as catalyzed lacquer.

So how do you proceed if you have to do your finishing entirely from the products available at home centers?

It's not all that difficult, really. You're just limited in some of the decorative effects you can achieve – decorative effects you may not be interested in anyway because you're more than likely using the natural color and figure of the wood for most of your decoration.

With the limited choice of finishing products at home centers, you can still get all the following:

❯ Protection and durability ranging from minimal to the best possible
❯ A sheen ranging from gloss to dead flat
❯ Finishes ranging from amber to colorless
❯ A near-flawless finish resembling sprayed lacquer
❯ Elimination of blotching from stains
❯ A glaze substitute
❯ A grain-filling option
❯ The ability to block off problems in the wood.

Marketing

Before proceeding with how to accomplish these objectives, I want to explain how companies producing and marketing finishing

You don't have to go to specialty retailers to find finishing supplies; you can produce a quality finish from products readily available at home centers.

materials sell their products (how all companies probably sell their products, for that matter).

Finish companies target specific markets. Within any given category – oil stain, varnish, water-based finish, etc. – all companies' products are very similar, if not identical. But because stores and catalogs carry different brands, and because the marketing can sometimes make you believe some brands are somehow better than others, you may think you're getting inferior products at low-end, mass-consumer home centers when you're not.

For example, a big brand name in home centers is Minwax, while General Finishes and Behlen dominate in woodworking stores and catalogs, and Old Masters is popular in independent paint stores. There are also stores that feature Sherwin-Williams, Benjamin Moore, Pratt & Lambert, Varathane and many other brands.

In addition, some companies target just contractors, others target cabinet and fur-

niture makers, and still others (an entirely different group of companies) target refinishers.

Within any finish category – oil stain, glaze, varnish, lacquer etc. – all these companies make essentially the same thing. They all have access to the same raw materials, and the instructions for putting these raw materials together are available to everyone, even to you and me if we want them.

So there's nothing at all inferior about the finishing products available at home centers. There's only a limitation as to what's available.

From these limited choices, however, you have many possibilities for achieving the results you want.

Protection & Durability

You have control of the amount of protection and durability you get simply by how much you build your finish and by your choice of finish.

Protection means resistance to moisture

penetration into the wood – in liquid or vapor (humidity) form. All finishes provide better resistance the thicker they are, so the finishes that harden well and can be built up on the wood are capable of much better protection than finishes such as boiled linseed oil, 100 percent tung oil and blends of one of these oils and varnish, which don't harden.

Among the finishes that harden, oil-based polyurethane varnish provides the best resistance to moisture penetration and also the best durability – that is, the best resistance to being damaged by scratches, heat, solvents,

acids and alkalis. Polyurethane is almost as protective and durable as the best of the high-performance finishes used in industry.

Following polyurethane in declining order are alkyd (regular) varnish, polyurethane water-based finish, acrylic water-based finish, lacquer and shellac.

But even fresh shellac is considerably more protective and durable than the finishes that don't harden as long as you apply several coats. Because shellac loses a lot of hardness and water resistance as it ages, however, it's best to use it within a year of manufacture.

The date of manufacture is stamped on the bottom of the can.

Color

The color you get on the wood is partially contributed by the finish. Finishes differ in how much yellowing or "oranging" they add.

Amber shellac adds the most orange color. You can use this finish on pine, for example, to create the knotty pine look popular in the 1950s, or recreate the warmth common on oak trim and paneling original to early 20th-century houses.

Your choice of finish can have a big effect on the color you get, whether or not you have stained the wood. From the left, water-based finish darkens this walnut a little but doesn't add any color; lacquer adds a little yellowing; polyurethane varnish adds a little orange; and amber shellac adds a distinctly orange coloring.

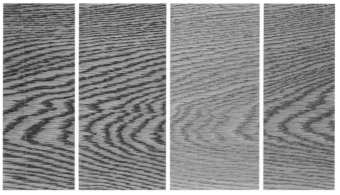

Boiled linseed oil and 100 percent tung oil add yellow coloring to the wood initially but then darken significantly as they age. This oak board was finished with three coats of each finish more than five years ago. From the left are boiled linseed oil, 100 percent tung oil, wiping varnish (varnish thinned half with mineral spirits), and a half-and-half mixture of boiled linseed oil and varnish. Notice that the linseed and tung oils have oranged about the same and that the mixture of oil and varnish has darkened about half way between that of the oils and varnish alone.

Keeping in mind that the name of the color on the stain can is merely a manufacturer's interpretation, you can adjust any stain by mixing. You can even mix two or more stains of different brands as long as you stay within one type: oil or water-based. Here, I'm increasing the reddish tint in a "walnut" stain by adding some "mahogany."

You can achieve any sheen you want just from the gloss and satin varieties of varnish, water-based finish and lacquer offered in home centers. To get a sheen in between the gloss and satin, mix the two. To get a sheen flatter than the satin, pour off some of the gloss (as I'm doing here) from a can of satin in which you have allowed the flatting agent to settle, then mix the two to get what you want.

Boiled linseed oil and 100 percent tung oil have a slight yellow color to begin with, then they yellow, or rather orange, significantly as they age. You can use either of these finishes under any other finish to achieve this oranging as long as you let the oil cure well first. A week or two in a warm room should be adequate.

Oil-based varnishes, lacquer and clear shellac also have a slight yellow tint, which may darken a little with age. But the finish most significant for color is water-based, both polyurethane and acrylic. These finishes aren't, and don't, yellow at all. They are "water clear."

So you would choose a water-based finish for light woods such as maple or ash, or for white pickled woods, if you don't want them to have a yellow tint. You would probably choose one of the other finishes for darker woods because water-based finishes usually make these woods appear "washed out" unless you apply a stain underneath.

Sheen

It's rare that home centers provide finishes with sheens other than gloss and satin (shellac comes in gloss only), but you can use these two to achieve any sheen you want.

Sheen is the amount of gloss, or reflection, in a finish. If no flatting agent is added – that is, there's nothing at the bottom of the can that has to be stirred into suspension

You can use aerosols as an alternative to a spray gun to achieve a level surface. Aerosols are available in polyurethane and water-based finish in addition to lacquer and shellac. To get a thicker build with less expense, brush two or three coats, then sand the surface level up to #400 grit then spray a couple of coats with the aerosol.

To eliminate brush marks (shown on the left), thin the finish a quarter to a half with the appropriate thinner then brush it. If you want to speed the build, brush two or three full-strength coats, then sand the surface level up to #400 grit and apply a couple thinned coats.

before application – the finish produces a gloss, or sharp image clarity. Manufacturers create satin and flat finishes by adding a flatting agent, which is usually silica. The more flatting agent added, the less reflective the finish.

To get a sheen in between that of gloss and satin within any finish type – varnish, lacquer or water-based – simply mix the two (after stirring the satin, of course). To get a sheen flatter than the satin, let the flatting agent settle (don't let the store clerk shake the can) and pour off some of the top. What is left will be much flatter. You can then mix these to get something in between if you want.

Because it is the top, or last, coat applied that is responsible for determining all of the sheen, you can change the appearance simply by applying another coat with a different sheen.

Avoiding Flaws

Spray guns can be used to produce nearly flawless, meaning almost perfectly level, surfaces. But you can achieve the same without a spray gun simply by thinning the finish or using an aerosol. The thinner (meaning "thinned") the finish the better it levels and the faster it dries.

Better leveling means no brush marks. Faster drying means reduced dust nibs.

You can thin any finish to get it to level better, but the easiest to use are the varnishes. All home centers carry already thinned alkyd and polyurethane varnishes. These are sometimes labeled "Wipe-On Poly," but also "tung oil," "tung oil finish" or "tung oil varnish." In no cases do these products, which I call "wiping varnish" because they're easy to wipe on wood, have anything to do with tung oil, but they produce wonderful results nevertheless.

There are three good ways to apply a wiping varnish: wipe or brush it on the wood and wipe off all the excess; wipe or brush it on and wipe off some or most of the excess; brush it on and leave it. The more you leave the greater the build, but the longer time dust has to settle and stick to the finish.

To get a thick build with fewer coats, brush several full-strength coats of alkyd or polyurethane varnish, sand the surface level up to #400-grit sandpaper, then apply several coats of wiping varnish and wipe off some or most of the excess. You can make the wiping varnish yourself by thinning the same finish you're brushing by half with mineral spirits, or you can use one of the already thinned brands.

You can also use an aerosol for your finishing. Aerosols are now available in oil-based polyurethane and water-based finish in addition to lacquer and shellac, but they are relatively expensive. Instead of building all your coats with the aerosol, you can brush a couple coats, sand out the brush marks, then use the aerosol of the same type of finish to apply level final coats.

Whatever finish you're applying and however you're applying it, always watch it in a reflected light to spot runs as they develop and respread or rewipe to remove some of the excess.

Whatever method you use to get a level surface, rub it lightly with a folded brown paper bag after the finish has hardened to remove minor dust nibs and make the surface feel smoother.

Blotching

Blotching is uneven, and usually ugly, coloration caused by stains penetrating unevenly.

To avoid blotching on softwoods such

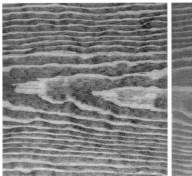
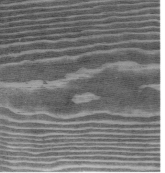

The easy way to eliminate blotching in pine is to apply a gel stain as I have done to the right half of this pine board. The left side is stained with a liquid stain. Gel stains are so effective on pine they should be called "pine stain."

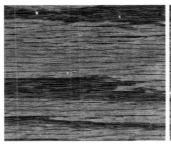
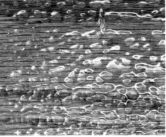

Fish eye (cratering) is one of the most serious problems in refinishing. It's caused by silicone from furniture polishes getting into the wood and causing the new finish to wrinkle when applied. One easy way to avoid fish eye is to block it with a first coat of shellac, applied here to the left side of the board. The only new-wood use for shellac as a first coat is over resinous knots in softwoods such as pine.

as pine, use a gel stain. This is a stain thickened enough so that it doesn't penetrate. Gel stains ought to be called "pine stain" because they are so effective at eliminating blotching in pine.

On hardwoods such as cherry, birch, maple and poplar, it's more effective to use a washcoat. This is any finish thinned to about a 10 percent solids content. Lacquer is used in industry, but the type sold in home centers is varnish or a blend of oil and vanish labeled "wood conditioner" or "stain controller." You can make your own by thinning any full-strength varnish or blend of boiled linseed oil and varnish with two parts mineral spirits.

When you apply this washcoat, be sure to let it cure at least six hours in a warm room, better overnight, or it won't be very effective. This is different than the directions on the cans, which usually say to apply the stain within two hours.

There is no need to apply a washcoat to woods such as oak, ash, walnut and mahogany that don't blotch.

Glaze Substitute

Colored glazes are used to add highlighting, antiquing or create faux graining over at least one coat of finish. Glazes are rarely available in home centers, but you can substitute a gel stain with excellent results. Glazes and gel stains are essentially the same thing anyway – a thickened stain.

To do glazing, brush or wipe the glaze or gel stain over at least one coat of finish then remove all the color you don't want using a rag, brush, sponge, graining tool (usually available at home centers), steel wool or any other tool that produces the results you want.

A typical use of glaze on cabinets and furniture is to leave it in recesses to add three-dimensional depth or an antique look. Be sure to apply at least one coat of finish over the glaze after it has dried to protect it from being scratched or rubbed off.

Pore Filling

Some woods look better with their pores filled to create a "mirror-flat" surface. Mahogany is the best example.

Products called "paste wood filler" or "grain filler" (not the same as wood putty or wood filler) designed to achieve this look are rarely available at home centers. But you can achieve the same result by sanding a number of coats of finish down to the deepest level of the pores. You can sand a little between each coat, or you can sand more after you have applied all the coats.

Because we all apply finishes differently, you will have to experiment on scrap to determine the number of coats necessary so you don't sand through.

For the easiest sanding between coats, use stearated sandpaper. Norton "3X" and 3M "Tri-Mite" and "Sandblaster" are all stearated. This means they contain a soap-like lubricant that reduces clogging. You can use your hand to back the sandpaper when sanding between coats, but you should use a flat sanding block on flat surfaces when sanding many coats level.

For the easiest sanding after a number of coats, use black, wet-dry sandpaper with a mineral-oil, mineral-spirits or mixed mineral-oil/mineral-spirits lubricant. Begin sanding with a grit sandpaper that levels efficiently without creating larger than necessary scratches (for example, #320 or #400 grit) then sand to finer grits if they are available.

It finer grits aren't available, apply one more coat of thinned finish (so it will level well), spray with an aerosol, or rub the surface with #0000 steel wool. You can use a wax, oil or soap-and-water lubricant with the steel wool to reduce the scratching and improve the smoothness.

Problems in the Wood

Of all the finishes, shellac is easily the most effective for blocking off problems in the wood. The most common problem in new wood is resinous knots in pine and other softwoods. The resin can bleed into the finish and cause it to remain tacky and not cure.

In old (refinished) wood, the most common problems are fish eye (cratering or ridging) and odors from smoke or animal urine. Shellac blocks all these problems so you can then successfully apply any finish over it. If you are using varnish or water-based finish, it's best if you use dewaxed shellac, sold in most home centers as "SealCoat."

To make your own dewaxed shellac, pour off or decant the shellac from a can of Bull's Eye Clear Shellac after the wax has settled to the bottom. It will take a long time for this to occur on its own, so don't shake the can when you buy it, or thin the shellac with at least two parts denatured alcohol in a glass jar (so you can see it) to get it to settle faster.

If there are no problems you need to block off, there's no reason to use shellac as a first coat.

Conclusion

Somehow, a lot of unnecessary mystique is introduced into wood finishing. In reality, however, it is quite simple. This is most evident when you realize all the possibilities available from just the few products stocked by home centers.

The Deterioration of Furniture

How 'Antiques Roadshow' is contributing to it.

One of the most watched PBS programs is the "Antiques Roadshow," which has been broadcast since 1996. The format features some of our nation's foremost antiques experts and appraisers explaining to a nationwide audience the monetary value and some of the history of the objects shown. These objects include almost everything you can think of that is old or antique, ranging in size from jewelry to large pieces of furniture. (As applied to furniture, the term "antique" is variously defined as at least 100 years old or pre-industrial, which usually means 1840s or earlier. So I'm using the phrase "old or antique" to be sure to include everything that might appear on the show.)

The "Roadshow" tours a dozen or so cities each year, bringing many of its stable of about 150 appraisers to each. (The appraisers work without pay and cover their own expenses; side benefits created by the national television exposure usually give back many times over.) Thousands of people line up at each venue to have two or more objects appraised. The most interesting appraisals are filmed for later use on the television broadcast.

The format of the "Roadshow" is very entertaining. The show could stand on its own just for this quality. But it has another very important enticement: It appeals to the "win-the-lottery" fantasy of most people. In the majority of cases, the people shown on the "Roadshow" are pleasantly surprised and often elated to learn that their object is worth far more than they thought – often in the thousands of dollars. Maybe there's also something in the viewer's attic that is worth a lot of money? Maybe the viewer will find that he or she has "won the lottery" with what was previously thought to be junk.

The "Roadshow" is also educational. I know many professional refinishers and antique dealers who watch to learn. But most (and maybe all) complain about the misleading message that is being sent concerning furniture. It's the pivotal message of the entire show, the message everyone

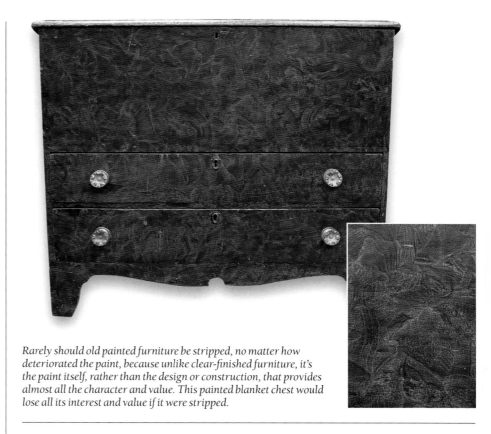

Rarely should old painted furniture be stripped, no matter how deteriorated the paint, because unlike clear-finished furniture, it's the paint itself, rather than the design or construction, that provides almost all the character and value. This painted blanket chest would lose all its interest and value if it were stripped.

associates with the "Antiques Roadshow": "Don't refinish!" Refinishing reduces the value of furniture, it is alleged, sometimes by thousands of dollars.

It's my contention that this message misleads the public about the appropriateness (or inappropriateness) of refinishing. The message indirectly causes serious damage to old and antique furniture and will result in the disappearance of much of it unless the message is changed.

Furniture requires a finish in good shape to protect the wood from moisture exchange and to make the wood look nice. Furniture with joint failure, peeling veneer, warps and splits – all caused by excessive moisture exchange – and furniture that looks bad because of a deteriorated and ugly finish, often ends up in an attic, basement, garage or barn where it further deteriorates. Or it is tossed out.

How Furniture Deteriorates

Furniture deteriorates as a result of exposure to moisture, light and abuse.

Moisture affects the wood. Contact with water and changes in humidity cause wood to expand and contract across the grain, but not significantly along the grain. When boards are joined perpendicularly, as they almost always are to make furniture, stress develops in the joints because of contrary wood movement in the parts. As the glue ages and becomes brittle, this stress causes the glue to give way. The joints then loosen and separate.

The same happens with veneer, which was often glued perpendicularly to a solid-wood substrate or laid over a frame-and-flush-panel substrate. The veneer separates or cracks, especially over the joints.

Exposure of only one side of wood to water also causes warping and splitting, a poorly understood phenomenon, which I explain in "Tabletops & the Need to Refinish" at the end of this chapter.

Moisture-vapor exchange (higher humidity in the air leading to higher moisture content in the wood, and vice versa) has always been a problem. But it has become worse in modern, tightly constructed buildings because of the impact of central heating. In the winter, interior humidity conditions become much drier than previously, so the variations between summer and winter are greater. The result is increased wood movement.

The easiest way to keep moisture exchange to a minimum is to keep the finish in good shape. (The other way is to maintain a constant humidity, which is usually not possible outside of a museum setting.) A finish doesn't completely stop moisture penetration, but it slows the penetration significantly. A deteriorated finish is pitted with microscopic voids that allow moisture in liquid or vapor form to pass through. An old, deteriorated finish offers almost no barrier to moisture penetration.

While the deterioration of the wood in furniture is caused primarily by moisture exchange, the deterioration of finishes results primarily from exposure to light.

A finish will eventually dull, become brittle and crack simply because of exposure to oxygen, but this takes a very long time. Exposure to ultraviolet light, especially from sunlight and fluorescent lighting, accelerates this deterioration considerably. The finish on a piece of furniture placed near a window in direct sunlight will dull and crack far sooner than a finish placed in a dark corner across the room.

Finishes can also deteriorate from abuse, of course. Abuse in the form of scratches and rubs removes finishes and may even damage the wood.

No matter how a finish deteriorates, the end result is increased moisture exchange in the wood, reduced functionality and increased ugliness. And, with rare exceptions, this deterioration leads eventually to the disappearance of the furniture if nothing is done to reverse it.

The Misleading Message

Some very old furniture has survived in good condition, but the instances of this happening are rare. The furniture that has done so, however, is worth more than furniture that has had to be refinished. People will pay more for things that are rare.

How does some furniture survive for hundreds of years with its original finish in good condition? Consider this scenario as an example.

A bureau (chest-of-drawers) is made for a wealthy New England family in 1790. It is used by that family for a couple decades then passed down to one of the children who remains in the family house. But the bureau is no longer "modern" and is relegated to a dark corner in a guest bedroom where it is rarely used. The house and bureau remain in the family for 200 years, after which the bureau is sold and enters the antiques market – with a finish that is a little dull but otherwise in near-original condition.

The circumstances necessary for furniture to survive in near-original condition are that it receive little exposure to bright light and be rarely used or moved.

As chance would have it, the furniture appraisers who appear on the "Roadshow" deal primarily with this type of furniture in their own businesses. There is a small but very enthusiastic market for furniture with old or original "surfaces." It is therefore natural for these appraisers to compare the value of an object that has been refinished with one that hasn't. Had the furniture survived in near-original condition, it would be worth much more.

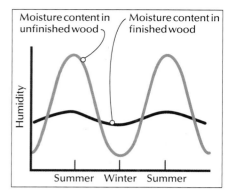

A finish in good condition reduces the swelling and shrinking of wood by slowing the exchange of moisture in and out of wood. This graph represents a hypothetical situation.

But I rarely hear the appraisers explain survivability on the "Roadshow." Instead, they say things like, "Had this furniture not been refinished, it would be worth many thousands of dollars. But it was refinished, so now it's worth only a few thousand dollars."

To the unsophisticated viewer this evaluation says, "Furniture loses value when it is refinished."

It's rarely explained that furniture is seldom refinished unless it needs to be. And if the furniture needs to be refinished and it isn't, it may not survive. The appraisers should be saying, "This piece was refinished, which is good because it surely needed to be. In this condition, it's worth "X" dollars. Had it been one of those rare pieces of furniture that survived with its original finish in good condition, it would be worth this much more. You should be happy that someone cared enough to refinish the furniture so you have the opportunity to enjoy it."

Or, in cases of badly deteriorated finishes on pieces with no special provenance, the appraisers should say something like, "The finish on this piece is in very poor condition and is no longer serving its protective purpose. The furniture would be worth more refinished."

As chance would also have it, most of the leading museums in the country have an interest in keeping furniture in their collections in the same condition as when it was acquired – often with a very deteriorated finish. (Museums spend a lot of effort controlling humidity.) The purpose is so the furniture can be studied for original techniques, adhesives and finishes used.

Therefore, when a museum curator or conservator is asked by a consumer maga-

Light destroys finishes. Direct sunlight and fluorescent light are the most damaging. The 100-year-old drawer front on the left is badly crazed except where the finish was protected from light by the hardware. There, the finish is in near-perfect condition. The backside of the walnut cabinet on the right sat next to a west-facing window for 10 years. The finish is peeling and the color is faded where the sunlight hit.

zine to comment on the appropriateness of refinishing, the response is almost always, "Refinishing is bad." The museum professional is thinking of his or her own needs, not those of the general public. The result is that the "Roadshow's" message is reinforced.

More sophisticated dealers and collectors don't object to refinishing. The market for old and antique furniture in deteriorated condition is very small. Most people want their furniture to look good, which usually means refinished, or at least restored as I describe below in "Rejuvenating Old Finishes." This has been brought home to me on a number of occasions when I've visited high-end antique stores, especially in the Northeast. I've walked through shops containing hundreds of pieces of furniture from the late 18th and early 19th centuries, every one of which has been refinished at some point in its life, usually fairly recently.

The shop owners explain to me that there isn't a market for "crusty craze." People want their furniture to look nice. Or as one dealer at one of the most prestigious New York City stores said when I asked about the influence of the "Antiques Roadshow": "Our customers know better."

The Other Side

There's another side to this issue. An old or original finish makes it easier to determine the

The decision of whether to refinish, rejuvenate or leave alone varies with each piece of furniture (and also with the desires of the owner). At right is an early 19th-century bow front bureau with a badly damaged finish, including significant missing color. As is, the piece is very unattractive. The choice would probably be to refinish, or possibly to rejuvenate using the amalgamation technique, hoping to move some of the color around to fill in. (Nothing would be lost if amalgamation didn't produce good results because refinishing is the other choice; it could still be done.) On the right is the arm of a painted Windsor chair from about the same period, with clear patterns of wear. It would be a shame to remove, or try to amalgamate and respread, the paint. The wear adds to the character and value.

authenticity of a small percentage of antique furniture. There are fakes and restorations at all levels of the market, and crusty old finishes, which are difficult if not impossible to replicate, provide a high degree of insurance against fraud. Even old dirt in cracks and recesses is helpful. An original or at least very old finish makes authentication easier and sales better for a few high-end dealers.

This desire for old, deteriorated and even dirty surfaces could be consciously or unconsciously motivating the appraisers on the "Roadshow."

It could well be argued that this is fair, that there is a legitimate authentication rationale for not refinishing no matter how bad the condition of the finish. But even if you accept this rationale, it doesn't apply to the vast majority (somewhere north of 99 percent) of old and antique furniture. The mantra, "Don't refinish," should not be promoted on a television show targeted at the general public without constant explaining. The current practice is having a harmful effect.

Reprinted from Woodwork, *August 2006.*

Rejuvenating Old Finishes

There are three ways to deal with an old, deteriorated finish: You can leave it as is, doing no more than possibly apply some paste wax; you can strip and refinish; or you can rejuvenate or "restore" whatever finish is left. The decision is always made on a case-by-case basis. No method is right for all furniture.

In many cases, an old finish surface has an attractive aged coloring that will be lost if the finish is stripped and a new one applied. Refinishing makes furniture look new and can cause it to lose some of its charm. On the other hand, if the finish is unattractive and no longer performing its function of slowing moisture exchange, something should be done. There are a number of techniques you can use to rejuvenate an old finish that will maintain the color while at the same time improve the overall appearance. Here is a list of techniques, advancing

from least to most intrusive, effective and difficult to pull off.

❯ Apply a commercial "restorer," such as Howard's Restor-A-Finish. This will add shine, and sometimes color, to scratches for a short time.

❯ Apply paste wax. Wax will add a semi-permanent shine without highlighting cracks in the finish (as liquid polishes do). But wax won't improve resistance to moisture exchange in any significant way. Use a colored paste wax to add color in scratches and dings.

❯ Clean the surface with soap and water and/or mineral spirits before applying wax or a restorer. There are two types of dirt, water-soluble and solvent-soluble, so you may need to use both types of cleaner.

❯ Apply a coat or two of finish. You can use any finish, including shellac (French polish), varnish (including polyurethane varnish), water-based, or lacquer, but be careful with

lacquer because the thinner in it may blister the finish if applied really wet. In all cases, applying thinned coats produces better, more level, results. Oil is not as effective as a hard, film-building finish and could darken the wood unevenly and undesirably as the oil ages and darkens.

❯ Abrade the surface before applying restorer, paste wax or finish. Use sandpaper if you want to level the surface. Steel wool and Scotch-Brite pads merely round over unevenness. Abrading removes the top surface, which serves doubly to clean dirt. Don't abrade through any color, whether in the wood or in the finish, or you may lose control and end up having to refinish.

❯ Amalgamate the finish and respread. This can be done only with shellac and lacquer. Wipe or brush an appropriate solvent over the surface to soften or liquefy the finish, then smooth it level.

Tabletops & the Need to Refinish

It's a widespread myth among woodworkers that the way to reduce, and maybe even prevent, warping is to finish both sides of the wood. I don't have any objection to finishing the underside and inside, but doing so isn't going to have any significant impact on warping; the moisture content of the wood is going to adjust to the surrounding atmosphere anyway. It's keeping the finish on the exposed side in good shape that makes the biggest difference.

Have you ever noticed that warps in tabletops, deck boards, siding, floorboards and even cutting boards are almost always concave on the top or exposed side? And that this is the case no matter which side of the wood (heartwood, sapwood or quartersawn) is up or out, or whether one or both sides of the wood is finished?

The explanation is that the top or exposed side was wetted and allowed to dry repeatedly over a long period of time and the finish (or paint) wasn't in good enough shape to prevent the water from getting to the wood. The continued wetting and drying of just one side caused compression shrinkage (or "compression set").

Compression shrinkage is a technical term used by wood technologists to describe a condition in which the cylindrical cells of cellulose in wood are not allowed to expand when moisture is absorbed, so they get compressed into oval shapes. Compression shrinkage explains how screws work loose in wood, and why wooden handles become loose in hammers and hatchets. It also explains splits in the ends of boards and checks in the middle of boards in addition to warping.

When water enters wood, the cellulose cell walls swell. If the wetting is only on one side and the thickness of the wood prevents the cells from expanding, they become compressed into oval shapes. When the wood dries, the cells don't resume their cylindrical shapes and that side shrinks a little. Each time the one side is wetted and dries out it shrinks a little more. Repeated wetting and drying of one side eventually leads to that side cupping, and if the cycle continues long enough, the wood splits and checks.

Tabletops are commonly wiped with a damp cloth to clean spills and sticky dirt. If the finish is allowed to deteriorate to the point where it no longer prevents water

Tabletops are often exposed to spills or wiped down with a damp cloth. If the finish is deteriorated, water can get into the wood and, over time, cause enough compression shrinkage to warp it concave. This type of warp has nothing to do with which side of the wood (heartwood, sapwood or quartersawn) is up or whether the finish was applied to one or both sides.

Wood floors are often kept clean by wet mopping, and if the finish isn't kept in good shape the boards will cup due to compression shrinkage. Every floorboard throughout this second-floor apartment has cupped, and the boards were, of course, laid randomly.

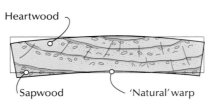

Antique plainsawn wood can be expected to have shrunk and warped around the rings as the surrounding conditions in buildings have become drier over the last 150 years. Most antique tabletops were made with the heartwood up because it's the better side, with more good wood exposed. So it would be expected that old tabletops would bow rather than cup. But the opposite has happened in almost all cases. The fact that the underside was not finished can't possibly have anything to do with the warping.

penetration (or if the finish is too thin to prevent water penetration), warping and eventual splitting result. More than any other furniture surface, the finish on tabletops needs to be kept in good condition.

Compression shrinkage has been well understood by wood technologists for decades, but none of them carried it to its logical conclusion to explain warping until Carey Howlett did so in a paper he presented to the Wooden Artifacts Group of AIC (The American Institute for Conservation of Historic and Artistic Works) in 1995. You can read the paper online at http://aic.stanford.edu/sg/wag/1995/WAG_95_howlett.pdf.

Interestingly, understanding the cause of warps in tabletops leads to the counter-intui-

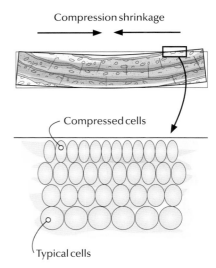

Wood is composed of cylindrical cells of cellulose that are compressed into oval shapes when the wood is exposed repeatedly to cycles of wetting and drying out. The compression becomes permanent, and if the exposure is to one side only, the wood warps and eventually splits. Spills and exposure to damp washcloths are the primary causes of warping in tabletops.

tive but effective method for correcting warps. Hold the board in clamps across the grain to keep the wood from expanding. Then wet the convex side, usually the bottom side of tabletops, many times, letting it dry thoroughly after each wetting. The convex side will slowly shrink, bringing the board flat.

2

Wood Preparation

Rules for Sanding Wood

Material and finish choice help dictate grit progression.

The objective of sanding wood is to remove mill marks, which are caused by woodworking machines, and to remove other flaws such as dents and gouges that may have been introduced in handling. The most efficient method of doing this is to begin sanding with a coarse enough grit sandpaper to cut through and remove the problems quickly, then sand out the coarse-grit scratches with finer and finer grits until you reach the smoothness you want — usually up to #150, #180 or #220 grit.

This is a very important concept because it gets past all the contradictory instructions about which sandpaper grits to use. Conditions vary.

For example, a board that has been run through a planer with dull knives will require a coarser grit of sandpaper to be efficient than you'd need with typical veneered plywood or MDF that has been pre-sanded in the factory. You can finish-sand both of these surfaces with #180 grit, for example, but you might begin with #80 grit on the solid wood and #120 grit on the plywood. It would be a total waste of time and effort to begin with #80 grit on the pre-sanded veneered wood (and you would risk sanding through). So you don't want to begin with too coarse a grit because it will cause you more work than necessary sanding out the scratches.

There's also no fixed rule for how to progress through the grits. Sanding is very personal. We all sand with different pressures, number of passes over any given spot and lengths of time.

Unquestionably, the most efficient progression is to sand through every grit — #80, #100, #120, #150, #180 — sanding just enough with each grit to remove the scratches of the previous grit. But most of us sand more than we need to, so it's often more efficient to skip grits.

You'll have to learn by experience what works best for you.

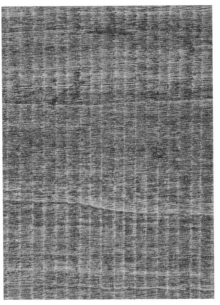

The primary reason you need to sand wood is to remove the washboarding and other mill marks caused by machine tools. On this board, the washboarding, which was caused by a planer and has been highlighted with stain, is particularly severe. I think it would have been most efficient to begin sanding with #80 grit.

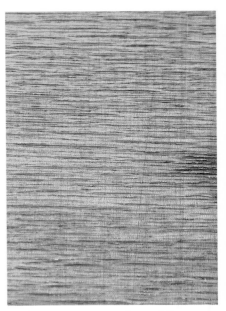

Sanding cross-grain tears the wood fibers so the sanding scratches show up much more, especially under a stain. The best policy is to always sand in the direction of the grain when possible. The scratching that does occur is then more likely to be disguised by the grain of the wood.

Random-orbit sanders are more efficient than vibrator sanders, but they still leave cross-grain marks in the wood. I refer to these as "squigglies." The best policy is to sand them out by hand in the direction of the grain after sanding to the finest grit, usually #180 or #220, with the sander. Doing this is especially important if you are staining.

Sanding finer than #180 or #220 is wasted effort in most cases, as explained in the text. In fact, the finer the grit the wood is sanded to, the less color a stain leaves when the excess is wiped off. In this case, the top half was sanded to #180 grit and the bottom half to #600 grit. Then a stain was applied and the excess wiped off.

How Fine to Sand

It's rarely beneficial to sand finer than #180 grit.

Film-building finishes, such as varnish, shellac, lacquer and water-based finish, create their own surfaces after a couple of coats. The appearance and feel of the finish is all its own and has nothing any longer to do with how fine you sand the wood.

Oil and oil/varnish-blend finishes have no measurable build, so any roughness in the wood caused by coarse sanding telegraphs through. But these finishes can be made ultimately smooth simply by sanding between cured coats or sanding each additional coat while it is still wet on the surface using #400 or #600 grit.

Only if you are staining or using a vibrator ("pad") or random-orbit sander does sanding above #180 grit make a difference.

The finer you sand, the less stain color will be retained on the wood when you wipe off the excess. If this is what you want then sand to a finer grit. If it isn't, there's no point going past #180 grit. The sanding scratches won't show as long as they are in the direction of the grain.

Sometimes with vibrator and random-orbit sanders, sanding up to #220 grit makes the squiggly marks left by these sanders small enough so they aren't seen under a clear finish. Sanding by hand in the direction of the grain to remove these squigglies then becomes unnecessary.

In all cases when sanding by hand, it's best to sand in the direction of the wood grain when possible. Of course, doing this is seldom possible on turnings and decorative veneer patterns such as sunbursts and marquetry.

Cross-grain sanding scratches aren't very visible under a clear finish, but they show up very clearly under a stain. If you can't avoid cross-grain sanding, you will have to find a compromise between creating scratches fine enough so they don't show and coarse enough so the stain still darkens the wood adequately. You should practice first on scrap wood to determine where this point is for you.

Three Sanding Methods

Other than using a stationary sanding machine or a belt sander, which will take a good deal of practice to learn to control, there are three methods of sanding wood: with just your hand backing the sandpaper, with a flat block backing the sandpaper and with a vibrator or random-orbit sander.

Using your hand to back the sandpaper can lead to hollowing out the softer early-wood grain on most woods. So you shouldn't use your hand to back the sandpaper on flat surfaces such as tops and drawer fronts because the hollowing will stand out in reflected light after a finish is applied.

The most efficient use of sandpaper for hand-backed sanding is to tear the 9" x 11" sheet of sandpaper into thirds crossways, then fold each of these thirds into thirds lengthways. Sand with the folded sandpaper until it dulls, flip the folded sandpaper over

The most efficient use of sandpaper when backing it with just your hand is to tear the sheet into thirds crossways and then fold one of the thirds into thirds lengthways. Flip the thirds to use 100 percent of the paper.

The most efficient use of sandpaper when backing it with a flat sanding block is to tear the sheet into thirds crossways then fold one of the thirds in half. Hold it onto the block with your thumb and fingers as shown here. Flip the folded sandpaper for a fresh surface, then open up the sandpaper and wrap it all around the sanding block for a third fresh surface.

to use the second third, then refold to use the third third. This method reduces waste to zero and also reduces the tendency of the folds to slip as you're sanding.

If you are sanding critical flat surfaces by hand, you should always use a flat block to back the sandpaper. If the block is hard (wood, for example), it's best to have some sort of softer material such as cork glued to the bottom to improve the performance of the sandpaper. (I find the rubber sanding blocks, available at home centers, too hard, wasteful of sandpaper and inefficient because of the time involved in changing sandpapers.)

I made my own sanding block. Its measurements are $2^3/4$" x $3^7/8$" x $1^1/4$" thick, with the top edges chamfered for a more comfortable grip. Any wood will work. I used sugar pine because it is very light in weight.

To get the most efficient use of the sandpaper, fold one of the thirds-of-a-sheet (described above) in half along the long side and hold it in place on the block with your fingers and thumb. When you have used up one side, turn the folded sandpaper and use the other. Then open the sandpaper and wrap it around the block to use the middle.

Most woodworkers use random-orbit sanders because they are very efficient, easy to use, and they leave a less-visible scratch pattern than vibrator sanders due to the ran-domness of their movement. For both of these sanders, however, there are two critical rules to follow.

First, don't press down on the sander when sanding. Let the sander's weight do the work. Pressing leaves deeper and more obvious squigglies that then have to be sanded out. Simply move the sander slowly over the surface of the wood in some pattern that covers all areas approximately equally.

Second, it's always the best policy to sand out the squigglies by hand after you have progressed to your final sanding grit (for example, #180 or #220), especially if you are applying a stain. Use a flat block to back the sandpaper if you are sanding a flat surface. It's most efficient to use the same grit sandpaper you used for your last machine sanding, but you can use one grit finer if you sand a little longer.

Removing Sanding Dust

No matter which of the three sanding methods you use, always remove the sanding dust before advancing to the next-finer grit sandpaper. The best tool to use is a vacuum because it is the cleanest. A brush kicks the dust up in the air to dirty your shop and possibly land back on your work during finishing.

Tack rags load up too quickly with the large amount of dust created at the wood level. These sticky rags should be reserved for removing the small amounts of dust after sanding between coats of finish.

Compressed air works well if you have a good exhaust system, such as a spray booth, to remove the dust.

It's not necessary to get all the dust out of the pores. You won't see any difference under a finish, or under a stain and finish. Just get the wood clean enough so you can't feel or pick up any dust when wiping your hand over the surface.

How Much to Sand

The biggest sanding challenge is to know when you have removed all the flaws in the wood and then when you have removed all the scratches from each previous grit so you can move on to the next. Being sure that these flaws and scratches are removed is the reason most of us sand more than we need to.

A lot of knowing when you have sanded enough is learned by experience. But there are two methods you can use as an aid. First, after removing the dust, look at the wood in a low-angle reflected light – for example, from a window or a light fixture on a stand. Second, wet the wood, then look at it from different angles into a reflected light.

For wetting the wood, use mineral spirits (paint thinner) or denatured alcohol. Avoid mineral spirits if you are going to apply a water-based finish because any oily residue from the thinner might cause the finish to bead up. Denatured alcohol will raise the grain a little, so you'll have to sand it smooth again.

Random-orbit sanders are easy to use and efficient for smoothing wood. To reduce the likelihood of the squigglies these sanders produce, use a light touch. Don't press down on the sander; let its weight do the work.

Prevent, Remove & Disguise Glue Splotches

Nothing is more agonizing than discovering a glue splotch during staining.

There's no finishing problem more frustrating than glue splotches. You spend countless hours cutting, shaping, smoothing and joining pieces of wood only to have your work discolored where glue from squeeze-out or dirty hands seals the wood so stain and finish can't penetrate. The wood under the splotch doesn't change color while all around it the wood is darkened.

Avoiding this common problem is easy with one or more of the following four steps:

❯ Keep the glue from getting on the surface of the wood in the first place.

❯ Wipe the glue off the surface while it's still wet.

❯ Identify areas of dried glue and remove them before applying a stain or finish.

❯ Remove or disguise the glue splotch after it has occurred.

Preventing Glue Splotches

Glue squeeze-out is a good thing when gluing boards edge to edge, because it's evidence you've applied enough glue and enough pressure with your clamps. This type of squeeze-out is seldom a problem, however, because you'll remove all traces of it when you plane, scrape or sand the surface level.

It's the squeeze-out from cross-grain joints, such as stiles and rails, and legs and aprons, that causes problems because it's hard to sand or scrape a 90° joint without leaving unsightly scratches.

The most obvious way to prevent cross-grain glue squeeze-out is to apply no more glue to the joint members (mortise and tenon, dowel and hole) than necessary to make a good glue bond. This is hard to do when working fast, however, because it's difficult to avoid getting too much glue in the joint when you're even more concerned about not

Glue squeeze-out is a particularly thorny problem when a joint meets at a 90° angle, such as a table leg to an apron. And because the apron is set back, it's easy to miss the squeeze-out during sanding.

getting enough to make a strong bond. The trick is to create spaces within the joint for excess glue to collect, giving you more leeway for how much glue you can apply.

To create these spaces, make your mortise or dowel hole a little deeper than necessary, chamfer the end of the tenon or dowel (most commercial dowels come this way), and chamfer the front edges of the mortise or dowel hole. When you then slide the joint together, excess glue will collect in the cavities before squeezing out.

To keep your hands clean of glue while gluing up, keep a damp cloth and a dry cloth nearby. If you do get some glue on your hands,

wipe it off quickly with the damp cloth, then dry your hands with the dry cloth so you don't cause grain raising.

Removing Wet Glue

The best time to remove excess glue is while it's still wet by wiping with a cloth dampened with the solvent or thinner for the glue – water in most cases. To totally prevent glue splotching, however, you'll have to soak the wood and wipe it dry several times so you thin the glue so much that not enough is left in the wood's pores to cause a problem. You'll then have to sand to level the raised grain.

Some people remove glue squeeze-out by letting the glue dry just enough so it holds together and can be peeled off. This is a quick and easy way to remove most of the glue, but some will still remain in the pores and will have to be sanded, scraped or scrubbed out.

Identifying & Removing Glue

Once the glue has dried, it's usually difficult to see on the surface of the wood. To highlight these areas, wet the entire surface with water or mineral spirits, which will soak deeper into unsealed wood and make it darker. The areas that are sealed with glue will be easy to indentify because they will be lighter.

Water raises the grain of wood, so if you use water, you'll have to let it dry then sand the wood smooth again. This procedure is called sponging or dewhiskering, and it's a good step to take anyway if you plan to use a stain that contains water.

Alternatively, there are commercial products you can add to white and yellow glues before use that will make them show up under a UV (black) light.

When you've identified the problem areas, remove the glue by scraping, sanding or scrubbing with a solvent for the glue.

You can break down white, yellow and hide glues with water. Hot water works best. You can add some white vinegar ("white" so you don't stain the wood) to the water to speed the process even more.

A trick you may not be familiar with is using a solvent to soften white and yellow glues. The advantage of using a solvent is that it doesn't raise the grain.

Xylene (xylol) and toluene (toluol) work best. Xylene is the solvent in products such as Oops! and Goof Off sold to remove latex paint spatter. Latex paint and white and yellow glues are the same chemistry. You could, of course, use one of these commercial brands instead of xylene. Acetone and lacquer thinner are also somewhat effective.

You can dissolve contact cement with acetone or lacquer thinner, and you can thin epoxy and polyurethane glues with acetone until they have cured. Then you'll usually have to resort to sanding or scraping.

If the wood is oak, walnut, mahogany or one similar in porosity, you'll need to scrub the area with a toothbrush or soft bristle brush in the direction of the grain to help remove all the glue from the pores. Then wipe the surface dry.

After cleaning all the glue off the surface, sand it with the same grit sandpaper you used elsewhere. You need to remove all raised grain and make the sanding scratches uniform, or differences in color may show up when you apply a stain. Doing this is not so critical if you're not staining.

If you scrape or sand the glue off the surface, finish up by sanding with the finest grit sandpaper you've used elsewhere to make the scratch pattern uniform. Again, you don't have to be as careful if you're applying only a clear finish.

Correcting Problems

For those cases where you don't discover the glue splotch until after you've applied the stain, sand or scrape off the glue through the stain and restain that area or leave the splotch and disguise it later, after you've applied a coat of finish.

If you sand or scrape off the glue, you may have problems blending that area with the surrounding wood. Be sure to sand the damaged area to the same grit as elsewhere before applying more stain. If the damaged area still shows, try sanding the entire part (leg, rail, tabletop) while the surface is wet with stain, then wipe off the excess.

If the part you've wet-sanded is a little lighter than other parts, wet-sand again with a coarser-grit sandpaper. Most stains lubricate sandpaper, which reduces the coarseness of the scratching and could be the cause of the lighter coloring.

If wet-sanding doesn't solve the problem, you'll have to strip the stain using paint stripper or the thinner for the stain. Then resand

If you leave the dried glue wet with water for a while, it will turn white and be easy to scrub off.

the wood and begin again with the staining step. You don't have to remove all the color from the wood if you're restaining with the same stain, but you do need to get the remaining color fairly even.

An alternative solution you can use with all film-building finishes (not oil because it's too thin) is to disguise the splotch after you've applied a coat of finish in the same way you would disguise a wood-putty repair, a burn-in repair or a rub through.

Begin by drawing in the grain using pigment suspended in a shellac or padding-lacquer binder and a very fine artist's brush. You can also use pigment in varnish (the same as thinned oil paint or glaze), but you'll have to allow a day's drying time between coats.

When you have the grain lines connected to the grain in the surrounding wood, rub lightly with #0000 steel wool to soften the lines and apply a thin barrier coat of finish so the lines won't get smeared during the next step. Then color the areas in between the grain lines with either pigment or dye in a binder. When you have the splotch disguised, continue applying coats of finish.

To avoid squeeze-out it helps to design your joints so that excess glue has a place to collect. Chamfering the ends of your tenons or using dowels with chamfered ends will help.

A good way to find glue seepage or fingerprints is to wet the surface of the wood with water or mineral spirits. These will soak deeper, darkening the wood more than the glue does. Water raises grain; mineral spirits doesn't.

Instead of removing dried glue seepage, you can disguise it by painting between coats. Begin by drawing in the grain lines to connect with the stained wood on either side. Then apply a thin barrier coat of finish and color in the wood between the grain lines.

3

Wipe-on
Finishes

What is Oil?

Understanding just a little chemistry will teach you a lot about this finish.

At a wood-finishing seminar I once taught, a participant asked, "What is oil?" The question caused me to remember my own confusion a number of years ago. The term "oil" can seem confusing because there are many very different finishing products labeled and marketed (or mis-marketed) as oil.

Here's an explanation of oil.

The Nature of Oil

You've probably noticed that some oils stay liquid forever while others get sticky after a while and still others dry completely. The explanation is that some oils have more reactive sites than others, and it is at these sites that the molecules in oil form a chemical bond, or "crosslink", or "hook up," when exposed to air (more specifically, to oxygen in the air).

Oils that never dry have very few or no reactive sites; oils that dry only to a sticky state have a few reactive sites; and oils that dry completely to a soft film have sufficient reactive sites to make curing possible.

I find it helpful to picture the method of drying as Tinker Toys on a molecular scale. The sticks in the Tinker Toys represent the chemical bonds, or crosslinks, at the reac-

Here are four common oils. Mineral oil is a non-drying oil. It remains liquid forever. Walnut oil is a semi-drying oil. Linseed oil and tung oil are drying oils. They turn from a liquid to a soft solid with the introduction of oxygen.

tive sites. The more "sticks," the tighter the network and the better the drying.

The two large families of oils used in finishing are mineral oil and vegetable oil.

Mineral Oil

Mineral oil (or with an added scent, baby oil) is distilled from petroleum and has no reactive sites, or sticks. So mineral oil never dries.

A number of companies sell mineral oil labeled to make it seem more exotic. Examples include mystery oil, butcher-block oil, and sometimes "teak" oil. If an oil product sold as a wood finish stays liquid no matter how long you leave it exposed to air, then it's almost surely mineral oil.

If you apply mineral oil to wood and wipe off the excess so the surface isn't smeary, the oil that remains continues to penetrate. This may take a very long time, so what you experience over several months is the wood losing its color and looking drier until eventually it looks raw.

If you continue applying mineral oil to the wood, eventually you "fill it up" so that the surface remains in a semi-permanent oily state. The surface feels oily and smudges when you touch it.

Washing at any point along the way removes the surface oil, of course, leaving the wood drier and more colorless.

Mineral oil is ineffective as a protective or decorative finish for wood.

Vegetable Oil

Vegetable oils are pressed from plant seeds and nuts and are made up of a glycerol molecule with three fatty acids attached. This compound is called a "triglyceride," a term you're probably more familiar with in the context of blood tests and what is more or less healthy to eat.

There are many different fatty acids, each containing from zero to four reactive sites. Sometimes all three fatty acids attached to a glycerol molecule are the same, but usually they are mixed. So the best way to figure the number of reactive sites in any given triglyceride or oil is to use averages.

Oils with fatty acids containing an average of zero-to-one reactive site per fatty acid don't crosslink enough to ever dry. So these oils, which include olive, castor and coconut, are similar to mineral oil. In the context of wood finishing, they are called "non-drying" oils.

Oils with an average of one-to-two reactive sites per fatty acid dry better. But the drying takes a very long time, often never getting past the sticky state. These oils are called "semi-drying" oils. Examples include walnut, soybean (soya) and safflower oil.

Oils with fatty acids containing an average of two or more reactive sites dry fully to a soft film and are called "drying" oils. The most common examples are linseed oil (pressed from seeds of the flax plant) and tung oil

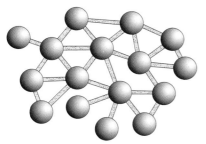

The drying of oils can be represented by Tinker Toys. Upon exposure to the oxygen in air, the molecules of oil crosslink or "hook up" to from chemical bonds (represented by the sticks). When enough of the molecules have crosslinked, the liquid oil changes to a soft solid.

(pressed from nuts of the native Chinese tung tree). Drying occurs faster when metallic driers are added.

These driers, which are often sold separately as "Japan Drier," are catalysts that speed the introduction of oxygen into the oil. (Lead was once used as a drier in wood finishes, but it isn't anymore.)

Driers are commonly added to raw linseed oil to create "boiled" linseed oil. Driers aren't added to tung oil because they can cause it to take on a frost-like appearance when dry.

A myth persists in the woodworking community that finishes with driers added are unhealthy for contact with food or children's mouths. This is not the case as long as the finish has fully dried; the rule of thumb for drying is 30 days, but the time can be reduced significantly in warmer temperatures.

The difference between linseed oil and tung oil can be explained quite easily as the difference in the number reactive sites, or sticks, on their respective fatty acids. Linseed oil has an average of about two reactive sites on each fatty acid, whereas tung oil has an average of about three.

With more reactive sites, tung oil dries significantly faster than raw linseed oil – but not as fast as boiled linseed oil with the driers added. Tung oil also dries to a tighter Tinker Toy network than either raw or boiled linseed oil, so tung oil is more water resistant.

Oil/Varnish Blend

Linseed oil (rarely tung oil because it's much more expensive) is often combined with varnish to create an oil/varnish blend. Blends of oil and varnish are very popular finishes with woodworkers.

You can easily make your own blend, of course, by mixing any varnish, including polyurethane varnish, with boiled linseed oil and/or tung oil. This is what Sam Maloof did to make his popular "Maloof finish." To make spreading easier, you can add mineral spirits (paint thinner) to thin the finish. Begin with one-third oil, one-third varnish and one-third mineral spirits, and adjust from there to your liking.

Adding a drying oil, which dries soft, to varnish, which dries hard, prevents the mixture from hardening. So oil/varnish blends have to be applied like straight oil. All the excess has to be wiped off after each application or the result will be a soft, gummy finish.

Only a miniscule build can be achieved with any of these "oils," which is the reason linseed oil, tung oil, and blends of oil and

varnish offer much less moisture resistance than do finishes that cure hard and can be built up to greater thicknesses.

But the thin build makes these finishes easy to repair. Simply apply another coat of oil. You don't need to use the same brand – or even the same type of oil. For that matter, as long as the surface is clean and totally dry, you can apply any finish over an oil finish.

Some suppliers of oil/varnish blends make pretty ridiculous claims for their products – that they make the wood harder, protect the wood from the "inside" or provide some other magical effect. In fact, these blends do nothing to wood; they simply crosslink and cure like any straight drying oil or varnish.

Make your own oil/varnish blend by mixing some boiled linseed oil and/or tung oil with varnish. A higher ratio of varnish increases scratch, water and stain resistance and raises the gloss. A higher ratio of oil slows the drying so you have more application time. Add mineral spirits to make the finish easier to spread.

Unfortunately, many finish manufacturers label varnish thinned about half with mineral spirits "oil," usually "tung oil." Varnish is about as different from oil as two finishes can be. Varnish, even when thinned, dries hard, so each coat can be left wet on the surface to create as thick a film build as you want. Oil and blends of oil and varnish have to have all their excess removed after each coat or they will dry gummy.

Commercial brands of oil/varnish blend are widely available and very popular with woodworkers because these blends are easy to apply and produce very pleasing results with little risk of problems.

Oil Finishes: Their History & Use

Here's how to cut through all the confusion about oil, tung oil and wiping varnish.

Finishing is a mystery to most woodworkers, but it's not because finishes are difficult to apply. All that's involved in applying a finish is transferring a liquid from a can to the wood using one of three very easy-to-use tools: a rag, a brush or a spray gun.

Finishing is a mystery largely because of the confusion created by manufacturers in their labeling, and there's no better example of this than the mislabeling of various "oil" finishes.

The Background

Before the growth of the consumer market in the 1960s and 1970s there was little confusion about finishes. There were fewer products available and most were bought and used by professionals who were fairly knowledgeable about them. Manufacturers helped by listing ingredients, something very few do today.

Boiled linseed oil was available, of course, and was used by many amateurs who sometimes added varnish to it to make the oil a little more durable. To make the mixture easier to apply, they thinned it with turpentine or mineral spirits so the proportions were about one-third linseed oil, one-third varnish and one-third thinner.

Linseed oil, which is pressed from the seeds of flax plants, and blends of linseed oil and varnish, are easy to apply. Wipe, brush or spray the finish onto the wood; keep the wood wet with the finish for five to 10 minutes, or until it stops soaking in; then wipe off the excess and allow the finish to cure overnight at room temperature.

The next day, sand lightly to smooth the raised grain. Then apply one or two more coats, allowing overnight for each coat to cure. Be sure to wipe off all the excess after each coat, and leave rags spread out to dry so they don't heat up and spontaneously combust.

This top group of finishing products are oil and varnish blends. They are easy to apply, but they cure soft. As a result, the necessarily thin coats don't provide much protection. This bottom group of finishing products are actually wiping varnishes. They are thinned down varnishes, and are as easy to apply as the above oil and varnish blends. However, they can be built up thicker so they offer more protection.

Although boiled linseed oil and oil/varnish blends are easy to apply, they cure soft, so they have to be left too thin on the wood to be protective or durable. The growing consumer market created a need for something better. Shellac, varnish and lacquer were, of course, available at every paint store, but these finishes don't have the mystique of oil, and they require brushing or spraying which makes them more difficult to apply than oil.

Oil/Varnish Blend

One replacement was prepackaged oil/varnish blend. This didn't add anything to what was already being used, but manufacturers made consumers think it did by labeling their products with enigmatic names like Danish oil (made by squeezing Danes?), antique oil (just for antiques?) and Velvit oil.

Then they attached misleading marketing phrases to the product such as "contains resin," "protects the wood from the inside" or "makes the wood 25 percent harder" to make consumers think they were buying something more than simply a repackaged oil/varnish blend.

Tung Oil

A second replacement was a product labeled "tung oil." This oil, which is pressed from the nuts of a tung tree, was introduced to the West from China around 1900. It was useful for making superior, water-resistant varnishes, especially for outdoor use.

But tung oil is too difficult for most people to use by itself as a finish. You apply tung oil just like linseed oil or oil/varnish blend, but you have to sand tung oil after every coat, not just after the first, and it takes five to seven coats, allowing two to three days drying time between each, to achieve a smooth, attractive sheen.

Tung oil comes from China, however, so it has a certain mystique. Because few people really knew what tung oil was anyway, many manufacturers began packaging varnish thinned about half with paint thinner and labeling it "tung oil," "tung oil finish," or "tung oil varnish." Others further muddied the waters by calling their thinned varnish Val-Oil, Waterlox, Seal-a-Cell, ProFin or Salad Bowl Finish.

Thinned varnish (more appropriately called "wiping varnish") can be applied just like boiled linseed oil or oil/varnish blend, or it can be applied with a brush like regular varnish. It makes an excellent finish because it looks good after only two or three coats, cures much more rapidly than oil or oil/varnish blend, and can be built up to a thicker, more protective film because it cures hard.

Wiping varnish is an improvement in protection and durability over boiled linseed oil and oil/varnish blend, but the only thing new about it is the misleading name on the can. Anyone can make their own wiping varnish by thinning any oil-base alkyd or polyurethane varnish enough so it is easy to wipe on the wood.

The Difference Between Oil & Varnish

To help understand the differences in these products, you need to know the difference between oil and varnish.

Oil is a natural product. Some oils, such as linseed oil and tung oil, turn from a liquid to a solid when exposed to oxygen, so they make effective finishes. But these oils cure slowly to a soft, wrinkled film if they are applied thick, and this makes it necessary

for you to remove all the excess after each coat. You can't build oil finishes to a thicker, more protective coating.

Varnish is a synthetic product made by cooking a drying oil, such as linseed oil, tung oil or modified soybean (soya) oil, with a resin, the modern synthetic versions being polyurethane, alkyd and phenolic. Varnish cures relatively rapidly to a hard, smooth film if it is applied thick, so you can leave the excess if you want to achieve a more protective coating.

Varnish is as different from oil as bread is from yeast (an ingredient in bread). It makes no more sense to call a varnish "oil" than it would to call bread "yeast," and manufacturers do everyone a great disservice by doing so.

How to Tell Which You Have

Because you can't trust the labeling, you have to know how to determine the difference between these products yourself.

Linseed oil is always labeled linseed oil, so far as I know. There are two types: raw and boiled. Raw linseed oil takes weeks to

cure. Boiled linseed oil has driers added to make it cure in about a day with the excess removed. I know of no interior use for raw linseed oil.

Real tung oil is labeled 100 percent tung oil and has a very distinct odor that clearly separates it from wiping varnish and oil/varnish blends, both of which have a varnish-like smell. Only if you are willing to go through the extra work for the increased water resistance in a non-building finish should you use real tung oil.

Linseed oil and tung oil are always sold full strength, so if "petroleum distillate," "mineral spirits" or "aliphatic hydrocarbons" is listed as an ingredient, this is a clue that the finish is either wiping varnish or oil/varnish blend. To tell the difference between these two you'll have to pour some of the finish onto a non-porous surface, such as the top of the can or glass, and let the finish cure for a couple days at room temperature. If it cures fairly hard and smooth, it is wiping varnish. If it wrinkles badly and is soft, it is a blend of oil and varnish.

Both of these brands are labeled "tung oil," but they are clearly very different. Old Masters is really tung oil. It cures soft and wrinkled, so it can't be built up on wood for better protection. McCloskey is thinned "wiping" varnish. It does cure hard, so it can be built up to provide excellent protection.

Both of these finishes are represented on the can as "oil," but the overspill on the tops tells a different story. ProFin on the left is clearly a wiping varnish. Bush Oil on the right is an oil/varnish blend because it dries soft and wrinkled and it isn't labeled "linseed oil" or "tung oil."

How to Apply Oil

It's simple: Wipe, wait, sand, repeat.

Oil is the easiest of all finishes to apply with good results. Simply wipe or brush the oil onto the wood (or pour on the oil and spread it around), let the oil soak in for a few minutes, then wipe off all the excess before it dries.

This direction applies to all types of oil and all blends of oil and varnish. The only thing you can do wrong is not wipe off the excess. (If a little oil "bleeds" back out of the pores after you have wiped off the excess, continue wiping every 30 minutes or so until the bleeding stops.)

If you are using a non-drying oil such as mineral oil, there is no need to apply multiple coats except after several weeks or months, or whenever the surface begins to appear dry.

If you are using a semi-drying oil (such as walnut oil), a drying oil (such as boiled linseed oil or tung oil), or a blend of oil and varnish, the best procedure is to allow each coat to dry before applying the next. Each additional coat then adds a tiny bit of build to what is already there, which improves the moisture protection to the wood. The second and sometimes third coats also improve the sheen (that is, shine) to make the wood look better.

Unfortunately, some of the most popular brands of oil/varnish blends instruct to apply the second coat 45 minutes after the first. The second coat then merely mixes with the first because it hasn't had time to dry. There's no improvement in protection or sheen.

As a general rule, you should allow each coat to dry overnight in a warm room before applying the next. But with tung oil, it's best to wait several days between coats because it takes longer to dry.

Walnut oil, raw linseed oil and some proprietary brands, such as Tried & True (based on raw linseed oil with no driers added), take a very long time to dry, sometimes weeks, so they have questionable use as wood finishes. They owe their survival as wood finishes primarily to the continued existence of the "food-safe" myth—that is, that oils with driers

1 Sand the wood to remove mill marks and other flaws. Sand with a grit sandpaper (usually #80, #100, or #120 grit) that removes the problem efficiently without creating unnecessarily deep scratches. Then sand up through the grits to #180 or #220 grit, removing the scratches created by each previous grit.

2 Apply a wet coat of any oil or oil/varnish blend to the wood with a cloth or brush. Allow the finish to penetrate a few minutes and apply more oil to any spots that dry due to penetration. Then wipe off the excess finish. (No benefit is gained by heating the oil first or rubbing it "into" the wood; the oil penetrates all that it can on its own.)

3 For subsequent coats, wait until the previous coat has dried, then sand with very fine sandpaper (#400 or #600) just enough so the surface feels smooth. Follow by applying another coat like the first and wipe off the excess.

You can also apply a wet coat of finish first, then sand the surface lightly while it is still wet, as I'm doing here. The oil serves as a lubricant for the sandpaper, creating a slightly "softer" sheen and smoother feel. The sanding dust isn't a problem because you're wiping off all the excess. (Using very fine sandpaper to sand between or within coats produces the same ultra-smooth results as pre-sanding the wood to #600 grit, but with much less work.)

Apply additional coats after each previous coat has dried until you don't notice any improvement. Usually two to four coats are all that are necessary, but you can apply as many coats as you like. To reduce scratches to the surface, you can apply paste wax after the finish has dried.

added to them are unsafe to eat off of.

The drying of all oils (all finishes for that matter) can be accelerated by raising the temperature. You can do this by turning up the heat, putting the object under a heat lamp or, if the object is small, putting it in an oven set on low for a short time.

CAUTION: With any drying oil, or blend of drying oil and varnish, hang the rags you use or drape them over the edge of a trash-can or table to harden. Drying oils have the potential to spontaneously combust if rags are piled up so the heat that is created in the drying can't dissipate.

The Basics of Wiping Varnish

Its durability and ease of use make searching out this hard-to-identify finish worth it.

All of these finishes are wiping varnish. If you shop at a home center or paint store, you will find the brands on the left. If you shop at a woodworking store or from a woodworking catalog, you will find the brands on the right. All of these finishes are essentially the same. They are varnish thinned enough with mineral spirits so they are easy to wipe on the wood.

O f all finishes available, none offers as much protection and durability with as little difficulty in application as wiping varnish.

With wiping varnish, you can achieve a run-free, brush-mark-free, air-bubble-free, and almost dust-free finish, which after several coats is very protective against moisture penetration, and resistant to scratches, heat and solvents. And you can do this with no more effort than wiping or brushing on the finish, and either leaving it, or wiping off some or all of the excess.

No other finish offers all of these great qualities. The only finish that competes is gel varnish, but it's messy to apply, not as water resistant, and it can't be built up as fast on the wood without leaving brush marks. Wiping varnish is arguably the single best finish for most amateur woodworking projects.

What is Wiping Varnish?

Wiping varnish is simply common oil-based varnish (any type, including alkyd varnish, polyurethane varnish or spar varnish) that is thinned enough with mineral spirits (paint thinner) so it is easy to wipe on wood. You can easily make your own.

The name, which I coined in 1990, and which has been adopted by most writers and teachers of wood finishing, makes sense because the purpose of thinning is to make the varnish easy to wipe.

You may already be using wiping varnish and not realize it because it isn't sold under that name (maybe because that would give away the simplicity of the finish). It's sold under many different brand names, and few indicate what the finish really is.

This is the problem with wiping varnish and the reason it isn't widely recognized as one of the best finishes for anyone not using a spray gun. Manufacturers obscure the true nature of the finish by their misleading, and sometimes outright deceptive, product labeling. They want you to think they are selling you something different and special.

What is Varnish?

Varnish is a very common finish that is appreciated for its terrific moisture, scratch, heat and solvent resistance. No matter how new you are to woodworking, you have probably used some type of varnish or oil-based paint, which is varnish with pigment added.

One way to identify varnish is by the thinner and clean-up solvent listed on the container. This is mineral spirits, which is usually identified by its more all-inclusive name, "petroleum distillate," though Minwax and General Finishes use the more obscure technical term, "aliphatic hydrocarbon." The only other finishes that thin and clean up with mineral spirits are oil, blends of oil and varnish, and wax. None of these finishes cure hard, so they can't be built up thick on the wood like varnish can.

All types of varnish are made by cooking an oil with a resin. (This is done in controlled

To tell if a finish that thins with mineral spirits and is sold as oil or labeled with some uninformative name is wiping varnish, put a puddle on top of the can and let it cure. If it cures hard and smooth within a day or two, it is wiping varnish. If it takes a lot longer and finally cures soft and wrinkled, it is oil or a mixture of oil and varnish.

Each of these finishes is a type of varnish. You can thin any one of them with mineral spirits to make a wiping varnish. The wiping varnish will have the characteristics of the varnish you use.

conditions; you shouldn't try it yourself because of the fire hazard.) The oil, which is usually linseed oil, tung oil or modified soybean (soya) oil, makes it possible for the finish to cure in contact with the oxygen in air. The resin, which is usually alkyd or polyurethane, provides the hardness in the finish.

The most popular type of clear varnish is polyurethane vanish. It is the most protective and durable of the varnishes. That is, it is the most resistant to moisture penetration, and it is the most resistant to being damaged itself by coarse objects, heat or solvents.

Spar or "marine" varnish is also widely available. Its unique quality is increased flexibility created in the manufacturing process by including a higher ratio of oil to resin. Spar varnishes are meant to withstand the greater shrinkage and swelling of wood placed outdoors. Sometimes this varnish contains UV absorbers to resist damage from sunlight.

If the varnish is not labeled "polyurethane" or "spar," it is probably alkyd varnish. Alkyd is the workhorse of the varnish resins. Almost all varnishes contain some alkyd, including polyurethane varnish. Oil paints are almost always made with alkyd resin and are often called "alkyd paint."

These are the common types of varnish on the market. You can thin any of them with as much mineral spirits as you want. The more mineral spirits you add, the less "solids" the varnish contains and the thinner each layer of finish will be on the wood. (In some parts of the country it is illegal to thin varnish because of VOC laws, and some brands of varnish reflect this by telling you not to thin their varnish; but you can't harm any varnish by thinning it.)

No finish is perfect in every way, and varnish is no exception. Varnish has two critical flaws: It cures slowly and it has a fairly thick or viscous consistency.

The slow curing gives dust a lot of time to settle and become stuck, and runs and sags have a lot of time to develop on vertical surfaces.

The thickness is responsible for brush marks and bubbles curing in the finish because it doesn't flatten out well and bubbles don't pop out easily.

As a result, varnish is actually the most difficult of all finishes to apply with near-perfect results. But there is a way around the problem: Thin the varnish so it cures faster (the thinner film combines faster with oxygen in the air), levels better and releases bubbles easier.

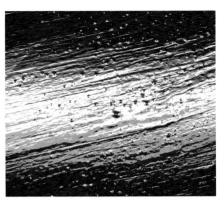

Full-strength varnish is a difficult finish to apply with near-perfect results because it cures slowly and is relatively viscous. The slow curing creates time for dust to settle and become embedded, and for runs to develop. The thickness makes brush marks likely and increases the possibility of bubbles curing in the finish.

The product made by thinning varnish is "wiping varnish."

History of Wiping Varnish

Wiping varnish has been very popular with amateur woodworkers and refinishers for at least 35 years, but few have actually known that it was wiping varnish they were using. The finish was made popular in the late 1960s and early 1970s by Homer Formby. He traveled the country doing demonstrations of his new miracle finish, "Tung Oil," at shopping malls and antique clubs, and he made a number of infomercials that were broadcast on television.

Few people were familiar with tung oil, which has its origins in China, so the exoticness of the name and source made the finish seem special. Formby was a master salesman.

But he wasn't selling tung oil. He was selling thinned varnish that he labeled "Tung Oil Finish." This finish is still available and the oil used to make the varnish isn't even tung oil. It's modified soybean oil.

It's important to note that even if this finish were made with tung oil – that is, tung oil cooked with a resin to make varnish – it still wouldn't be "tung oil." It would simply be varnish made with tung oil instead of some other oil.

Formby made contact with a very large number of people, however, and his mislabeled wiping varnish was a very good finish. So he won a big following and created a market for finishes labeled "tung oil." Soon other manufacturers joined in with their own "tung oils." Some made their varnish

like Formby did – by cooking alkyd resin with modified soybean oil. Others cooked real tung oil with one of the resins.

Some misunderstood what was happening and actually sold real tung oil in its raw state and this really created problems. Incorrectly labeled or not, thinned varnish is an excellent finish because it cures hard. Tung oil doesn't cure hard, so it can't be built up on the wood without being sticky and gummy.

Moreover, unlike boiled linseed oil, which will produce an evenly attractive satin sheen after just two or three coats, tung oil requires five or more coats to produce an equivalent satin sheen. And each coat requires several days to cure and then has to be sanded smooth before the next is applied. Tung oil is a difficult finish to apply effectively, and many people who have tried it have been very dissatisfied.

Despite the difficulties with real tung oil, the market for a thinned varnish finish had been established. So as time passed, other manufacturers marketed their own versions of wiping varnish. Unfortunately, many of the manufacturers further confused the marketplace by labeling their finishes with non-informative names such as Waterlox, Seal-a-Cell, Salad Bowl Finish, Val-Oil, ProFin and more.

The result is that no one using one of these brands now knows what finish they are using if they do no more than read the label. But all of these brands, being wiping varnish, are easy to use, and they produce excellent results.

Does It Get Hard?

With all the confused labeling from manufacturers, how can you tell if a product is wiping varnish or some mixture of varnish and oil – an oil/varnish blend? It's simple. If the finish meets these three criteria, it's wiping varnish:

❯ It thins and cleans up with paint thinner. ("Mineral spirits," "petroleum distillate" or "aromatic hydrocarbon" will be listed on the container.)

❯ A puddle on top of the can, or on any non-porous surface such as glass, gets hard within a day or two.

❯ It is watery thin. (Full-strength varnish and polyurethane meet the first two criteria, but they are relatively thick, like syrup. They are also labeled "varnish" or "polyurethane," and wiping varnish is not.)

Curing hard is the critical characteristic because it makes it possible to leave each coat of wiping varnish wet on the surface – as wet and thick as you want as long as the finish doesn't puddle or run. You can build coats one on top of another to achieve an even thicker coating for better protection of the wood against moisture.

Confusion is caused because wiping varnish is often sold or marketed as "oil," and it is sometimes included in the same category as oil in books and magazine articles. But neither oil nor blends of oil and varnish cure hard unless you leave them for many months or years, and then only if they are applied very thin. So all the excess oil or oil/varnish blend has to be wiped off after each application or you will end up with a sticky, gummy mess. Oil and oil/varnish blend are about as different from wiping varnish as any finish can be.

Some years ago, I saw a woodworking magazine article that compared a large number of "wipe-on" finishes for characteristics such as viscosity, dry time, penetration and solids content (ratio of finish to thinner). Some of the finishes in the comparison were wiping varnishes. Others were oil/varnish blends.

The article was virtually useless as an aid to choosing a finish because the characteristic that matters most, "Does it cure hard?" wasn't included. You will never make sense of "wipe-on" finishes and overcome the confusion caused by misleading labeling until you understand this distinction.

If a finish thins with mineral spirits, cures hard, and is watery thin, it is wiping varnish. If a finish thins with mineral spirits, is in liquid form (it isn't wax), and cures soft, it is oil or a mixture of oil and varnish. There aren't any other possibilities for a finish that thins with mineral spirits.

Make Your Own

You don't, of course, have to buy pre-packaged wiping varnish. You can easily make your own. If you do, you can choose which type of varnish to use, polyurethane, spar, or alkyd, and you can also choose between gloss and satin.

After choosing a varnish, turn it into a wiping varnish by thinning it with mineral spirits. (You can also use turpentine, but there is no advantage, and turpentine is more expensive and has a more pungent odor.)

To recreate a commercial wiping varnish, thin the varnish 50/50 with mineral spirits. To get a faster build, thin the varnish less. The less you thin the varnish, however, the more you increase the possibility of brush

To make your own wiping varnish, add mineral spirits to any varnish. The more thinner you add, the better the finish will level and the less dust it will collect. But the thickness of each coat will be less. Begin by thinning with one part mineral spirits to two or three parts varnish, and adjust from there to your satisfaction.

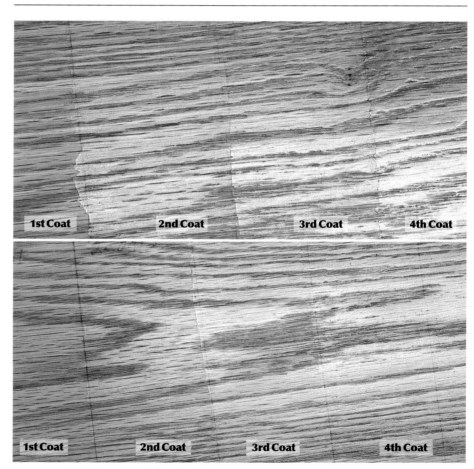

You can see the differences in the build of four coats of varnish thinned with 25 percent mineral spirits (top) and 75 percent mineral spirits (bottom). Each coat was brushed on and not wiped off. The lower the percentage of mineral spirits the greater the build of each coat, but the more likely you are to get brush marks and dust nibs.

marks and bubbles curing in the finish. You also increase the amount of dust that can stick to the finish because a thicker film (after the thinner evaporates) takes longer to cure.

I suggest you begin with one part thinner to two or three parts varnish and see how it feels to you. You can always adjust the ratio as you are applying the finish.

Applying Wiping Varnish

Practice makes perfect.

The advantage of grouping all thinned varnishes as a category of finish, called "wiping varnish," (similar to other categories such as shellac, lacquer and water-based finish) is that it allows us to discuss uniform application procedures that apply to every brand.

So here are step-by-step instructions using scrap wood and homemade wiping varnish. If you would like to follow along, you will need the following supplies, most of which are available at a home center.

> A quart of gloss, oil-based polyurethane varnish (approximately $8).

> A quart of mineral spirits, also known as paint thinner (approximately $5).

> A clean, wide-mouth glass jar with a lid (from your kitchen).

> Latex or other type of protective gloves (approximately $2 for 10 pair).

> Lint-free rags such as old, clean T-shirts, cheesecloth or Scott Rags, which are paper rags in a box or on a roll (approximately $2 for the roll).

> A sheet of #400-grit sandpaper (approximately $4 for a packet of three).

> A 2' x 2' or larger, sheet of ½" or ¾"

Above is everything you need to make and apply wiping varnish, which is simply alkyd or polyurethane varnish thinned about in half with mineral spirits. By first practicing on scrap, you'll feel more comfortable when you tackle the real project.

veneered plywood or MDF. Any hardwood veneer is OK (from your scraps, a wood supplier or one of many cabinet shops that often throw away pieces this size).

> A brown paper bag (from the supermarket).

The procedure is detailed in the following pictures.

1 *To made your own wiping varnish for this exercise, pour approximately equal amounts of oil-based polyurethane and mineral spirits into a wide-mouth jar.*

2 *Be sure to stir the thinned polyurethane or the two parts will remain separated.*

3 Before applying the finish, sand the surface of the panel to #150 or #180 grit with the grain. (If you use a random-orbit sander, finish off by sanding in the direction of the grain with #180 grit to remove the sander swirls. Back the sandpaper with a flat sanding block.) Remove the dust with a vacuum if possible so you don't brush the dust into the air. You can also use a tack rag, but you will load it up pretty quickly. Then pour some of the wiping varnish onto the wood and wipe it all over the surface with one of the types of rags. You could also brush on the wiping varnish, but pouring and spreading is much faster.

4 After thoroughly wetting the surface, wipe off all the excess wiping varnish with a dry rag. (I seldom use cheesecloth, and I often use the Scott Rags. Here I'm using an old, clean T-shirt.) There's no need to scrub dry; simply wipe to remove the wetness. Let this first coat dry for four to six hours or overnight.

5 Sand the surface lightly using #400-grit sandpaper until the finish feels smooth. It shouldn't take much, usually not more than one or two passes everywhere. There's no reason to use a flat block to back the sandpaper. For the most efficient use of the sandpaper, tear off a third of a sheet crossways, and fold it into thirds lengthways. This gives you three faces for easy handling.

6 Remove the sanding dust with a vacuum or a tack rag. Finish by wiping over the surface with your hand. You'll feel if any dust remains and your hand will pick it up. You can wipe your hand on your pants to clean it.

7 For the second coat, we'll leave a little more finish on the surface, though you could apply all coats in the manner of the first. The downside of the first method is that the build will be slow, but each coat will be almost perfect. Instead of using a brush for the second coat, fold one of the rags to create a flat side. Here I'm using a Scott Rag.

8 Just as with the first coat, pour some of the wiping varnish onto the surface and wipe it around with the folded cloth.

9 With the surface wet, begin wiping in the direction of the wood grain to get an even thickness that is slightly more than damp but not as wet as when brushing. If you have poured too much finish onto the surface, remove some with a dry cloth and continue spreading with the folded cloth. Move your head to catch a reflected light on the surface to see what's happening so you can correct problems. This is critical for achieving good results. Let this coat dry for four to six hours or overnight (the finish dries faster in warmer conditions). Clearly, each coat has to be kept very thin on vertical surfaces to avoid runs and sags.

10 When the finish is dry, sand the surface lightly with #400-grit sandpaper to remove dust nibs and other problems. (There are always dust nibs when you apply the finish damp or wet.) Sand just enough so the surface feels smooth.

11 If anything should go wrong during application – for example, using a dirty cloth that leaves lots of dust in the finish – you can remove the uncured finish for quite some time by wiping over with a cloth wet with mineral spirits. You won't remove or damage the coat underneath.

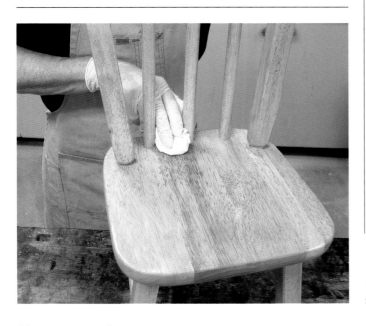

12 You can apply as many coats as you want, until you get the look you want. You can experiment with how much finish you leave on the surface with each coat. Once you have built a noticeable thickness, the finish will be glossy. If you would rather have a satin sheen, dull the surface with #0000 steel wool and apply a last coat or two using gel varnish (also sold as neutral-gel stain) in the same manner as the first coat of wiping varnish. Wipe off all the excess. No matter how clean you get the air in your shop there will always be some dust nibs. An easy way to remove them without changing the sheen is to rub lightly using a folded brown paper bag. Wait to do this until the finish has cured enough so you no longer smell the paint thinner with your nose pressed against the surface. You'll be amazed at how effective this is.

13 On three-dimensional surfaces, you have to remove all the finish, similar to the way the first coat was applied, to avoid rag tracks (like tiny brush marks) drying in the finish. Here I'm wiping off excess finish between the spindles on this child's chair.

Gel Varnish

The (almost) perfect compromise.

Most woodworkers do their finishing with one of two wipe-on/wipe-off finishes: oil/varnish blend or wiping varnish.

Oil/varnish blend is a thinned mixture of boiled linseed oil or tung oil with alkyd or polyurethane varnish. You can buy it commercially (often labeled "Danish oil") or you can make your own—for example, one part oil, one part varnish and one part mineral spirits.

Wiping varnish is alkyd or polyurethane varnish thinned a quarter to a half with mineral spirits to make the finish easy to wipe on and off the wood. You can buy it commercially (rarely labeled for what it is) or you can make your own by thinning any varnish or polyurethane.

Both finishes are easy to apply and produce near-perfect results. But they differ significantly in sheen and water resistance.

Oil/varnish blend produces a pleasing satin or "rubbed" sheen, but the finish is too thin to be water-resistant. This is because all coats have to be thoroughly wiped off or the finish dries tacky.

Wiping varnish can be left in thicker applications because it dries hard. So it can be built up enough to produce excellent water resistance. But wiping varnish produces a gloss sheen many woodworkers find objectionable. (Of course, you could always rub the final coat with fine steel wool or other abra-

Gel varnish is thick in the can, but it spreads easily because of its thixotropic quality.

sive to lower the sheen, but doing this adds a complication most woodworkers would rather avoid.)

Gel varnish, which is also available as gel polyurethane, can be thought of as a compromise. It produces an attractive satin sheen similar to an oil/varnish blend but with better water resistance, and it is almost as easy to apply. It also has a very low odor, which makes it especially user-friendly for home workshops.

If you've ever applied a gel stain, you're familiar with gel varnish. It's exactly the same, just without the pigment colorant.

Gel varnish has been around for decades,

but it gets much less attention than the other two finishes and it is often difficult to find. It is sometimes labeled "natural" gel stain when the manufacturer intends it for thinning or reducing the color intensity of its colored gel stains. But it is the same as a gel varnish.

What is Gel Varnish?

Manufacturers change the consistency of liquid alkyd or polyurethane varnish to that of a gel by incorporating a thixotropic additive. You are quite familiar with products that have been made thixotropic. They include ketchup, mayonnaise, many facial creams and salves, and latex wall paint.

All these substances appear thick in their containers. Once on the bread, face or wall, however, they spread easily. This is because thixotropic substances have the added characteristic of responding easily to a shearing force, such as brushing, wiping or spreading. When the shearing stops, the substance returns quickly to its thickened state.

A good example is latex wall paint. The paint appears thick in the can but stirs and pours easily. It also spreads easily under a roller. But as soon as the roller is past any given point on the wall, the paint thickens so that the protruding nibs created by the nap hold their shape and don't run down the wall.

Here are four brands of gel varnish. Notice that some are polyurethane varnish rather than alkyd varnish and some are packaged in squat cans that make it easier to get to finish near the bottom with a cloth.

Gel varnish is the same. It appears thick in the can, but it spreads easily. It also retains the ridges left by a brush or cloth, so almost all the excess has to be wiped off after each application.

The thixotropic additive in gel varnishes gives them a satin sheen.

Just as with all varnishes, gel varnishes can be applied over any stain as long as it is dry.

Applying Gel Varnish

Gel varnish applies almost exactly like oil/varnish blend. Wipe or brush the finish onto the wood and wipe off the excess before the finish dries.

There are two minor exceptions. Because gel varnish doesn't soak into the wood like oil/varnish blend, there's no reason to continue wetting the surface until the soaking-in stops. In other words, there's no benefit to leaving the finish wet on the surface for any length of time. You can wipe off immediately.

Also, gel varnish dries much faster than oil/varnish blend. So on large surfaces you have to move rapidly. You may even have to divide the object into sections and finish each before moving on, or get a second person to wipe off while you apply. (Bartley's brand dries noticeably faster than the others I've tried.)

You'll learn the drying characteristics of the gel varnish you're using very quickly. But if some dries too hard to wipe off while you're learning, simply remove it within a short time by wiping with a rag soaked with mineral spirits then adjust your application method when reapplying the finish.

Just as with any finish, it's important to sand the surface smooth after the first coat (the sealer coat) and after each additional coat unless the surface feels perfectly smooth – that is, no dust nibs. Unless you have an unusually rough surface, use #320- or #400-grit stearated sandpaper. The most widely available brands are Norton 3X and 3M Sandblaster.

Gel varnish is almost the perfect compromise between oil/varnish blend and wiping varnish, but not quite. Though a pleasing satin sheen can be achieved in three or four coats, it takes a great many coats to produce a completely water-resistant film. Even though you can usually apply two, and maybe even three, coats in a day because of the rapid drying (more rapid in warmer temperatures), getting this degree of protection can still take many days and be a lot of work.

To apply a gel varnish, simply wipe it on the wood like you would an oil/varnish blend. You can use a brush to help get the thickened varnish into recesses and inside corners, but wiping is much faster on level surfaces. You can wipe in any direction.

Use a cloth to remove the excess gel varnish before it begins to harden, which it does much faster than liquid varnish. To aid in getting the varnish out of recesses and inside corners, use a dry brush as I'm doing here.

So to speed the goal of good water resistance on a critical surface such as a tabletop, apply several coats of wiping varnish and leave most or all the excess of each to build a thickness. Then follow with one or two coats of gel varnish to get a satin sheen.

Be sure to sand between coats of wiping varnish to remove dust nibs, and rub the last coat before applying the gel varnish with #000 or #0000 steel wool to dull the finish in the pores and other recesses. You can also sand this coat. But the sandpaper won't get in the pores to dull them, so some gloss may show through.

The most difficult surfaces to coat with gel varnish are those with three-dimensional recesses such as carvings, turnings and mouldings because of the difficulty getting the finish into and the excess out of the hollows. If you are struggling with a cloth, switch to a brush. To remove excess, use the brush dry. A cheap throwaway "chip" brush works well.

Just as with oil/varnish blend, gel varnish is very easy to repair if it gets scratched or damaged. Simply clean the surface, sand out any roughness, and apply another coat. You can use any brand.

In contrast to the gloss sheen of wiping varnish (applied on the left half of this panel), gel varnish (right half) produces a satin sheen. This is due to the thixotropic additive, which also gives the varnish its thickness and easy spreadability.

Wax Finishes & Polishes

Although a poor finish when used alone, wax excels as a polish.

Wax has been used for centuries as a finish and polish on furniture and other wooden objects, but it is still a very misunderstood material.

Wax is derived from all three classes of natural materials – animal, vegetable and mineral – and some waxes are made synthetically. The practical difference in these waxes is hardness, which corresponds to their melting points: the higher the melting point, the harder the wax. For example, carnauba (pronounced "car-NOO-ba") wax has a higher melting point (about 180 F) and is harder than beeswax (150 F), which has a higher melting point and is harder than paraffin wax (130 F).

As it turns out, a melting point of about 150 F is best for wax applied to wood or used as a polish. Higher melting-point waxes are too hard to buff out; lower melting-point waxes smudge too easily. So manufacturers using a hard wax such as carnauba commonly blend it with a softer wax such as paraffin.

Because of this blending, all the liquid- or paste-wax products sold for application as wood finishes or polishes develop about the same hardness as beeswax when the solvent evaporates. The differences in these products are in color (if some is added) and in the evaporation rate of the included solvents – petroleum-distillates such as mineral spirits, and turpenes such as turpentine and citrus. The faster the evaporation rate the sooner the wax is ready to buff off.

To get a paste wax with hardness characteristics not available commercially, you could make your own by dissolving any wax or waxes in mineral spirits or turpentine (and adding a colorant if you like). Heating the wax and solvent in a double boiler, so as not to cause a fire, will speed the dissolving.

Wax as a Finish

Until modern times, woodworkers were limited in the choices they had for a finish

Wax is a time-honored polish for wooden furniture, but after centuries of use, it is still a widely misunderstood material.

because of availability; as wax was widely available, it was often used.

But wax isn't a good finish because it's too soft to be built up enough to protect against water. A drop left on a wax finish for even a few seconds penetrates the wax, raises the grain of the wood and causes the spot to turn white, which can be difficult to repair. You'll have to abrade off the damage with sandpaper or steel wool, best with the aid of a mineral-spirits or naphtha lubricant.

(Don't confuse water repellency with water resistance. Water beads on a waxed surface because of surface-tension differences. Beading doesn't mean the water isn't penetrating into the wood below.)

Wax's weak water resistance doesn't prevent it from being a good finish choice for decorative objects – such as carvings and turnings – that won't be handled much. In fact, uncolored wax is the only finish that leaves wood looking entirely natural; the wax just adds shine. For turnings, solid wax sticks are available that make the wax easy to apply while the wood is spinning on the lathe.

It's often suggested that you can improve water resistance by applying a coat of shellac or another finish under the wax. Of course you can do this, and of course it makes for a more protective finish. But it's inaccurate to label this a wax finish. It's the other finish with a wax polish applied on top!

You can use colored rather than clear wax when there are nicks, scratches or recesses you want to color. For example, the gap in this wedged through-tenon would show up white if clear wax were applied.

To avoid a smeary appearance on a waxed surface, change often to clean cloths or lamb's wool pads when you buff. Not doing so will result in your just moving the excess wax around rather than removing it.

Buffing off the excess wax is hard work. It's always good to have help.

Wax as a Polish

Though wax is not very functional as a finish, it is excellent as a polish over another finish. Unlike liquid furniture polishes, wax provides long-lasting shine and scratch resistance without smear (as long as the excess is buffed off). In addition, if the wax includes a colorant, the product can be used to fairly permanently color in nicks and scratches so they become less noticeable.

Because it's the finish underneath that provides protection for the wood, wax's weak water resistance is not a factor. You won't get a white water mark unless that finish has deteriorated. If that's the case, waxing the finish won't help much.

To maintain a wax polish, apply more wax when you can no longer buff up a shine in the existing wax. On tabletops in constant use, this might be as often as every couple months, but on other objects, it might be as seldom as once every year or two.

You don't need to worry about wax buildup. The solvents in each new coat of liquid or paste wax dissolve the existing wax, making one new mixture; wax can't build unless you just don't buff off the excess after each application. Wax doesn't build in layers; it builds because you leave it thick.

Just as the solvents in a new coat of wax dissolve the existing wax, the solvents in liquid furniture polishes also dissolve wax. So it's best to dust a waxed surface with a damp cloth or chamois rather than with furniture polish so you don't remove the wax.

Applying Wax

Wax is very easy to apply – the effort comes in buffing off the excess.

To apply wax, put a lump of paste wax on a cloth, wrap the cloth around the wax, then move the cloth over the surface in any direction pressing just hard enough so the wax seeps through the cloth and coats the surface. The idea is to cover the surface entirely but deposit as little wax as possible, so removal will be easier.

Alternative application methods include dampening the cloth with water, brushing the wax into recesses and applying the wax with #0000 steel wool. Using steel wool combines the application step with that of dulling the finish surface, so use steel wool only when your intention is to abrade the surface.

To remove the excess wax, rub with a soft, clean cloth just after the wax has dulled because of solvent evaporation. At this point the wax should offer a slight resistance to your cloth. If there's no resistance, you've wiped too soon and you may be removing all of the wax, or you've waited too long and the wax has hardened too much.

On non-flat surfaces such as carvings, use a shoe brush for buffing. At any point if you have problems, you can apply more wax to resoften the existing wax, or you can remove all the wax by wiping with paint thinner or naphtha, then start over.

The biggest problem in wax removal is smearing, which is caused by continuing to buff with a cloth or lamb's wool pad (on an electric buffer) that is already loaded with wax. Instead of transferring wax from the surface to the cloth, you're just moving the wax around. To eliminate smearing, change often to a clean cloth or lamb's wool pad.

Of course, you can leave a smear intentionally if you want. This is commonly done by antique dealers, and the smeared-wax look has become popular. Just be aware when using a colored wax that the color has the potential of rubbing off on clothes.

For non-flat surfaces or any surfaces with recesses that are difficult to get into, use a paint brush to apply the wax and a shoe brush to buff it.

4

Film-building Finishes

Shellac & Sealing Wood

Overpromotion has made finishing unnecessarily complicated.

Shellac is available in orange (amber) and blonde (clear) colors. Orange shellac, whether already dissolved in a can or in flakes for you to dissolve, still contains its natural wax. Blonde is usually available either with wax (Bulls Eye Shellac) or without wax (Bulls Eye SealCoat) in its already dissolved form, and is always dewaxed in flake form.

Shellac was once the most widely used wood finish in the world. Now it's commonly promoted in woodworking magazines as a sealer, often as the "best" or "universal" sealer, even though virtually no cabinet shop or furniture factory, and very few professional woodworkers, use it in this way.

How did this happen? How was shellac transformed, actually diminished, from being the most popular topcoat finish to becoming just a "sealer," the first coat? And why is it that shellac is represented so positively as a sealer in amateur woodworking circles when virtually no large users of finishes think of it this way?

A Little History

From the 1820s until the 1920s almost all furniture made in the United States (and in Europe) was finished with shellac. It was then replaced by nitrocellulose lacquer in factories because lacquer was cheaper and its drying can be controlled better with lacquer thinner, a very versatile solvent.

But shellac continued to be used extensively by painters finishing woodwork and floors and by amateur woodworkers until the 1960s and '70s. If you are old enough, you surely used shellac as a finish in shop class in high school.

Four things happened in the 1960s and '70s that transformed shellac from a finish to a sealer.

> Polyurethane was introduced as a very durable "no wax" floor finish, and many people decided they wanted that durability on their woodwork, cabinets and furniture also.

> Homer Formby achieved success selling his thinned varnish (Formby's Tung Oil Finish), which he labeled and misrepresented as tung oil, to amateur woodworkers.

> Woodworking magazines began promoting Watco Danish Oil, an oil/varnish blend, as an easy-to-apply wood finish for woodworkers.

> Zinsser "Bulls Eye," the largest (now almost a monopoly) supplier of shellac, didn't defend the finish for its quite adequate water-resistant qualities. Instead, the company, which specializes in sealers and primers, reduced the finish to a sealer in its marketing – even enlisting several prominent woodworking writers to help promote it in this way.

Sanding sealers, which powder when sanded as shown above, are available for varnish and lacquer because these finishes gum up sandpaper when sanded.

All types of shellac tend to gum up sandpaper when sanded, especially if the shellac hasn't fully hardened. So there's no reason to use shellac as a sealer if your goal is easy sanding.

So shellac was replaced as a finish in the amateur woodworking community by polyurethane, various brands of thinned varnish ("wiping varnish") and various brands of oil/varnish blend, all quite legitimate finishes in their own rights. Shellac became a sealer in the minds of most woodworkers.

What is a Sealer?

The first coat of any finish you apply to wood stops up the pores so the next coat doesn't penetrate. It just bonds to the first coat. So this first coat is logically called the "sealer" coat. Every finish can serve as a sealer if it is applied as the first coat.

Note that a sealer for clear finishes serves a different purpose than a primer for paint. Paint is loaded to the maximum with pigment to provide the best "hiding" possible. A good paint is one that covers and conceals in one coat. The effect of loading the paint with pigment is that not enough "binder" remains to glue the pigment particles to each other and to the wood. This is because wood is rough and porous and requires more binder to achieve a good bond than does a smooth surface such as an already-coated one.

So a primer is simply paint with less pigment and more binder. You can tell this is true by the poor hiding qualities that primers exhibit – they don't conceal what's underneath as well as paint does. Additional ingredients may be added to primers, of course, including mildewcides and preservatives, but these additives are there to provide a special function. They aren't what make the product a primer.

Now contrast paint and primers with a topcoat finish, which is 100 percent, or nearly 100 percent, binder. It bonds perfectly well to wood. There's no need for a separate product to improve the bond. There's no reason to use shellac for a better bond because the finish itself bonds just as well.

So what do products labeled or marketed as sealers do? Two things: They make sanding easier and they block, or "seal off," problems in the wood. (There's also a third type of sealer for professionals using a catalyzed finish. They might use a special "vinyl" sealer for various reasons. But amateurs rarely use catalyzed finishes, so I'm not discussing vinyl sealers here.)

Easier Sanding

When you apply a coat of any finish to wood, fibers get raised and locked in place, which makes the surface feel rough. This roughness should be sanded smooth so additional coats go on smoothly.

But common alkyd varnish and nitrocellulose lacquer (not polyurethane varnish or water-based finish) are difficult to sand because they gum up the sandpaper. So manufacturers produce a special product called "sanding sealer," which is the varnish or lacquer itself with soap-like lubricants included to make the finish powder when sanded.

The problem with sanding sealers is they interfere with the bond of the finish to the wood, actually weakening it. You're better off not using a sanding sealer unless you're finishing a very large project (for example, a set of kitchen cabinets) and don't want to fight the sandpaper constantly gumming up.

There's a good way around using sanding sealer anyway. You can thin the first coat of finish half with the proper thinner (mineral spirits for varnish or lacquer thinner for lacquer). This thinned coat will dry harder more quickly because it is thinner on the wood. It will be easier to sand smooth than a full coat of finish.

Shellac isn't as difficult to sand as varnish and lacquer, but it gums up sandpaper much more than sanding sealer. You wouldn't choose shellac for easy sanding.

Problems in the Wood

Shellac becomes useful when there's something in the wood you want to block off because it interferes with the drying or leveling of the finish, or produces an unpleasant odor. In fact, no finish is as effective at blocking off problems as shellac.

But if you build furniture or cabinets, you rarely have problems you need to block off. Almost all the problems for which shellac is useful occur when refinishing previously finished wood.

Refinishing problems include fish eye (the finish bunching up in ridges) caused by silicone oil from furniture polishes having penetrated into the wood, poor bonding due to residual wax from paint strippers, and odors from smoke or animal urine. Professional refinishers often use shellac as a barrier coat to overcome these problems.

The only common problem you might experience finishing new wood is getting varnish or lacquer to dry over the resin in pine knots, or getting varnish to dry over the oily resin is some exotic woods. Shellac will seal off this resin so you can apply these finishes without problems. Resin problems don't exist in common hardwoods.

Sealing is the simplest of concepts: The first full coat of any finish does it, and there's no reason to use a special product unless you have a problem you need to solve – making sanding easier, or sealing off oil, resin, wax or an odor in the wood.

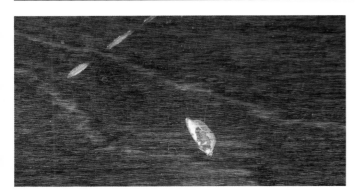

A weakness of sanding sealer is that it can crumble under finish topcoats when struck by a blunt object if the sanding sealer is applied thick. Sanding sealer weakens the strength of the finish film, so it's better to not use it except in production situations with many objects.

Shellac is extremely useful as a barrier against problems in wood that are commonly encountered when refinishing. This oak has a very bad case of silicone contamination, which causes fish eye (left). A sealer coat of shellac (right) "seals off" the silicone so a lacquer finish can be sprayed on top without problems.

The Many Faces of Varnish

Despite their names, many of your finishing products simply are a form of varnish.

You are surely familiar with varnish. It is one of the oldest and most widely available wood finishes, and it is a very popular finish with amateur woodworkers. Varnish is easy to brush, and it provides excellent protection for wood surfaces and resistance to scratches, heat, solvents and chemicals.

You may not realize it, but varnish is packaged and sold under many different names, some with no indication that the product is simply varnish. If you count all the supposedly different finishing products that are actually just varnish, you probably have a shelf full. Here are the eight categories of varnish:

> Alkyd varnish
> Polyurethane
> Spar varnish
> Marine (boat) varnish
> Wiping varnish (sold under many different names)
> Salad bowl finish
> Wood conditioner
> Gel varnish

Varnish is made by cooking a hard resin with an oil that has the ability to cure when exposed to oxygen. The resins used are alkyd, polyurethane and phenolic. The oils used are linseed oil, tung oil, modified soybean (soya) oil and modified safflower oil. The cooking combines the resin and oil chemically to create something different from either.

It's easy to tell that a product is varnish. If it thins with mineral spirits (usually labeled "petroleum distillate") and cures hard, then it is varnish. No other finish both thins with mineral spirits and cures hard.

(Linseed oil, tung oil and blends of varnish and oil thin with mineral spirits, but they cure soft and they usually wrinkle. So to tell if a finish is varnish or if it is oil or a blend of the two, pore a puddle of the finish on the top of the can or on another non-porous surface and check it after it has cured.)

Eight Categories of Varnish

Here is an explanation of each of the eight categories of varnish.

Alkyd varnish is the common varnish available at paint stores and home centers. It is meant for interior use and is made with alkyd resin, cooked with one or more of the oils. It is always labeled "varnish," so far as I know. There are some varnishes made with phenolic resin and also labeled "varnish," but these are rare. Phenolic resin yellows significantly more than alkyd resin.

Polyurethane is varnish made with both alkyd and polyurethane resins (called uralkyd), and it is usually made with modified soybean oil so there is relatively little yellowing. Polyurethane is more durable than "varnish," and it is almost always labeled "polyurethane." Some manufacturers use variations on the term, such as "Defthane" and "Varathane."

Spar varnish is meant for exterior use and is made with a higher ratio of oil to resin than interior varnish. This makes it more flexible to withstand the greater wood movement outdoors.

Marine (boat) varnish is spar varnish with ultraviolet-light absorbers added to resist penetration by UV light. (Many marine varnishes are made with phenolic or polyurethane resin and tung oil because these provide the best water resistance.) There is a big difference in the amount of UV absorbers added to products labeled or marketed "marine" varnish. The products sold in home centers and most paint stores have very little of the absorber added, so they are only a little more effective against sunlight than spar varnish. The marine varnishes sold in boat marinas are by far the more effective against UV light. They are also more expensive.

Wiping varnish is a category of varnish thinned about 50/50 with mineral spirits. You may very well have several brands on

Varnish is the only finish that both thins with mineral spirits and cures hard. All of these products are varnish. From the left: alkyd varnish, polyurethane, spar varnish, marine varnish, wiping varnish, salad bowl finish, wood conditioner and gel varnish.

your shelf without realizing they are all the same. Wiping varnishes are usually alkyd resin cooked with one of the oils, but some are made with polyurethane resin, and the wiping vanish "Waterlox" is made with phenolic resin.

You can easily make your own wiping varnish from any of the above four categories of varnish. Making your own gives you control over the viscosity. Add less thinner than manufacturers do to achieve a better build with each coat. Add more thinner to improve flow out and leveling.

Salad bowl finish is simply a wiping varnish. The implication in the name is that it is safe for contact with food and for small children who might chew on the finished wood. It is safe of course, once it has cured, but so are all the other varnishes and wiping varnishes.

The safety concern is the metallic driers used to speed the drying of the finish. Lead was once used and it isn't safe. But lead isn't used anymore. It takes several driers to replace the lead, and there are only a few driers available. So all varnishes use essentially the same driers. There is no difference in the safety factor of any of these driers. All are safe.

I find it amazing that people who buy into the food-safe myth consider salad-bowl finish safe and other varnishes unsafe. The only issue is that the finish be fully cured. Press your nose up against the hardened finish and take a whiff. If you can't smell anything, the finish is cured.

Wood conditioner (or "stain controller") is sold to prevent blotching and is an alkyd/soybean-oil varnish thinned with about two parts mineral spirits to one part varnish. Again, you can easily make your own. Wood conditioner is the varnish variety of what professional finishers call a "washcoat." Professionals commonly use lacquer thinned a little over half with lacquer thinner. Because varnish has a higher solids content (less thinner) than lacquer to begin with, varnish needs to be thinned with two parts thinner to make an equivalent product.

The problem with wood conditioner is that the directions on many of the brands are wrong. You need to let the varnish cure hard before it becomes effective at blocking the penetration of a stain into the wood. This usually takes six to eight hours (better overnight) depending on the temperature. Curing can't happen in the two hours or less claimed by some manufacturers unless you put the coated object in an oven.

Wiping varnish is any full-strength varnish thinned about half with mineral spirits so it's easy to wipe on wood. All of these products are wiping varnish – though, as you can see, many are labeled to make you think they are something else.

Gel varnish is commonly made with alkyd resin and one of the oils, but it's sometimes made with polyurethane resin. The finish is given a gelled thixotropic quality (like mayonnaise or latex wall paint) in the manufacturing process so that it becomes easy to wipe on the wood. You have to wipe off most of the excess to avoid severe ridging. Gel varnish is very popular with amateurs because, like wiping varnish, it can be applied to produce a smooth, ridge-free result without an expensive spray gun.

Both of these finishes are commonly referred to as "oil" in woodworking magazines. But it's clear from the way the finishes cured on the tops of the cans that Waterlox is varnish.

You can brush any of the varnishes I've discussed, including the polyurethane shown here. But brushing and leaving a gel varnish can cause severe ridging.

Wiping varnishes are very popular with amateur woodworkers who don't own spray equipment because these finishes are so easy to apply.

The Case for Shellac

Long neglected by wood-workers in favor of oil and varnish finishes, this gift from the insect world is a great finish for home woodworkers. Here's why.

Shellac in flake form is available in various colors and grades. Across the top from left is dewaxed blonde shellac, orange shellac with the wax unremoved and crudely refined button shellac. Across the bottom is dewaxed garnet shellac, dewaxed extra-dark (ruby-red) shellac and totally unrefined seed lac.

Today, shellac is the most under-appreciated of all finishes, but this hasn't always been the case. Until the 1920s, when lacquer was introduced, shellac was the primary finish used in furniture factories and small woodworking shops. It continued to be the favored finish of professionals finishing interior wood trim and floors, and of hobbiests finishing everything, until the 1950s and '60s.

Now shellac is rarely used as a finish except by makers of reproduction furniture and refinishers of high-end antiques. This is terribly unfortunate, because shellac is still one of the best finish choices for most woodworking and refinishing projects.

What is Shellac?

Shellac is a natural resin secreted by insects called lac bugs, which attach themselves to certain trees native to India and South Asia. Suppliers buy the resin and sell it as flakes, or dissolve it in alcohol and package the solution in cans for you to purchase.

Natural shellac is very dark and is processed to lighten the color. Orange (amber) shellac is your best choice when you want to add warmth to wood. A lot of old furniture and woodwork was finished with orange shellac. Bleached shellac (sold as "blonde" or "clear") is best when you want to maintain the whiteness of a pickling stain or the natural color of light woods such as maple, birch and ash. You can mix orange and bleached shellac to achieve an in-between color.

Natural shellac contains about 5 percent wax and will produce excellent results; but dewaxed shellac, whether pre-dissolved or in flake form, is more water-resistant. You can remove wax from regular shellac by letting the wax settle and then decant the liquid.

Shellac is a very old finish, so it has an old measuring system based on the concept "pound cut." One pound of shellac flakes dissolved in one gallon of alcohol equals a one-pound cut. Two pounds in one gallon is a two-pound cut; one pound in a quart is a four-pound cut; and so on.

Zinsser Bulls Eye amber and clear shellacs that you buy at the paint store contain wax and are three-pound cuts, which is very thick for brushing or spraying. Zinsser Bulls Eye ClearCoat shellac is dewaxed and a two-pound cut, still fairly thick for brushing or spraying. Thin these shellacs with denatured alcohol (shellac thinner) if needed to reduce brush marks and orange peel. (You shouldn't use methanol as a thinner unless you have a good exhaust system because methanol is very toxic.)

Shelf Life

Shellac's single biggest disadvantage is that it has a very short shelf life. Shelf life means the length of time a finish stays good in the can. You should avoid using shellac that is too old.

Shellac begins to deteriorate as soon as it is dissolved in alcohol. This is true whether you do the dissolving yourself or the supplier does it, and it occurs even if the shellac is kept in a sealed container.

The deterioration occurs slowly and is not noticeable for a while. After six months or so, you will begin to notice a slight difference in the drying rate compared to freshly made shellac. After a year the slower drying becomes quite obvious. After several years the applied shellac will remain noticeably softer for months. You can dig your fingernail into it while you can't into freshly made shellac. Eventually, the shellac will never fully harden.

Five problems can occur if you use deteriorated shellac:

> The shellac will scratch easier.

> It will also water spot more easily.

> The finish won't ever attain the same gloss as that produced by freshly made shellac.

> It will be difficult to sand between coats because the shellac is too soft, and it won't produce an even sheen if you rub it out after the last coat.

> If you use the shellac as a barrier coat under another finish, that finish may wrinkle or crack.

The generally accepted shelf life for dissolved shellac is six months for bleached shellac and one year for orange shellac. These times will vary depending on how the flakes are stored, how old the flakes were when they were dissolved, and how the liquid shellac has been stored. The warmer the storage conditions the more rapidly shellac deteriorates. In addition, because shellac is a natural resin, there may be some slight variations from one year's crop to the next.

If you make your own shellac, date the container so you know when the resin was dissolved. If you buy shellac already dissolved, check that there is a date of manufacture on the can. Be wary of bleached shellac more than six months old and orange shellac more than one year old if you intend to use the shellac on a critical surface such as a tabletop.

Dissolve Your Own

Though it's a little more work, you have much more control over the drying rate of shellac if you dissolve your own. Freshly made shellac dries faster and harder than any shellac you can buy in a can. You also have less waste, because you can dissolve just the amount you need for a project. You won't ever have to discard old, deteriorated shellac.

To dissolve shellac flakes add denatured alcohol to the flakes to produce the pound cut you want.

Be sure to stir the shellac every hour or so or it will lump on the bottom and be hard to break up.

It's always a good idea to strain the shellac to remove dirt and other foreign matter. In my experience, straining isn't so necessary, however, with blonde shellac because it's usually very clean.

Shellac Pros & Cons

Advantages:

❯ Much more water- and scratch-resistant than oil or oil/varnish-blends, which cure too soft to be built up on wood.

❯ Better dust-free results than varnish or polyurethane which cure very slowly.

❯ Less polluting, less of a health hazard and less smelly than varnish, polyurethane or lacquer.

❯ Easier to apply and richer-looking than water-based finishes.

❯ Easier to clean (with ammonia and water) than all other finishes.

Disadvantages:

❯ Not water or scratch resistant enough for surfaces such as kitchen cabinets and tables that take a beating.

❯ Available only in gloss sheen.

❯ Tends to ridge at the edges of brush strokes.

❯ Slowly deteriorates after being dissolved in alcohol.

To dissolve flake shellac, add enough denatured alcohol (ethyl alcohol that has been made poisonous so it is not taxed as a liquor) to the flakes to make the pound cut you want. Or make a higher pound cut and thin it later. For your first attempt I recommend you make a two-pound cut, which is thin enough so the shellac dissolves quickly and easily.

You can make a small amount of two-pound-cut shellac by adding one pint of denatured alcohol to a jar containing one-quarter pound of shellac flakes. Always use a jar or other non-metal container, because metal reacts with the shellac causing it to darken.

Stir the mixture several times over a period of a couple hours to keep the flakes from solidifying into a lump at the bottom of the jar. And keep the jar covered so the alcohol doesn't absorb moisture from the air. Too much moisture in the shellac will cause it to blush (turn milky white).

To speed the dissolving, grind the flakes into a powder or place the jar of shellac and alcohol in a pot of hot water.

When the flakes are totally in solution, remove impurities by straining the shellac through a paint strainer or loose-weave cheesecloth into another jar, and write the current date on that jar so you know when the shellac was made.

Orange shellac will keep in flake form for many years, but bleached shellac won't. If the flakes are stuck hard together in a lump and don't dissolve in the alcohol, throw the flakes out and begin again with fresh flakes. Just as with cans of already dissolved shellac, it's best to buy the flakes only as you need them.

Applying Shellac

To brush shellac, remember that alcohol evaporates rapidly, so you must work fast. Use a good quality natural- or synthetic-bristle brush, or a foam brush if your project is small, and brush in long strokes in the direction of the grain if at all possible. Work fast enough on your project to keep a "wet edge," and wait until the next coat to fill in missed places if the shellac becomes tacky.

Spraying shellac is no different than spraying other finishes. Just as thinning shellac reduces brush marks during brushing, thinning reduces orange peel while spraying.

However you apply the shellac, allow the first coat to dry for about two hours, then sand with #320- or #400-grit stearated (dry-

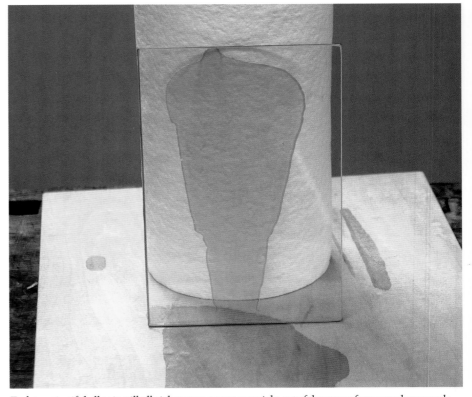

To determine if shellac is still all right to use, pour some right out of the can or from your homemade preparation onto a piece of glass or other non-porous surface. Give the shellac several seconds to spread out. Then lean the glass almost vertical, and let the shellac run down and off the bottom. The objective is to get a uniformly thin layer of shellac. Let the shellac dry for an hour or two at room temperature. It should then be hard enough to resist fingerprinting. After drying overnight, the shellac should be hard enough so you can't indent it with your fingernail.

lubricated) sandpaper just enough to remove dust nibs and raised grain. Use a light touch to reduce sandpaper clogging and to avoid sanding through.

Remove the dust and apply a second coat. Add more alcohol to the shellac if you're getting severe brush marks or orange peel, or if air bubbles are drying in the film. The alcohol will extend the "open" time and allow the bubbles to pop out. There is no limit to the amount you can thin shellac, but thinning may result in your having to apply more coats to get the build you want.

Apply as many coats as necessary to achieve the look you want. Each new coat dissolves into the existing coat, so there's no need to sand between coats except to remove dust nibs or other flaws. To see flaws such as runs and sags before they dry in the film, arrange your work so you can see a reflected light in the area you're finishing. Then brush out the flaws before they dry.

If the humidity is high, or if there's too much water in the alcohol you've used to thin your shellac, it may turn milky-white. This is called "blushing" and is caused by moisture

settling in the finish. Wait for a drier day to do your finishing. You can usually remove existing blushing by applying alcohol on a dry day or by rubbing with an abrasive, such as a Scotch-Brite pad or steel wool.

If, at any time, you create problems you can't remove without creating greater problems, strip the finish with alcohol or paint stripper and begin again. In between coats you can store your brush by wrapping it in plastic wrap or hanging it in a jar of alcohol. You can clean the brush easily by washing it in a half-and-half mixture of household ammonia and water. You can reclaim brushes with hardened shellac by soaking in alcohol.

When you have applied the desired number of coats (three is minimum in most cases), you can leave the finish as is. Or you can level it using #320-grit and finer sandpaper and a flat backing block, then rub it to the sheen you want using Scotch-Brite pads, fine steel wool or abrasive compounds such as pumice and rottenstone. If the rubbed finish shows finger marks too easily, apply paste wax or a silicone furniture polish.

An Array of Lacquers

Many finishes are known by this one name.

In common speech and among those in the professional finishing trade the term "lacquer" usually refers to nitrocellulose lacquer. But there are many other finishes that go by that name.

When referring to one of these, it's best to use a modifying word, or words, to distinguish it from nitrocellulose.

These other lacquers include water-white lacquer, urethane-modified lacquer, vinyl lacquer, brushing lacquer, CAB-acrylic lacquer, crackle lacquer, pre-catalyzed lacquer, post-catalyzed lacquer, padding lacquer, water-based (or waterborne) lacquer and Oriental (Japan or Chinese) lacquer.

Here's an explanation of these lacquers, all of which, except padding and Oriental lacquer, are available in various sheens ranging from gloss to flat.

Nitrocellulose Lacquer

Nitrocellulose is the first modern lacquer. It was used as a plastic as early as the late 19th century (for example: movie film and brush handles). After World War I it came into wide use as a finish.

The impetus was the growth of the automobile industry and the large stocks of gunpowder (cellulose nitrate) left over from the war.

The automobile industry had been using varnish, which dries very slowly, to finish cars. The introduction of fast-drying, pigmented nitrocellulose lacquer removed the bottleneck at the finishing stage of production.

By 1930 most furniture manufacturers had shifted to lacquer from shellac.

Nitrocellulose lacquer is made with cellulose nitrate and a modifying resin (usually alkyd or maleic) that improves build, flexibility and adhesion. An oil-like plasticizer (modified castor oil was used originally) is added for further flexibility.

The raw ingredients are dissolved in lacquer thinner, which is unique among

When poured into glass jars, it's easy to see the different colors of lacquers. On the left in nitrocellulose, which is made with fairly orange modifying resins. In the middle is water-white lacquer, which is made with fairly colorless modifying resins. The color that exists is supplied mostly by the nitrocellulose. On the right is CAB-acrylic lacquer, which is totally colorless.

finish solvents because it is composed of half-a-dozen or more individual solvents that evaporate at different rates. The manufacturer controls the drying speed of the lacquer by its choice of solvents.

The most unique characteristic provided by lacquer thinner is resistance to runs and sags on vertical surfaces. The individual sol-

Because lacquer thinner is made up of individual solvents that evaporate at different rates, it's possible to spray relatively heavy coats of any finish thinned with lacquer thinner onto a vertical surface with no runs or sags. This is one reason finishers love spraying lacquer.

vents are chosen to evaporate quickly one after another immediately after the lacquer is propelled from the spray gun – so that by the time the finish settles on the surface it is already beginning to thicken.

No other finish solvent or thinner provides this characteristic.

Closely Related Lacquers

Water-white, urethane-modified, vinyl and brushing lacquers are all made with cellulose nitrate and are closely related to nitrocellulose lacquer.

Water-white lacquer is made with a lighter-colored modifying resin, usually more expensive coconut alkyd or acrylic. So this lacquer yellows less and costs more.

Urethane-modified lacquer uses urethane alkyd to add a little more heat, scratch and alcohol resistance. This lacquer isn't widely available or used.

Vinyl lacquer is made with a modifying vinyl resin to improve adhesion and water resistance. This finish doesn't harden as well as other lacquers, but it performs well under catalyzed finishes, so it is usually sold as "vinyl sealer."

Brushing lacquer is simply nitrocellulose lacquer made with slower evaporating lacquer-thinner solvents. The finish dries slowly enough to be brushed, but the non-sagging characteristic common with spray lacquers is lost.

CAB-acrylic Lacquer

Cellulose/acetate/butyrate and acrylic resins dissolve in lacquer thinner and are considerably more expensive than cellulose nitrate. But they are non-yellowing, so they are used to make a totally colorless lacquer.

The usual reason for choosing CAB-acrylic is to finish light-colored woods such as maple, or to finish over white pickling stain.

Crackle Lacquer

Crackle lacquer is nitrocellulose lacquer made with more pigment than there is finish to bind all the pigment particles together. As the finish dries and shrinks, it cracks and separates, revealing the layer below.

To create this finish, apply a coat of colored nitrocellulose lacquer and follow with a different-colored crackle lacquer. You can control the size of the cracks, and the "islands" in between, by varying the amount of thinner, and the speed and spray distance of the gun, as well as the amount of finish that's sprayed on the piece – but no more than one coat.

Because the crackle layer is crumbly, you should always apply a clear coat on top.

Pre- & Post-catalyzed Lacquers

Catalyzed lacquer is made with only a small percentage of cellulose nitrate. The bulk of the finish is another resin entirely – melamine or urea formaldehyde. These resins are combined with alkyd resin to cure very hard and scratch resistant when an acid catalyst is added.

The cellulose nitrate is added to make the finish more user-friendly. Without it the product is called conversion or catalyzed varnish.

The defining difference between pre- and post-catalyzed lacquer is that the manufacturer adds the catalyst to the pre-; you add it to the post-. Pre-catalyzed lacquer is therefore more user friendly, but it often cures slowly and has a shelf life of six months to a year or two.

Padding Lacquer

Padding lacquer is not lacquer at all but shellac thinned in solvents that dissolve lacquer. The name causes a lot of confusion.

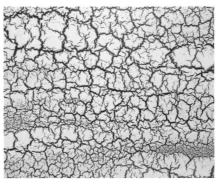

Crackle lacquer contains more pigment than the lacquer can bind together. So when the finish dries and shrinks, it cracks and separates to reveal the layer below. You can create very interesting and attractive effects by varying the amount of thinner, the speed you move the spray gun and the distance you hold the gun from the surface.

When furniture manufacturers shifted from shellac to lacquer in the 1920s, they found that touching up nicks and rubs using shellac and the French polishing method wasn't as successful as it had been when shellac was the finish. Shellac dissolved in alcohol doesn't bite as well into a lacquer finish.

So manufacturers added some lacquer solvents to shellac and changed the name to padding lacquer to distinguish the product.

Water-based Lacquer

Water-based finish is entirely different from any of the lacquers discussed above. It's related more closely to latex paint and white and yellow glue. Unfortunately, some manufacturers insist on calling their water-based finishes lacquer (or varnish or polyurethane), which creates confusion among consumers.

A water-based finish is an emulsion of acrylic and sometimes acrylic/polyurethane resin. The finish dries initially by water evaporation, then forms a hard film when the droplets of emulsified resin stick together as the very slow solvent evaporates.

Besides the water raising the grain of the wood and slowing the drying, the most important difference between water-based finishes and true lacquers is in application. Water-based finishes don't contain lacquer thinner so they run and sag easily on vertical surfaces.

Oriental Lacquer

The original lacquer is a natural resin harvested from trees in east Asia, primarily Japan and China. So this lacquer is commonly called Japan or Chinese lacquer. It is totally unrelated to any of the lacquers discussed above.

When exposed to very high humidity, Oriental lacquer crosslinks to form a hard, durable film. The natural reddish color is often enhanced with pigments.

Oriental lacquer has been used since before recorded history. Beginning in the 15th century, furniture and other objects with this highly decorative finish were imported to Europe, and European craftsmen tried with varying degrees of success to imitate it with the resins they had available. Their efforts are often called "japanning."

By dissolving their lacquer finish in slower-evaporating lacquer-thinner solvents, manufacturers make a lacquer that dries slowly enough to be brushed. But the slow drying cancels out the benefit of reduced runs and sags on vertical surfaces. So on these you need to stretch the finish out with your brush so the build isn't too thick.

Why Water-based Finishes Aren't Catching On

Many woodworkers are frustrated by water-based finishes. Learn to use them properly and you'll reach for them more often.

Water-based finishing products get a lot of attention in magazines and at trade shows, but these products still don't sell all that well. Most woodworkers seem reluctant to give up their familiar oil, varnish, shellac and lacquer finishes.

I think the reason for the poor sales, especially to amateur woodworkers, is the excessive hype that has raised expectations beyond what water-based products can produce. When you've been led to believe that a stain or finish "doesn't raise the grain," is "equivalent to lacquer," or is "as durable as oil-based polyurethane," but discover otherwise when you use it, you become skeptical of the product and retreat to what you know and feel comfortable with.

Water-based finishing products have plenty going for them, especially for amateur woodworkers, so they should sell quite well without all the hype.

Two qualities are critical: Water-based products don't stink and make you feel bad; and water-based products are easy to clean from brushes (not so easy from spray guns, however). The proof of the significance of these two qualities is demonstrated by the overwhelming popularity of latex paint, which is water-based finish with pigment added, vs. oil paint. Almost everyone uses latex paint on interior trim, kitchen and bathroom cabinets, and outdoor furniture when there is no question that oil paint would perform better. Reduced smell and easy cleanup rule with people working at home!

Other advantages you might find attractive are a reduced level of polluting solvents, reduced fire hazard and absolutely no yellowing. For the amount of finishing material you

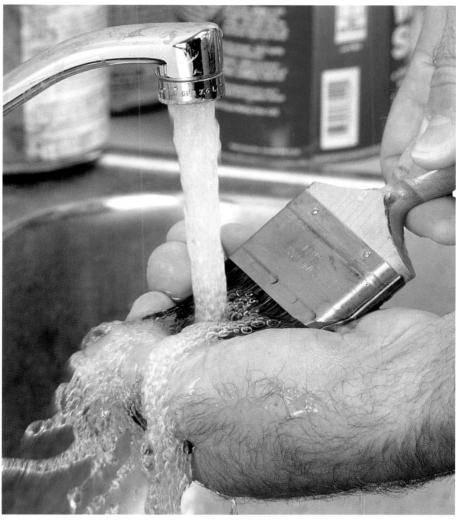

Water-based finishes have the unique advantage over oil-based finishes of easy soap and water cleanup.

probably use, the first two are minor issues. But the non-yellowing quality can be a real benefit when you're finishing light or pickled woods. Water-based finishes are the only finishes that are totally non-yellowing.

For all their good qualities, however, water-based stains and finishes are still a relatively new technology. In contrast to other stains and finishes, improvements are still being made in the raw materials used, and some manufacturers are faster at picking up on them than others. So, if you're unhappy with the results you get from one brand, try

another before giving up on the entire class of products.

Disadvantages

The rarely mentioned disadvantages are the problem, of course, because you have to know what they are or you can't overcome them.

The first problem is in the naming of the products. Manufacturers often give water-based finishes the same names as totally different products that have been around for years – polyurethane, lacquer and varnish. The intent is to make you feel comfortable with the product, but the effect is opposite. The misleading naming sets expectations that can't be fulfilled and causes confusion because you are led to believe there are significant differences (water-based varnish vs. water-based lacquer, for example) when there aren't. The names are chosen for the market being targeted.

All water-based products should be labeled as "water-based," "waterborne," "aqua," or some other obvious water-indicating name right up front so you don't have to read the fine print to determine what the product is.

Other significant problems common to all water-based products are grain raising, fast drying and poor bonding over oil-based products. Let's take each in turn.

Grain Raising
Despite some manufacturers' claims to the contrary, all water-based products raise the grain of wood. How could it be otherwise? They contain a lot of water.

There are two ways to reduce the grain raising of a stain or finish. The first is to pre-wet the wood with water, let the wood dry for several hours or overnight, then sand it with fine-grit sandpaper just enough to make it feel smooth. Don't sand any deeper than necessary or you may cut into new wood that will raise again when you apply the stain or finish. In practice you can't eliminate grain raising totally because you can't sand evenly enough, but you can reduce it significantly.

The second is to reduce the depth the stain or finish penetrates. There are several ways to do this. Use a thicker stain or finish, one that has been slightly gelled; dry the wood very quickly with heat lamps and air movement; or spray the stain or finish in a light mist coat, so it flashes dry quickly. None of these methods eliminates grain raising

If you miss the fine print, you can always tell if a finish is water-based by removing the lid. Water-based finishes are white in the can.

totally, and each is less effective when the humidity is high.

Without a way to totally eliminate grain raising, you have to deal with it. If you aren't staining the wood, the easiest way is to simply sand off the raised grain after the first coat of finish – the same procedure you use with other finishes. Try to apply enough finish so you don't sand through, but sanding through seldom causes a problem as long as there isn't any stain.

If you are staining the wood, you can "bury" the grain raising caused by a water-based stain. This is what most cabinet shops and factories do. Apply enough finish so you're sure not to sand through, then sand the surface level and apply another coat or two. To learn how much sanding it takes to sand through, practice on scrap wood by sanding through intentionally.

Fast Drying
Fast drying is an advantage when applying a finish because it reduces dust nibs, but it's a disadvantage when applying a stain. Most water-based stains are difficult to apply evenly on large surfaces because they dry too fast to get the excess wiped off.

There are several tricks you can use to get an even color on a large surface. Spray the stain evenly and leave it. Spray the stain and wipe it off quickly. Wipe on the stain with a large soaked rag, then quickly wipe off the excess. Stain small sections at a time. Have one person apply the stain and another wipe off right behind.

If you do get an uneven coloring due to some of the stain drying before you get it wiped off, quickly wipe over the entire area with a wet cloth to redissolve and respread the stain. However, be aware that this may lighten the color.

Bonding to Oil Stains
To avoid both the grain-raising and fast-drying problems of water-based stains, you can use an oil-based stain, but then you have to worry about the water-based finish not bonding well. To ensure a good bond, let the oil-based stain cure totally before applying the water-based finish. Curing time depends on the stain itself, the weather and the size of the wood's pores. For example, stain on oak will take longer to cure than on maple.

Some water-based finishes bond well over some oil-based stains before the stain has fully cured, but there's no way of knowing for sure without trying it. The variables are the resins and solvents used in the finish and how much oil is in the stain.

To test the bonding, apply the stain and finish to scrap wood. After allowing it to dry for a couple days, score the finish with a razor in a cross-hatch pattern. Make the cuts about 1/16" apart and 1" long. Then press some masking or Scotch tape over the cuts and pull it up quickly. If the finish has bonded well, the scored lines will remain clean and very little or no finish will come off on the tape.

Other Problems
Water-based finishes have other problems as well, but they aren't serious enough to make you change to another finish except in special situations. These problems include the following: greater sensitivity to extreme weather conditions; less durability than varnish or polyurethane (but more durability than shellac or lacquer); and greater difficulty repairing or stripping than shellac or lacquer.

The problems using water-based finishing products aren't insurmountable. But they're made more formidable by manufacturers who claim too much, mislabel their products and provide inadequate instructions for dealing with the special problems created by water.

Water-based finish (right) maintains the natural color of maple while oil-based varnish "yellows" the maple considerably.

Water-based finish "washes out" the color of dark woods such as walnut (right) while oil-based varnish gives them a warm glow.

Some Reflections on Sheen

Understanding how sheen works allows you to control the gloss on your finishes.

One of the most important qualities of a finish when it comes to appearance is sheen. A finish can vary from a gloss so high it reflects the sharp outline of an image to a sheen so dull that nothing is reflected. In determining how you want your project to look, you need to take its sheen into account.

One method of controlling sheen is to rub the last coat with abrasives of various grits. The coarser the grit the lower or flatter the sheen. The finer the grit the higher or glossier the sheen. The problem with rubbing is that it is a lot of work.

An easier method of controlling sheen, and the method most commonly used, is to choose a finish with the sheen already built in. Then all you have to do is brush or spray the finish onto the wood and the sheen will come about automatically.

A hundred years ago, before electric lighting, people preferred a gloss sheen because gloss reflects a lot of light and makes rooms appear brighter. Today, most people prefer a flatter sheen.

Manufacturers offer a variety of choices. Unfortunately, the words they use to describe these choices are vague: gloss, semi-gloss, satin, eggshell, rubbed effect, matte, flat and dead flat. There are no fixed definitions for these terms; so one manufacturers satin may be another's flat.

To be successful getting the sheen you want on your projects, you need to understand how the sheen-creating elements in a finish work and how you can manipulate them.

Flatting Agent

The stuff in a finish that creates all the sheens lower than gloss is called "flatting agent." It is a very fine silica product that settles to the bottom of the can and has to be stirred into suspension before using. Gloss has no flatting agent added and therefore nothing to stir.

Though silica is a more complex material than fine sand, it's often helpful to think of it as fine sand for the impact it creates at the surface of a finish. Here's the way silica works.

The manufacturer adds the amount of silica necessary to create a given sheen to an alkyd or polyurethane varnish, lacquer, catalyzed finish or water-based finish. All film-building finishes except, unfortunately, shellac are available with silica added. (It's not true as you sometimes hear that lacquer is always glossy.)

Just before using the product, you need to stir the silica into an even suspension throughout the finish. You can also shake the can, but this may not be as effective unless you have a mechanical shaker like those in paint stores.

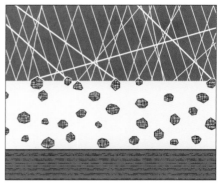

A finish with flatting agent added appears dull because of light being scattered off the micro-roughness at the surface of the film. This micro-roughness is created as the solvent evaporates by the finish "shrink-wrapping" around the particles of silica that lie at the surface.

With the silica in suspension, you brush or spray the finish onto the wood. You may notice that the finish goes on glossy. That is, it has a high reflective quality. But there will come a point within a short time (depending on the drying rate of the finish) when this gloss sheen flattens quickly across the surface.

The flattening is caused by the finish "shrink-wrapping" over the particles of silica that lie at the very surface of the film. This occurs as the solvent evaporates and the finish shrinks. The shrink-wrapping creates a micro-roughness at the surface that scatters light so the gloss is reduced. The higher the density of silica at the surface the flatter the sheen of the film finish.

A finish can have an infinite number of sheens depending on how much flatting agent (silica) is added. Above are examples of how the sheen, and resulting reflection, changes when flatting agent is added to gloss finish.

It's important to emphasize that the flattening is not caused by the silica particles embedded deep within the film as is commonly believed. Because of its nature, silica doesn't hinder the travel of light; it's as if the particles weren't even there. As a result, successive coats of a satin or flat finish don't make the finish flatter.

Because all the flattening occurs at the surface of the film, it's easy to rub a satin finish to a gloss using fine abrasives. Begin by removing the micro-roughness with very fine sandpaper, then rub with fine abrasive compounds.

Manipulating Sheen

As mentioned, manufacturers aren't very informative about the sheen of the products they sell us. First, their terminology is vague. (Among themselves, they use a more exact numbering system from 1 to 100, with 100 being perfect gloss; but they rarely share this information with us.) Second, they often give us only two choices.

What if you want a sheen that is flatter than anything offered in the store, or you want a sheen that is in between the two choices offered?

To create a flatter sheen, let the flatting agent settle to the bottom of the can (tell the paint clerk not to shake the can). Then pour off some of the gloss finish at the top into a second container. You will then have some gloss in one container and some flat in another. Blend these two until you get the sheen you want.

To easily create a sheen not available at a store, pour off some of the gloss from a satin or flat finish after letting all the silica settle to the bottom of the can. Then mix the two (gloss and very flat) until you get the sheen you want.

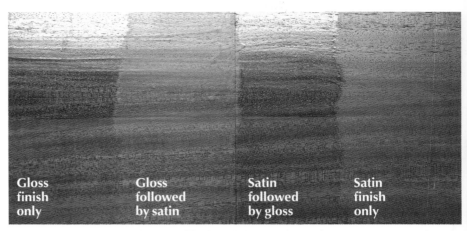

Gloss finish only

Gloss followed by satin

Satin followed by gloss

Satin finish only

All the sheen is created in the last coat of finish applied. Previous coats have no impact. Here's the proof. On the left half of this board, I brushed on three coats of gloss water-based finish. On the right half, I brush on three coats of satin water-based finish. Then I brushed satin water-based finish onto the right half of the gloss side and gloss water-based finish onto the left half of the satin side. The resulting glosses and satins are the same irrespective of what's underneath. The same would be the case no matter what type of finish I used.

Of course, you'll need to experiment by applying some of your blend to wood to see the sheen you are creating. Be sure to apply two coats because it's only the second coat that will produce an accurate sheen. It doesn't matter, of course, what you use for the first coat.

It's even easier if you want a sheen in between those of two products offered. Simply stir the flatting agent to put it into suspension, then mix the two.

Sheen Problems

Once you have determined the sheen you want and have a product that will produce it, problems are rare. The most common is not keeping the finish stirred. More rare, but also possible, is white specks appearing in the dried finish film.

It's not necessary to continually stir a flatted finish while brushing or spraying. But it is necessary to stir between coats.

If you are brushing, some of the flatting agent will have settled and the finish you are pulling off the upper level of the container will be glossier than you intend. If you are spraying, some of the flatting agent will have settled and the finish entering from the lower part of the spray-gun cup will be flatter than you intend.

Though it is rare, you may find tiny white specks in your dried finish and wonder where they came from. Unless you are using a dirty finish, it's most likely you have broken some clumps of dried silica away from the lip of the container. These clumps don't break up in the finish so they show up as white specks in the film.

There's no way to effectively strain these clumps because they are very small. It's best to toss the container and all the finish in it and begin again from a fresh can. You'll have to sand out the white specks from the dried film to remove them.

Even a flat finish goes on initially glossy. Flatting occurs fairly rapidly at the point when most of the solvent has evaporated. Here you can see that the thinner valleys in this brushed finish have reached that point while the peaks in the brush strokes have not.

5

Choosing a Finish

Tinker Toys, Spaghetti & Soccer Balls

The keys to understanding finishes.

Though you may use only one or two finishes in your work, you've surely wondered about the others and how they compare. You've probably even asked yourself if you shouldn't be using one of them instead.

To help answer this question, you may have tried to classify finishes by their resins—polyurethane, alkyd, acrylic, etc., but then realized that this isn't very helpful. Take polyurethane, for example. It is used in oil-based varnishes, water-based finishes, some lacquers and some two-part finishes. If you've used any two of these finishes, you know that they are very different.

A much better way to make sense of finishes, so you can choose intelligently among them, is to combine them into three groups by the way they cure, then associate each of the groups with the familiar objects—Tinker Toys, spaghetti and soccer balls. This may seem silly at first, but the objects make the groups easy to remember and the groups allow you to figure out the answers to most of your questions, even though you may never have used the finishes.

The Groups

The three groups are reactive, evaporative and coalescing.

Oil, varnish, and two-part finishes are reactive finishes because they cure by a chemical reaction that occurs in the finish when it comes in contact with oxygen (oil and varnish) or has a catalyst added (two-part finishes). Because the chemical reaction causes the molecules in the finish to join up or "crosslink," you can picture reactive finishes as Tinker Toys on a molecular scale that link up in a very large network.

Shellac, lacquer and wax dry entirely by the evaporation of their solvents (there is no chemical reaction and no linking up), so they are evaporative finishes. These finishes are made up of relatively large molecules that are long and stringy in shape, making the finishes resemble entangled, molecular spaghetti.

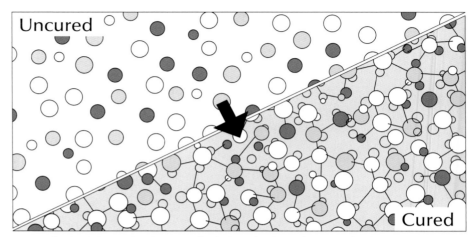

Reactive finishes (oil, varnish and two-part finishes) cure by chemical reaction after the thinner evaporates. On a molecular scale, these finishes resemble a gigantic Tinker-Toy-like network when cured.

Evaporative finishes (shellac, lacquer and wax) cure when the spaghetti-like molecules tangle after the solvent evaporates.

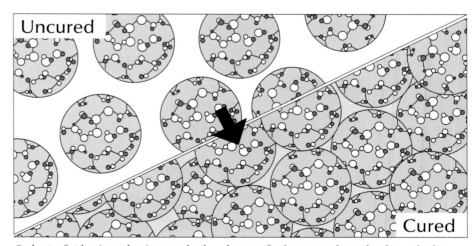

Coalescing finishes (water base) cure as droplets of reactive finish come together and stick to each other when the water, then the solvent, in the finish evaporate. The droplets resemble microscopic soccer balls containing Tinker-Toy-like networks of reactive finish inside each.

If you let all the water evaporate out of a pot of actual spaghetti, it hardens. If you then reintroduce water, the spaghetti first softens and becomes sticky, then the individual strands separate. The same happens to shellac with alcohol, lacquer with lacquer thinner and wax with turpentine or a petroleum distillate, only on a molecular scale.

Water-based finishes cure both by chemical reaction and liquid evaporation. Like latex paint and white and yellow glue, water-based finishes are composed of tiny droplets of finish suspended ("emulsified") in water and solvent. These droplets are very large compared to the molecules in the other finishes. Inside each droplet the finish molecules cure by chemical reaction, but the droplets themselves join only as a result of the water, then the solvent, evaporating.

You can picture the droplets of cured finish as microscopic soccer balls. As the water evaporates, the soccer-ball-like droplets approach each other, or "coalesce," so water-based finishes are classified as coalescing finishes. The small amount of organic solvent in these finishes then softens the outer surface of the droplets so they stick together when they come in contact. The solvent then evaporates and a film is formed.

Putting water back onto a cured water-based finish doesn't cause any damage, but a strong organic solvent such as alcohol or lacquer thinner will make the finish sticky, and dull it or dissolve it, just like the solvent does to evaporative finishes.

Using This Information

There are five characteristics you commonly look for in a finish.

> Protection for the wood (resistance to water and moisture-vapor penetration)

> Durability of the finish (scratch, heat, solvent, acid, and alkali resistance)

> Rubbing qualities (ease of rubbing to an even sheen)

> Reversibility (ease of repairing and stripping)

> Curing speed (ease of application without dust or sagging problems).

The Tinker-Toy-like reactive finishes – varnish and two-part finishes – are very protective and durable because the cross-linked molecules are difficult to penetrate or break apart. (Oil finishes offer very little protection or durability because they cure too soft and are left too thin on the wood.)

In contrast, the evaporative finishes – shellac and lacquer – allow some water

The Finishes

Even without the three groups to simplify the finishes, there are still only seven types of finishes to choose among:

> Oil, which includes raw and boiled linseed oil, 100 percent tung oil and blends of oil and varnish, commonly sold as "Danish oil" and "antique oil." The characteristic that unites these finishes is their inability to cure hard, which makes them functional only if you wipe off the excess after each application.

> Varnish, which includes all hard-curing finishes that thin and clean up with turpentine or a petroleum distillate such as paint thinner. Common polyurethane is a varnish, as are wiping varnishes and gel finishes.

> Two-part finishes, which, as the name indicates, are finishes that require the combining of two parts to cure. These include pre- and post-catalyzed lacquer (pre-catalyzed has the catalyst already added), conversion varnish, polyester, two-part polyurethane (both solvent-based and water-based) and epoxy.

> Shellac, the only finish that thins and cleans up with alcohol.

> Nitrocellulose, CAB-acrylic and water-white lacquers, which always thin and clean up with lacquer thinner and can be easily dissolved with lacquer thinner even after they're fully cured.

> Wax, which includes liquid, paste and solid, and always dissolves and thins with turpentine or a petroleum distillate. As with oil, you buff off all the excess to make the soft-curing wax functional.

> Water-based finishes, which include all finishes that thin and clean up with water except those that would be classified as "two-part" finishes.

In practice, you rarely have to choose among all seven types. You usually choose among four.

To begin with, you can eliminate wax from the seven (except for decorative objects such as turnings and carvings) because of its very weak protective and durability qualities. Wax is more often used as a polish on top of another finish to add shine and scratch resistance.

Of the remaining six types, you're usually limited to oil, varnish, shellac and water based if you aren't using a spray gun, because the other finishes dry too quickly to apply with a cloth or brush.

If you are using a spray gun, you normally choose between two-part finishes, shellac, lacquer and water base because you can achieve all the looks and durabilities you want much more quickly with these finishes.

Examples of the seven types of finish are (from left) oil, varnish, two-part finish, shellac, lacquer, water-based finish and wax. Other oils include boiled linseed oil and 100 percent tung oil. The Watco Danish Oil pictured is a mixture of oil and varnish. Polyurethane varnish is the most widely available of the varnishes. Others include alkyd varnish, spar varnish, gel varnish and thinned "wiping" varnish. Pre-catalyzed lacquer is the easiest of the two-part finishes to use. Post-catalyzed lacquer, and especially conversion varnish, are more durable. Shellac is also available in amber color and with the natural wax removed, called SealCoat. Flake shellac is available in a range of yellow and orange colors for you to dissolve yourself. Lacquer is also available as nitrocellulose lacquer and CAB-acrylic lacquer. Water-based finishes can be solely acrylic or a combination of acrylic and polyurethane. Brands of paste wax differ in solvent evaporation rate and in color. Most are clear, but some have pigment or dye added.

Comparing the Finish Groups

Groups	REACTIVE FINISHES (except oil) "Tinker Toys"	EVAPORATIVE FINISHES (except wax) "Spaghetti"	COALESCING FINISHES "Soccer Balls"
Finishes	Varnish; two-part finishes	Shellac; lacquer	Water based
Moisture Resistance	Excellent	Good	Good
Scratch Resistance	Excellent	Good	Very Good
Solvent, Heat, Acid & Alkali Resistance	Excellent	Poor	Poor
Ease of Repair & Stripping	Good (varnish) Poor (two-part finishes)	Excellent	Good
Ease of Rubbing to an Even Sheen	Poor	Excellent	Good
Ease of Dust-Free Application	Poor (varnish) Excellent (two-part finishes)	Excellent	Good

and moisture-vapor (humidity) penetration through the gaps where the spaghetti-like molecules bend around each other. And these finishes are easier to damage with coarse objects, heat, solvents, acids and alkalis because their molecules aren't held together by the strong ties common to reactive finishes.

(Like oil, wax is considerably weaker than shellac and lacquer because it's too soft and left too thin on the wood.)

The coalescing finish – water based – is resistant to abrasive damage because almost all the surface area is cross-linked inside the soccer-ball-like droplets. But where the droplets stick together, water and moisture vapor can penetrate – and heat, solvents, acids, and alkalis can cause the droplets to separate.

This is not to say that evaporative and coalescing finishes are weak finishes, only that they aren't as protective or durable as reactive finishes. If you want the best finish for a kitchen table, kitchen cabinets or office desk, it's a reactive finish (not oil). But this degree of protection and durability is seldom necessary for an entertainment center, most woodwork, or a bed.

The Trade Off

No finish can provide it all, however. There is a price to pay for protection and durability. Scratch resistance, for example, has the negative quality of making a finish difficult to rub to an even sheen using abrasives. Solvent

resistance means greater difficulty recoating, repairing and stripping. Heat resistance makes burn-in repairs less successful, and alkali resistance increases the difficulty of cleaning brushes and stripping.

At the sacrifice of better protection and durability, most refinishers and high-end furniture factories use lacquer instead of two-part finishes because of the reduced problems recoating and repairing, and because lacquer is easier to polish to a beautiful satin sheen.

Ease of Application

As a final lesson to be learned from the Tinker-Toy, spaghetti and soccer-ball analogy, consider that finishes are easier to apply the faster they dry and become dust and sag free. Fast-drying shellac, lacquer, catalyzed finish, and, to a lesser degree, water-based finish, are less likely to run, sag or collect dust than varnish. If you are one of the many woodworkers who use regular alkyd or polyurethane varnish for your finishing projects, you need to recognize that you're using the most difficult of all finishes to make look nice.

Ease of application is the reason factories that want the ultimate in protection and durability for objects such as office furniture and kitchen cabinets use catalyzed finishes instead of polyurethane, even though these finishes are still difficult to rub to an even sheen and to repair and strip. No finish has everything.

Conclusion

It's often difficult to keep all the characteristics in mind when choosing among finishes, especially if you haven't used them all yourself. You can overcome much of your lack of hands-on experience by using the mental pictures of Tinker Toys, spaghetti and soccer balls to help keep the differences straight.

Testing Wood Finishes

A few sample boards can save you from future finishing headaches.

To determine the relative scratch resistance of a finish, push the sharp edge of the cylindrical lead in various "B" and "H" architect's pencils forward on a finish. There's no need to use pressure. The next to hardest pencil that doesn't scratch the finish is the rating for that finish.

Finish manufacturers targeting the furniture industry and large professional finish shops provide a lot of information about their products. Unfortunately, the manufacturers who target amateur woodworkers and small shop professionals aren't as helpful.

In the end, we are often left to our own devices to figure out the characteristics of the finishes we are buying.

Here are some easy tests you can perform in your shop to determine the qualities of the finishes you're using. In most cases you'll want to do the tests on scrap wood. For the most accurate results let the finish cure at least a couple weeks in a warm room before performing the tests.

Scratch Resistance

The ability of a finish to resist damage from coarse or sharp objects is likely one of the most important qualities about which you're concerned.

To a large extent you can know the comparative scratch resistance simply from the type of product. For example, oil-based varnishes (including polyurethane varnish) and catalyzed finishes are much more scratch resistant than shellac and nitrocellulose lacquer, and a little more scratch resistant than acrylic and polyurethane water-based finishes.

But what about differences among brands within each finish type? Or what about the comparative difference between a water-based polyurethane and an oil-based polyurethane – that is, how much scratch resistance are you actually giving up by using a water-based polyurethane?

To determine a finish's scratch resistance, purchase a set of architect's drawing pencils ranging in hardness from about 2B (soft) to 5H (hard). Sharpen each pencil using a knife so you leave the sharp cylindrical edge of the lead intact. If you damage this edge, or

if it becomes worn, sand it flat, holding the pencil 90° to the sandpaper.

Beginning with one of the softer pencils, hold it as you would for writing and push it forward across the cured finish. Maintaining equal pressure, follow with pencils of increasing hardness until you find one that cuts into the finish. The hardness rating for that finish is the rating of the previous pencil – the hardest lead that doesn't cut.

Water Resistance

Another quality you may be looking for in a finish is water resistance. Keep in mind that a thickly applied finish is more water resistant than a thinner layer of finish. So testing won't be very revealing except on thin finishes such as oil or wax, or any film-building finish applied with just one or two coats.

To test for water resistance, make up a sample board with the same number of coats applied in the same manner as on your project. Then place a small puddle of water on the surface and cover it with a small metal or glass cup or jar to prevent evaporation. Check every 10 minutes or so until you notice cracks or discoloration in the finish. Rate the finish at the most recent previous time before the damage occurred.

The most vulnerable surface to water damage is the top edge of cabinet doors just below a sink. To test this surface, stand a finished sample door on a sponge lying in a pan of water. Check the finish around the edge every so often until cracks appear in the finish, the finish delaminates, or there is some discoloration that you can observe.

The relative water resistance of a thin finish can be determined by placing a small puddle of water on the finish and covering it to prevent evaporation. Check at regular intervals for damage.

Heat Resistance

Resistance to damage from hot objects is a very important quality for table and counter surfaces in kitchen and dining areas. Again, finish types tell you something. For example, oil-based polyurethane and catalyzed lacquer should pass almost any test. But shellac, lacquer and water-based finish will likely be vulnerable. There are two tests for heat resistance you can do at home.

To test for dry heat resistance, place a metal cup or pan containing water heated to just below boiling on a cured finish. Remove the cooled container after one hour and look for splits, indentations or discoloration in the finish.

To test a type of finish for wet heat resistance, do the same as above but this time place a cotton or cheesecloth wetted with the same hot water under the cup or pan. After an hour check the surface for splits in the finish or discoloration.

Chemical Resistance

Eating surfaces are also vulnerable to staining from a number of household liquids independent of the thickness of the finish. In other words, the finish itself may become stained. Common products that can cause a problem include vinegar, orange juice, lemon juice, grape juice, ketchup, mustard, coffee, tea, wine and 100-proof alcohol. (You can use denatured alcohol mixed half with water instead of liquor for the alcohol test.)

To test a finish for resistance to each of these liquids place a number of drops on the finish and sponge them off one at a time at short intervals (generally several minutes apart) until the finish under the drops becomes dull, discolored, shows cracks, or the wood underneath becomes stained.

The resistance of the finish to damage is rated at the last time before the damage appeared.

Yellowing

Yellowing can be a good or bad quality depending on the situation. Generally, darker woods and darker-stained woods look good under a finish that yellows because the yellowing makes the wood appear warmer. But yellowing often detracts from lighter woods or from woods that have been stained or "pickled" white or near white.

Acrylic water-based finishes don't yellow at all. Polyurethane water-based finishes yellow a tiny bit. Varnishes and oil/varnish blends yellow significantly, but the degree of yellowing will vary greatly among

Whether or not a finish is resistant to dry heat can be determined by placing a pot of hot water on a finished scrap board. Heat the water to just short of boiling and leave it for an hour. See if it causes any damage.

Many household substances can cause damage to a finish. To check the resistance of the finish you're using, place a number of drops of the substance, in this case ketchup, on the finish and sponge them off one at a time several minutes apart.

To determine the color of a finish, and thus the relative amount of color change it will add to the wood, pour a little of several finishes into jars and place them next to each other against a white background. Here I'm comparing two wiping varnishes. Waterlox is much darker and will make wood significantly darker than Minwax's Wipe-On Poly.

brands. Lacquers also vary among types and brands.

There are two tests you can perform in your home to determine the yellowing characteristics of various finishes. The first is for the color of the finish in liquid form and the second is for how much the finish continues to yellow as it ages.

To test for the color of a liquid finish, pour some into a glass jar or onto a glass plate and hold the glass against something white such as a piece of paper. It's easy to compare finishes when you place the test jars or plates next to each other.

To test for the amount a finish yellows as it ages, apply a coat or two to a piece of white plastic. After the finish has cured, cover part of it with paper or masking tape and leave the plastic in a normal room setting or in a window for several weeks.

Every few days remove the paper or masking tape and compare the color of the covered and uncovered parts.

Keep in mind that most woods darken with age, so some of the "yellowing" you may experience after application to wood could be associated with it rather than the finish.

Choosing a Finish for Color

Different finishes look different on different species.

There are many reasons to choose one finish over another. Usually the most important is for protection and durability – how well a finish protects the wood from moisture and how resistant the finish is to being damaged by coarse objects, heat and solvents.

Other significant factors include drying time (you don't want a fast drying finish if you're brushing) and odor (some finishes have a less irritating aroma than others).

There's also color. Finishes differ in color, or the amount of color, they add to wood. For example, clear paste wax adds the least amount of color and the least amount of darkening to wood. Wax adds a little shine, but otherwise leaves the wood looking very close to natural.

Water-based finishes don't add color either, but they do darken the wood noticeably. The lack of color can be an advantage on "white" woods such as maple or ash or a disadvantage on darker woods, making them look "washed out."

Nitrocellulose lacquer and blonde or clear shellac add a slight yellow/orange tint to wood. But not nearly as much as does orange or amber shellac.

(Shellac in flake form is usually labeled blonde and orange. In prepackaged liquid form the equivalent to blonde is "clear" or "SealCoat." The equivalent to orange is "amber.")

Oil-based varnish, including polyurethane varnish, and boiled linseed oil add a darker yellow/orange tint than lacquer or blonde/clear shellac. More significantly, varnish and oil continue to darken as they age – boiled linseed oil considerably more than varnish.

Mixtures of varnish and oil, often sold as "Danish Oil" or "Antique Oil," fall in between varnish and oil in their tendency to darken depending on the ratio of each that is included.

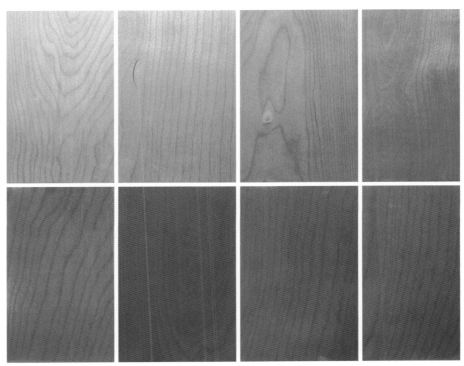

Seven finishes on maple. Top row from left: unfinished, clear paste wax, water-based finish, nitrocellulose lacquer. Bottom row from left: clear/blonde shellac, amber/orange shellac, polyurethane varnish, boiled linseed oil.

Seven finishes on oak. Top row from left: unfinished, clear paste wax, water-based finish, nitrocellulose lacquer. Bottom row from left: clear/blonde shellac, amber/orange shellac, polyurethane varnish, boiled linseed oil.

Seven Finishes

You'll find on these pages pictures of seven finishes (not including oil/varnish blends) on four different woods – maple, oak, cherry and walnut – to illustrate the differences in the amount of color each adds. Be sure to look closely at the woods in each of the pictures. The finishes have somewhat different effects depending on the wood.

I used the most commonly available finishes within each finish category for illustration. But there are exceptions within each of the categories. For example, though most brands of paste wax offer only a clear, some add pigment to produce colored paste waxes.

Though rare, some manufacturers of water-based finishes add a little dye colorant to make the finish better resemble the look of nitrocellulose lacquer. Information on the can or in the promotional literature will inform you of this.

Within the lacquer category, CAB-acrylic and water-white lacquers add considerably less color than does nitrocellulose lacquer. In fact, a good quality CAB-acrylic lacquer adds no color, similar to water-based finish. But it does bring out the richness of darker woods better than water-based finish.

In addition to clear/blonde and amber/orange shellac, some specialty suppliers offer a number of additional colors, including garnet, button and various shades of lemon.

Depending on the oils and resins used in manufacture, some varnishes darken wood more than others. For example, Waterlox, which is a popular wiping varnish used by woodworkers, is made with phenolic resin and tung oil, both of which are darker than the more common alkyd and polyurethane resins and soybean (soya) oil used to make most varnishes.

Though rarely used by itself as a finish, 100 percent tung oil darkens a little less than boiled linseed oil.

In choosing a finish for your project, you need to take into account a number of characteristics of the various finishes. One is the color the finish adds, or doesn't add, to the wood.

Seven finishes on cherry. Top row from left: unfinished, clear paste wax, water-based finish, nitrocellulose lacquer. Bottom row from left: clear/blonde shellac, amber/orange shellac, polyurethane varnish, boiled linseed oil.

Seven finishes on walnut. Top row from left: unfinished, clear paste wax, water-based finish, nitrocellulose lacquer. Bottom row from left: clear/blonde shellac, amber/orange shellac, polyurethane varnish, boiled linseed oil.

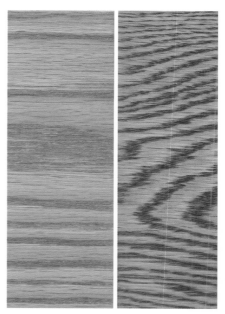

Boiled linseed oil (shown here on oak) and to a lesser extent varnish darken considerably as they age. On the left is freshly applied boiled linseed oil. On the right is boiled linseed oil that has aged about 10 years.

Finish Compatibility

Discover what finishing products work well together.

I'm sure you've come across cautions in woodworking books and magazines instructing you to "use a compatible product" – stain, filler, glaze, finish – and you've wondered, "What is compatible, and what isn't?"

The phrase, "use a compatible," is a "cover-my-behind" dodge used by authors who have little understanding of finishes. If you follow their procedures and then have problems, it must be your fault for using an "incompatible" product. The burden is on you to know what is compatible and what isn't.

So what is compatible with what?

Three entirely different situations can be referred to by the word "compatible":

❭ Mixing liquids with liquids

❭ Applying stains, fillers, glazes and finishes

❭ Coating over an existing finished or painted surface.

As I explain each of these, you will see that the issue of compatibility has been greatly exaggerated. In most cases, it's obvious which liquids mix. Almost any finishing product can be applied over any other as long as the previous is dry. And almost any finish can be applied over almost any old surface as long as it is clean and dull.

Mixing Liquids

Most products you use in finishing (or painting) are water-based or mineral-spirits-based. All water-based mix successfully, and all mineral-spirits-based mix successfully. But the two cannot be mixed together.

Wax mixed with varnish works well only if you wipe off all the excess after each coat, just as with wax mixed with oil.

It's easy to know when two products don't mix: They separate. For this reason it's wise to use a glass jar for mixing if you have any question, so you can see what's happening.

Just as all finishing products that thin with water can be mixed, so can all finishing products that thin with mineral spirits (paint thinner). Here I'm adding some stain of one brand to some polyurethane of another to make a "varnish stain," a stain that can be left a little thicker on the wood or over another coat of finish.

Applying Finishes

Almost any finishing product – stain, filler, glaze, finish – can be applied successfully over any other finishing product, except wax (including residue wax from paint strippers), as long as that product is dry. This includes every finish over boiled linseed oil, and water-based finishes over oil stains. You might need to give the oil-based product several days or a week to dry in a warm room, but once dry every finish will bond fine without problems.

Think of painting a piece of furniture you finished several years earlier with oil. You wouldn't hesitate using a water-based paint.

There are several fairly uncommon exceptions to this rule.

One is brushing a product that contains the solvent for an underlying stain. For example, if you brush a water-based finish over a water-soluble dye that doesn't contain a binder, you will smear the dye and cause the coloring to become uneven. The same is true if you brush lacquer over a lacquer stain. The lacquer-thinner solvent in the lacquer will dissolve the stain and your brush will smear it.

But there's no problem spraying because no smearing can occur.

If you need to brush a water-based finish over a water-soluble stain or lacquer over a lacquer stain – to match a color, for example – you can apply a barrier coat of shellac or varnish in between. Shellac is usually the better choice.

Another exception is applying lacquer over varnish, though I don't know why you would do this. The lacquer thinner in the lacquer may cause the varnish to blister. Spray light coats to begin with or apply a barrier coat of shellac.

Also, high-performance coatings such as conversion varnish, polyester and two-part polyurethane finishes have special rules for application. Few amateurs use these finishes, but if you do, be sure to follow the manufacturer's instructions.

Almost any finishing product can be applied over any other as long as the "other" is dry and the product you're brushing doesn't dissolve and smear the existing. I applied a water-soluble dye to this mahogany. Then I applied a thin shellac "washcoat" as a barrier so the water-based grain filler I used wouldn't dissolve and smear the dye. After the filler dried, I brushed polyurethane. I alternated water-based, alcohol-based and mineral-spirits-based without any problems because each previous product was dry.

The rule for coating successfully over an old surface is that the existing surface has to be clean and dull. So before applying another coat of finish to this 25-year-old lacquered cabinet door, I washed it with household ammonia and water. Ammonia cleans kitchen grease and dulls most finishes in one step.

The easy way to test the bonding of a finish is to scratch it with the edge of a coin. If you can scratch off a layer (as is the case here) rather than merely dent it, the finish isn't bonded well.

A more accurate method for testing adhesion is to make a half-dozen cuts into the finish in perpendicular patterns using a razor blade, with each cut about a millimeter apart and an inch long. Then press masking tape over the cuts and lift it quickly. If the edges of the cuts remain fairly clean, as they are here, the bond is good.

Coating an Old Surface

Almost any paint or finish can be applied over almost any old paint or finish as long as the surface is clean and dull.

It's pretty obvious how bonding problems could occur if you apply paint or finish over a greasy or waxy surface, or over a surface that is covered with dirt (such as a deck). So the first rule is that the surface be clean.

Because there are two types of dirt, solvent-soluble and water-soluble, there are two types of cleaner: petroleum distillate (mineral spirits and naphtha) and water, or soap-and-water. Petroleum distillate won't remove dirt on a deck, and water won't remove grease or wax.

Some strong cleaners, such as household ammonia and TSP (available at paint stores), will usually remove both, however. Also, abrading the surface with sandpaper, steel wool or an abrasive pad will usually remove both types of dirt, along with the top surface of the coating – paint or finish.

The surface also has to be dull to get a good bond. Liquids don't flow out and "wet" glossy surfaces well. Think of water beading on a car or glossy tabletop.

You can dull any surface using sandpaper, steel wool or an abrasive pad, and many times you can dull the surface adequately with one of the strong cleaners – a little household ammonia in a bucket of water or TSP in water. Depending on the paint or finish you're trying to dull, solvent-based "degreaser" and "liquid sandpaper" also often work. It won't hurt to try; you can always follow with an abrasive.

Besides "wetting," the reason a surface has to be dull is to create a "mechanical" bond between the new coating and the existing one. Dullness always indicates an uneven surface containing scratches, bumps or other irregularities that give the new coating something to lock into and grip. This is sometimes called "tooth."

There are three situations, however, where coating over an existing coating can be problematic.

The first is when using any finish that contains lacquer thinner. This solvent can cause any old coating, even lacquer itself, to blister. To avoid blistering, spray several light coats and let them dry thoroughly before spraying fully wet coats. Or apply a coat of shellac first then still spray a light coat of lacquer to begin with. Brushing lacquer is always risky because you can't brush light coats.

The second is when coating over a high-performance finish that has been applied in a factory or professional shop. Bonding can be weaker even with a clean-and-dull surface.

Also, water-based finish and latex paint don't bond as well to existing coatings as do solvent-based paint and finish.

Testing for a Good Bond

So you need to know how to test for a good bond. There are two ways.

The easiest is to press the edge of a coin into the newly applied coating after it has fully dried and drag the coin a few inches. You should just dent the surface, not separate the newly applied coating.

Another method is to use a razor blade to make perpendicular cuts into the coating about a millimeter apart and an inch long. Then press masking or other sticky tape over the cuts and pull it up quickly. The cleaner the cuts remain after removing the tape, the better the bond.

Of course, you should perform both these tests on an inconspicuous area or, better, on scrap wood.

Finishing the 5 Types of Wood

Organize all the woods into categories to determine the best finishing strategy.

Woodworkers choose among dozens of wood species for projects. Unless you've actually used many different woods and experienced how they machine, feel, smell and respond to stains and finishes, you probably find making an intelligent choice confusing. There needs to be some way to organize the woods so decisions are easier.

And there is.

To begin with, you can divide all the woods into five large categories: pine and related softwoods; coarse-grained hardwoods; medium-grained hardwoods; fine-grained hardwoods; and exotics.

Traditional furniture is rarely made of pine or exotics, so for simplicity's sake, let's reduce the categories to three: coarse-, medium- and fine-grained hardwoods. And to begin with, let's deal with just the five most common traditional furniture hardwoods: oak, walnut, mahogany, cherry and maple.

Importance of Grain

Grain is the most important indicator for identifying woods. Grain is the open pores or pitting in wood that give it texture. In finished wood you may have to look closely to see the grain because it may have been filled.

Most old furniture was made with one of these five woods, so identifying woods in antiques is fairly easy. If the grain is coarse, the wood is likely oak. If it is fine – that is, if there's no obvious pitting – the wood is probably cherry or maple. If there is pitting and it's finer and more evenly spaced than in oak, the wood is almost always walnut or mahogany.

To tell the difference between cherry and maple and between walnut and mahogany, the color of the heartwood is key. On an

Pictured are a number of woods woodworkers choose among for projects. Clockwise from the top are pine, oak, walnut, cherry, butternut, mahogany, ash, gum, soft maple, poplar, chestnut, teak, rosewood and ebony.

antique you may need to cut a sliver from an inconspicuous place to see its color. On newly milled wood, you can simply look at the color.

If the color of fine-grained wood has a reddish tint, the wood is cherry. If near white, it's maple. If the color of a medium-grained wood is charcoal gray, it's walnut. If reddish, the wood is mahogany.

Keep in mind that oak can have a very coarse grain when plainsawn, or less coarse when quartersawn. Quartersawn oak is usually easy to identify because of its medullary rays.

Additional Woods

Of course, wood identification becomes more difficult when more woods are added. Tradi-

tionally, chestnut, elm and ash were sometimes used instead of oak. Each is coarse grained but subtly different. You just have to learn to recognize these differences.

Butternut, hickory and pecan were also used, and their grain resembles walnut and mahogany. Color can help in identification. Butternut is tan; hickory and pecan are tan with a slight pink cast.

There are lots of fine-grained woods in addition to cherry and maple, including birch, poplar, gum, beech, yew and holly. Gum and beech have a color similar to hickory and pecan. Yew is light brown to reddish. The heartwood of poplar has a distinct greenish color, which ages to light brown. The others, and the sapwood of poplar, are near white.

To distinguish between these fine-grained woods, you need to recognize subtle differences in figure. Figure is primarily grain orientation, the appearance of which has a lot to do with the way boards and veneer are cut, but also small distinguishing characteristics such as the flecks in cherry, maple and beech.

Exotic Woods

Mahogany could be classified as an exotic wood because it grows in jungle areas. But mahogany has been used so extensively for so long, it makes more sense to classify it as a medium-grained wood along with walnut, hickory and pecan.

With the exception of teak and rosewood, exotic woods were rarely used until recently, and then usually just for decoration and veneer. Now a wide variety of exotic woods are used for bowl turning, decks and furniture.

Most of these woods are medium-grained, but many are very distinctive in color and figure and therefore fairly easy to identify once you have become familiar with them. I don't have any easy categories that will help.

Finishing the Five Categories

Here are some thoughts about finishing each of the five categories of wood.

The grain of walnut and mahogany are very similar. On unfinished wood you can use the color to tell the difference, but the colors can be very close on antique furniture due to the way the woods oxidize. I'm getting a look at the color of the raw wood on this antique piecrust table by cutting away a little sliver on the underside of a leg to determine that the wood is walnut, not mahogany.

Pine and related softwoods have a very pronounced grain – soft, absorbent, white spring growth alternating with hard, dense, orange summer growth. The spring growth absorbs stain well, but the summer growth doesn't. So staining these woods usually reverses the color, making the spring growth darker than the summer growth.

Pine also tends to blotch, which can be quite unattractive.

On the other hand, pine finishes well with any finish, though I don't like oil finishes because so many coats are usually required to bring the sheen of the spring growth even with that of the summer growth.

Like pine, fine-grained woods tend to

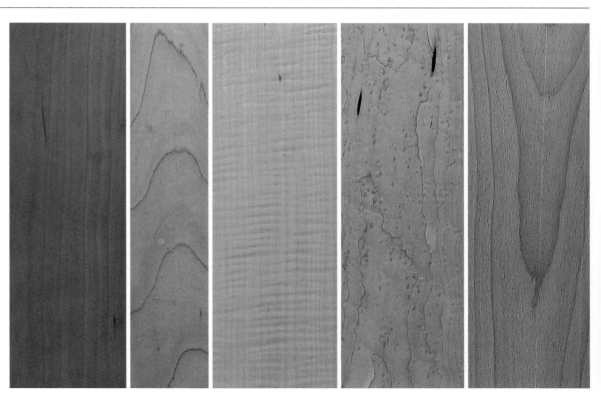

Woodworkers use a great many fine-grained woods. Examples include from the left: cherry, hard maple, curly maple, bird's eye maple and beech. As with most fine-grained woods, these tend to blotch, especially when stained. But the blotching is often considered attractive as with curly and bird's eye maple. Water-based finishes look especially good on the white woods but make darker woods such as cherry look washed out unless a stain is used.

blotch – often in an unattractive way. But sometimes, as with curly, bird's eye and mottled woods, the blotching is very attractive. You can reduce the blotching by applying a washcoat (thinned finish) before applying the stain, but the coloring will then be lighter.

All fine-grained woods finish well with any finish, but oil finishes require many coats for a nice appearance. Water-based finishes look wonderful on the white woods because they don't add any yellow/orange coloring, but they make cherry look washed out unless a stain is applied under the finish.

Medium-grained woods finish to look the most elegant of all woods as long as the pores are filled. This is one reason mahogany and walnut have long been considered the premier furniture woods.

All finishes except water-based look wonderful on these woods, and water-based also looks fairly good if a stain is applied under the finish.

All stains and finishes also look good on coarse-grained woods. Only quartersawn oak looks good filled. Plainsawn, coarse-grained woods look plastic, in my opinion, when filled. The filled areas are too wide.

Water-soluble dye stains don't color the pores well in coarse-grained woods. If you use a water dye, follow it with an oil-based wiping stain of a similar color, either directly over the dye or over a washcoat or sealer coat, to add color to the pores.

All stains and finishes (water-based with a stain applied underneath) also look good on exotic woods. The common finishing problem with these woods is getting an oil or varnish finish (not others) to dry in a reasonable time because of the natural oily resins many of these woods contain.

To overcome the problem, wipe the surface with naphtha or acetone just before applying the first coat of oil or varnish. Then apply the finish right after the solvent evaporates off the surface. Or apply a barrier coat of dewaxed shellac under varnish.

Three common examples of medium-grained woods used in woodworking are from the left: butternut, walnut and mahogany. These woods are widely considered the most elegant when their pores are filled. All stains and finishes can be used successfully.

Common coarse-grained woods include from the left: plainsawn oak, quartersawn oak, ash, chestnut and elm. All stains and finishes look good on these woods.

Solvents

Understanding Solvents & Thinners

Categorize by type to cut through confusion.

Finishing can't exist without solvents and thinners – even water-based stains and finishes contain them. If you understand a little about solvents and how they relate to one another, you'll have more control of your work. You'll be able to speed up or slow down the drying time of your finish to compensate for the weather, and you'll be able to manipulate the viscosity of your finish to make it flow better. You'll also be better able to choose the best solvent for cleaning in various situations.

Though the terms "solvent" and "thinner" often are used interchangeably (and I will sometimes use the more general term "solvent" here to refer to both), they are actually quite different. A solvent is a liquid that dissolves a solid, such as a cured finish, while a thinner is a liquid that thins a stain or finish already in liquid form. Sometimes a liquid solvent or thinner just thins a finish, and other times it both dissolves and thins a finish. (See "What Dissolves & Thins What" on the next page.)

Solvents are grouped in families. There are five families, not including the special ones used in paint-and-varnish removers: petroleum distillates, alcohols, ketones, esters and glycol ethers. Each family reacts with a finish in a different way.

Within each family, solvents differ primarily in evaporation rate, with some evaporating rapidly at room temperature and others evaporating very slowly or not at all.

Here's the easy way to understand solvents for wood finishes.

First, divide the solvents between the petroleum distillates, including turpentine, and all the rest. Because most of the solvents on the shelves are petroleum distillates, this reduces the rest to a number that's easy to handle.

Then make sense of the petroleum distillates and turpentine, all of which do essentially the same thing at different evaporation rates, and when this is done, deal with the rest.

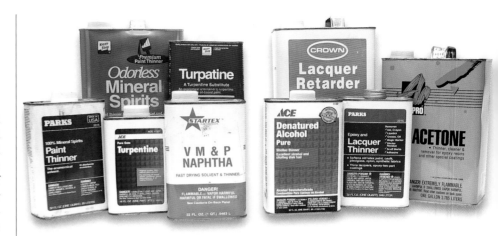

The easy way to makes sense of solvents is to divide them into petroleum distillates (left) and all the others (right). Once you have understood the petroleum distillates, all of which do essentially the same thing at different evaporation rates, it's easy to handle the rest.

Petroleum Distillates

Petroleum distillates are all distillations of petroleum. They include mineral spirits (paint thinner), naphtha, toluene, xylene and some "turpentine substitutes" such as turpatine and T.R.P.S. The primary use for these solvents in wood finishing is thinning waxes, oils and varnishes, including polyurethane varnish, and cleaning brushes. The solvents are also used to clean oil, grease and wax.

Turpentine is a distillation of pine tree sap. Before the mid-20th century, turpentine was widely used as a thinner and clean-up solvent for oil paint and varnish and also as a grease and wax cleaner.

With the growth of the automobile industry and its need for petroleum products, a large number of petroleum solvents were introduced and these have almost entirely replaced turpentine because they are less expensive and have less unpleasant odor. The only sector in which turpentine is still used in any significant quantity is fine arts.

To distill petroleum, it is heated higher and higher and the gases released at different temperatures are condensed into the various liquid solvents.

The first gas to come off is methane, which doesn't condense at room temperature, only at much colder temperatures. Then there's ethane, propane, butane, etc. Heptane and octane are used to make gasoline, a liquid

that evaporates very rapidly. Gasoline is sometimes used as a cleaner, but it is very dangerous because it is explosive. About 20 years ago the retired local sheriff in my town, an amateur woodworker, died of burns he received in an explosion while using gasoline for cleaning.

The solvents we use in wood finishing evaporate much more slowly than gasoline and are relatively safe to use, even with poor ventilation. But it's still unwise to use them in a room with a flame such as a pilot light.

Kerosene is also widely available, but it evaporates too slowly to be of much use in finishing. Mineral oil (also called paraffin oil) and paraffin wax don't evaporate at all at room temperature. Paraffin wax, in fact, is a solid at room temperature.

You may have noticed in using these solvents that the slower the evaporation, the oilier the liquid substance. Mineral spirits is oilier than naphtha, and kerosene is oilier than mineral spirits. Mineral oil is oil. Because none of these distillations damage finishes (except wax), and because oily substances are effective at picking up dust and adding shine to dull surfaces, petroleum distillates are widely used as the main ingredient in furniture polishes.

Mineral Spirits & Naphtha

The two most widely used finishing solvents are mineral spirits and naphtha. For our purposes, the principal differences between the two are evaporation rate and oiliness. Naphtha evaporates more quickly than mineral spirits and is "drier," that is, less oily. Naphtha is therefore better for cleaning all types of oily, greasy or waxy surfaces. Mineral spirits is better for thinning oils, varnishes (including polyurethane varnish) and oil-based paints because it leaves more time for the coating to level after brushing.

Naphtha is a stronger solvent than mineral spirits, but this is rarely significant in wood finishing. Mineral spirits is strong enough for any normal operation.

To better place turpentine among the petroleum distillates, think of it as having the solvent strength of naphtha but the evaporation rate and oiliness of mineral spirits. I don't know of any situation in wood finishing where this is important.

The nickname for mineral spirits is "paint thinner." Back in the early days of mineral spirits, before World War II, all paints were oil-based. So there was only one thinner for paint. The nickname made sense.

Today, with water-based paints and finishes in wide use, the name could be confusing to beginners. Paint thinner is used only with oil-based paints and finishes.

It's important to emphasize that mineral spirits and paint thinner are the same thing. Amazingly, there are manufacturers who try to trick you into paying more by labeling their containers "pure" mineral spirits and charging more.

The common naphtha available in paint stores is VM&P Naphtha. VM&P stands for

What Dissolves & Thins What

SUBSTANCE	DISSOLVES	THINS
Mineral spirits (paint thinner), naptha, turpentine	Wax	Wax, oil, varnish, polyurethane
Toluene, xylene	Dissolves wax; softens water-based finish, white & yellow glue	Wax, oil, varnish, polyurethane, conversion varnish
Alcohol	Shellac	Shellac, lacquer
Lacquer thinner	Shellac, lacquer, water-based finish	Lacquer, shellac, catalyzed lacquer
Glycol ether	Shellac, lacquer, water-based finish	Lacquer, water-based finish
Water	—	Water-based finish

"varnish makers and painters." Stronger and faster evaporating naphthas exist, but these are rarely sold to the general public.

Toluene & Xylene

Toluene, nicknamed "toluol," and xylene, nicknamed "xylol," are the strong, smelly, fast-evaporating and "dry" parts of mineral spirits and naphtha. These solvents are removed from mineral spirits and naphtha at refineries and sold separately as cleaners, and also as solvents for some high-performance spray finishes such as conversion varnish. Toluene and xylene are very effective as cleaners, but I find naphtha adequate for almost all situations.

Toluene evaporates a little more quickly than xylene, but this is significant only when using the solvent as a thinner.

The problem with these two solvents is that they are relatively toxic. They will affect your nervous system causing irritability and drunkenness, and in large doses could cause serious health problems. You should never use them in any sizeable quantity in a room without good exhaust.

One very interesting use for toluene and xylene is to soften latex paint. Using a dampened cloth (and solvent-resistant gloves) you can easily remove latex paint that has spattered off a paint roller, or even a full coat of latex paint, from any finish except water-

Any petroleum distillate or turpentine can be used to thin wax, oil or varnish, but mineral spirits (paint thinner) is best. It gives the finish time to level and is less expensive and has less unpleasant odor than turpentine.

Naphtha is usually better than mineral spirits for cleaning oily or waxy surfaces (including crayon marks) because it evaporates much faster. Naphtha also has more solvent strength than mineral spirits, which is sometimes helpful on old waxed surfaces such as this one.

based finish, without causing any damage to the underlying finish. In fact, the products sold specifically to do this, "Oops!" and "Goof-Off," are principally xylene.

Because white and yellow glues are the same chemistry as latex paint, you can also use toluene or xylene to soften and scrub these glues from wood when you have glue seepage or fingerprints that you didn't fully remove during sanding. You will need to use a toothbrush or soft brass wire brush to get the glue out of the pores.

Odorless Mineral Spirits

The mineral spirits left after the toluene and xylene are removed is sold as "odorless" mineral spirits. When understood this way, it's obvious that odorless mineral spirits is a weaker solvent than regular mineral spirits. But I've never found this to be a problem. It still appears to be strong enough to thin all common oils, varnishes and oil paints.

The disadvantage of odorless mineral spirits, of course, is that it is considerably more expensive because of the extra steps necessary to produce it. You may find the extra expense worth it, however, just to avoid the unpleasant odor of regular mineral spirits.

Turpentine Substitutes

The so-called turpentine substitutes are an interesting breed. My first question when I talk to the companies that produce them is, "Isn't that the role of mineral spirits?" (One company spokesman, identified as the "chemist," explained that these products were necessary because of all the protests against cutting down trees to make turpentine! Of course, trees aren't cut down; the sap is drained.)

Actually, these solvents seem to have similar characteristics to turpentine in that they have the solvent strength of naphtha but an evaporation rate closer to mineral spirits. So they are useful to fine artists but provide no special benefit to wood finishers.

These are all of the petroleum distillates used in wood finishing. Now for the other solvents.

Alcohol

Alcohol is the solvent for shellac. The solvent dissolves solid shellac flakes and thins the liquid shellac after dissolving. There are two alcohol types available at paint stores: methanol and denatured.

Methanol evaporates a little faster than denatured, but it is toxic and could blind or even kill you if you breathe too high a vapor concentration for too long. You shouldn't use it unless you have good ventilation in your shop.

Denatured alcohol is ethyl alcohol (the alcohol in beer, wine and liquor) that has been made poisonous so we don't have to pay liquor taxes to buy it. This is the alcohol you should use with shellac.

In situations where shellac is not the finish, alcohol has the further use as a felt-tip-pen ink remover. Dampen a cloth and wipe over the mark and you will remove it in most cases. You won't damage any finish except shellac as long as you don't soak the surface.

Lacquer Thinner

Lacquer thinner is the solvent and thinner for all the types of lacquer, including nitrocellulose, CAB-acrylic and catalyzed. It's the most interesting of the solvents because it's composed of half-a-dozen or so different individual solvents. Manufacturers vary these to control solvent strength and evaporation rate.

Solvents from five different families are used in lacquer thinners, including toluene, xylene and "high-flash" (meaning fast evaporating) naphtha from the petroleum-distillate family. The other four families are ketones,

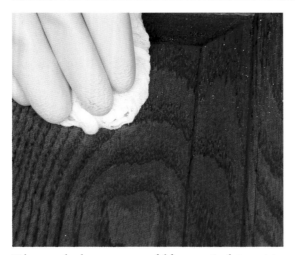

Toluene and xylene are very useful for removing latex paint spatter from all surfaces except water-based finishes. The commercial products Oops! and Goof Off are based on xylene and sold for this purpose.

Denatured alcohol is the best solvent for thinning shellac. It is much less toxic than methanol.

esters, glycol ethers and alcohols.

All the individual solvents from the ketone, ester and glycol-ether families dissolve lacquer on their own, but they evaporate at different rates. So manufacturers choose among them to make a thinner that evaporates in steps at the speeds they want. Alcohol doesn't dissolve lacquer on its own, but it does when in combination with these other solvents. So one or more of the alcohols is usually added to the mix to reduce cost.

The nature of lacquer is that it can be fully dissolved and still be too thick to spray efficiently. So to further thin the lacquer without adding expensive dissolving solvents, manufacturers add up to 50 percent toluene, xylene or high-flash naphtha to, in effect, "thin" the lacquer thinner.

By varying the solvents used, manufacturers can control the strength of lacquer thinner (automotive lacquers need a higher percentage of dissolving solvent) and the speed of evaporation. For example, lacquer retarders are made to evaporate slower so the lacquer stays "open" on the surface of the wood longer in order to eliminate blushing (turning white) in humid weather and dry spray (a sandy surface) in hot weather.

The purpose of using multiple individual solvents evaporating at intervals is to control the thickening of the lacquer on a vertical surface to reduce runs. The lacquer thickens quickly after being sprayed but enough of the slower-evaporating solvents remain so the finish has time to flatten out. Lacquer thinner is unique among solvents for having this characteristic.

A cheaper "clean-up" lacquer thinner is often available. It's made with a higher percentage of "thinning" petroleum-distillate solvents and doesn't dissolve lacquer well. You will have problems if you use this thinner for thinning lacquer.

Acetone & MEK

Only one of the families of active solvents in lacquer thinner (ketones, esters and glycol ethers) is commonly available in paint stores. This is the ketone family. The two fastest evaporating ketones, acetone and methyl ethyl ketone (MEK), are usually available.

Both make excellent cleaners, but keep in mind that they will damage and remove all but the most solvent-resistant paints and finishes.

Brush Cleaners & Deglossers

Brands of brush cleaner and deglosser (liquid sandpaper) vary greatly in their composition. Some are even water-based, but these work more slowly and are less effective than solvent-based.

You can usually substitute a brush cleaner for the mineral spirits or lacquer thinner you may otherwise use to clean your varnish, lacquer or water-based finish brushes. (It's easiest to clean shellac with household ammonia and water.) Brush cleaners are usually more expensive, however.

What is left unsaid about deglossers is that it matters greatly which paint or finish you're trying to clean and dull. Cleaning grease or wax is no problem, but high-performance paints and finishes such as UV-cured coatings, catalyzed lacquer, conversion varnish and even oil-based polyurethane are very solvent resistant. So it's rarely possible to dull them short of abrading with real sandpaper or steel wool.

Conclusion

Manufacturers are very creative in their labeling, so you could easily come across solvents with different names than the ones I'm using. But if you read the intended uses listed on the containers, you should be able to place them in one of the above categories.

Denatured alcohol is especially useful for removing felt-tippen marks. The solvent won't damage any finish except shellac, as long as you don't soak the surface.

Lacquer thinner is a blend of half-a-dozen or so solvents specially formulated for thinning lacquer. The blend allows for differing evaporation rates and for evaporation in steps to reduce runs on vertical surfaces.

Choosing a Spray Gun

Though a good finish can be achieved with other methods, guns are faster.

Spray guns are available in three configurations: siphon-feed with the cup under the gun, gravity-feed with the cup on top of the gun, and pressure-feed where the finish is fed to the gun through a hose connected to a separate pressurized pot. To illustrate the three configurations, I'm using the Apollo Atomizer spray gun, which is unique in that it can be set up in all three configurations and it can run off either a turbine or a compressor.

You don't have to use a spray gun to get good results. You can achieve a near-perfect finish using a rag or brush. For example: you can apply a wipe-on/wipe-off finish such as oil, wiping varnish or gel varnish; you can sand a brushed finish level and cover the sanding scratches with wiping varnish or gel varnish; or you can sand a brushed finish level and rub it to the sheen you want using fine abrasives.

But spray guns have some important advantages over brushing or wiping. The most obvious is application speed; applying a finish with a spray gun is much faster than brushing or wiping.

Spray guns also allow you to use fast-drying finishes to build a thickness rapidly with minimal dust nibs and make it possible to apply a finish film that is almost perfectly level (no orange peel) and to "tone" the wood.

Toning is spraying a finish with a little colorant (pigment or dye) added to tweak or adjust the color of the wood – whether stained or not. Toning can also be used to create highlights and other decorative effects.

The downsides of spray guns compared to brushes and rags are greater cost, increased waste because of lost overspray, and considerably more complexity keeping the tool in good operating condition.

So how do you choose a spray gun if you decide you want to take advantage of its benefits?

It's actually quite straightforward. First, you decide on your source of air: compressor or turbine. Second, you choose a spray-gun configuration: siphon-feed, gravity-feed or pressure-feed. Third, you decide on quality – that is, how much you're willing to pay.

And finally you choose a brand. Because competition keeps all manufacturers on the cutting edge of the technology, this is not as complicated as you may think.

Source of Air

Your first choice is between a gun that runs off a compressor and one that runs off a turbine.

It's important to emphasize that almost all compressor-supplied spray guns sold today produce the same soft spray, called HVLP, or High-Volume Low-Pressure, as do turbine-supplied guns. Practically speaking, there is only HVLP anymore.)

Choose a compressed-air spray gun if you already have a compressor that produces at least 7 or 8 CFM (about 2 horsepower) and has a 20-gallon or larger air-storage tank, or if you need a compressor to operate other tools such as a sander or nail gun.

Choose a turbine spray gun if you need portability or if you're short on space; turbines are small. Turbine spray guns are usually sold together with the turbine, but you can mix and match if you like because the connections are standard.

A compressor gives you more control over the air to the gun than a turbine does because you can increase the pressure as much as you want (though going over 10 pounds per square inch at the air cap breaks the definition of HVLP and can be illegal in some areas). But the air produced by a turbine is dry so there's no need to insert moisture-removing filters as there is with compressors.

Configuration

Spray guns that operate off each air source are available in three configurations: siphon-feed, gravity-feed and pressure-feed. All three work well, but for slightly different situations.

The siphon-feed configuration has a material cup attached under the spray gun. In the old high-pressure guns, a vacuum draws the fluid up through a tube into the air stream where it is atomized.

But high-volume air in HVLP guns doesn't create enough suction to do this. So the cup has to be pressurized through a tube running from the gun body to the cup. Some of the air is thus siphoned off from the airflow, which can cause poorer atomization and increased orange peel if the air supply isn't adequate.

Though most under-the-gun cups are now pressurized, manufacturers still call them siphon-feed.

Gravity-feed guns, with the cup on top of the gun, don't need to be pressurized. The fluid flows into the atomizing air stream by gravity alone. No pressure is needed, though some turbine-supplied guns do pressurize this cup to increase the fluid flow.

Having the cup on top of the gun has the advantage of eliminating the possibility of dragging the cup across a horizontal surface if you aren't careful.

But you can fit a siphon-feed spray gun into an interior cabinet space much easier than you can a gravity-feed gun, and a siphon-feed gun is more versatile because it can be converted to pressure-feed simply by replacing the cup with a connecting hose to a separate pressurized pot.

The pressure-feed system, with its separate pot that is pressurized by compressed air, is usually limited to production situations where a high volume of work is being finished. But not having a cup attached below or above the gun frees the gun to get into small spaces and even to be used upside-down. You may find that having these options is worth the extra effort involved in cleaning the pot and connecting hose.

Most turbine guns are siphon-feed. Gravity-feed guns seem to be more popular with finishers using compressors, probably because this is the configuration used by auto-body finishers. This is the bigger market, so most available compressor guns are gravity feed.

Quality

Just as with woodworking tools, always buy the best quality you can afford. Quality in

Quick-connect air inlets differ for compressor- and turbine-supplied spray guns. The air inlet on top is for turbine air; the one on the bottom is for compressed air.

Air hoses also differ for compressor- and turbine-supplied guns. The red air hose is for compressed air. The amber one with a larger diameter accommodates the high volume air produced by a turbine.

spray guns translates primarily to better atomization leading to reduced orange peel. It also means tighter control of the spray pattern, more accurately machined parts and the use of more damage resistant metals.

Brands

Once you've decided on quality, you need to choose a brand.

There's not a big difference among brands in any given price range. So the key factor you're looking for, after you've decided how much you want to spend, is service. You will usually get faster service from a local distributor than from mail order.

For compressed-air spray guns, I recommend you shop at a local auto-body supply store. In my experience, non-chain stores are more knowledgeable about spray guns than the national auto-parts chains.

Find out from the clerks which brands the local auto-body guys use and choose from among those brands. The clerks will understand the subtleties of these brands and the store will most likely stock parts.

These stores also carry very inexpensive "knock-off" spray guns, or you could buy one at a home center or Harbor Freight. These guns produce fairly good results, but the orange peel they produce is more evident because the atomization isn't as good.

For turbine-supplied spray guns, you should also look for a distributor in your area. Paint stores that target professional painters sometimes carry turbines and guns.

Otherwise, check web sites of the brands you're considering and choose from among those that give the most helpful information and easy parts ordering. Many woodworking suppliers carry one or more of these brands.

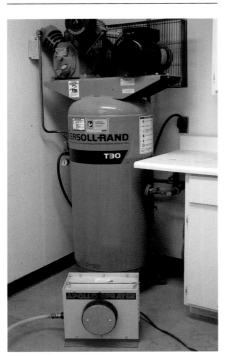

Compressors big enough to supply spray guns sometimes come with wheels but are otherwise not easily portable. Turbines are small and fairly light so they are very portable. This compressor is 5 hp, produces 15 CFM and has a 60-gallon tank. The turbine is three stage – the smallest that atomizes adequately.

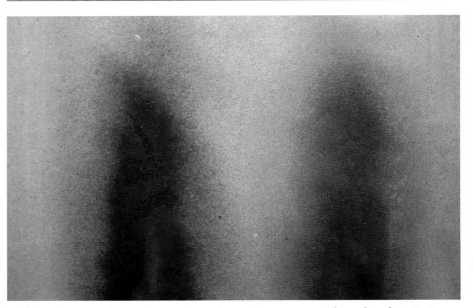

The biggest difference between inexpensive and expensive spray guns is the quality of atomization they produce. The finer the atomization of the liquid material, the more level the surface produced – that is, the more reduced the orange peel. The spray pattern on the left (made by an inexpensive spray gun) has a much poorer atomization than the spray pattern on the right, which was made by an expensive spray gun. This is evident from the much larger dots around the edges of the pattern on the left.

Setting the Air Pressure for a Spray Gun

With a simple test on brown paper or cardboard you can set the optimum air pressure for your spray gun.

Spray guns can run off a compressor or a turbine. With turbines the air pressure is established by the number of "stages," usually two, three or four. Each stage corresponds to about 2 psi. This seems ineffectively low, but it's made up for by a huge volume of air, giving rise to the name – High-Volume Low-Pressure (HVLP).

With compressors you have an infinite range of pressures you can use, and it is up to you to set this pressure so your spray gun is optimized for the best possible atomization. If you use too little pressure, you won't get the best atomization; you'll get orange peel. If you set the pressure too high, you'll waste finish or stain because of excessive bounce-back.

How do you determine the ideal pressure?

Some spray-gun and finish manufacturers provide a suggested air pressure for their products, and you may find this works just fine for you. But there are many variables manufacturers can't take into account. These include the actual finish or stain you're using if the suggestion comes from a spray-gun supplier, how much thinner you've added, the length of your air hose, and a particularly critical variable for home shops – temperature variations (liquids become thicker in cooler temperatures and require more pressure to atomize).

In addition, manufacturer-suggested pressures often don't specify whether they are measured at the compressor's regulator, the gun's air inlet, or at the air cap.

In order to adjust the pressure at the air inlet or air cap, you need a pressure gauge that attaches to these locations. Many spray-gun manufacturers supply an inlet air gauge with their gun. But the more accurate measurement, and the one that matters for complying

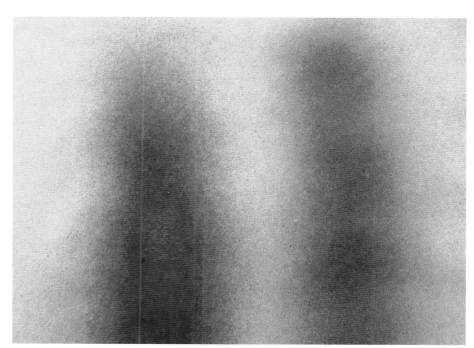

One method of optimizing the air pressure to a spray gun is to increase the pressure until the dots at the edges of the pattern no longer get smaller. Increasing the psi beyond this point only increases bounce-back. The air pressure on the left spray burst is 20 psi at the regulator. The air pressure on the right spray burst is 50 psi. The dots at the edges of the right pattern are significantly smaller and also more uniform in size than the dots at the edges of the left pattern.

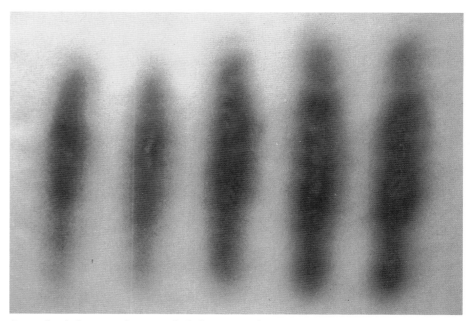

A second and often more obvious method of optimizing the air pressure to a spray gun is to increase the pressure until the pattern no longer gets wider. "When the pattern is right, the pressure is right." This picture shows increasing the air pressure in 10-psi increments from 20 psi at the regulator to 60 psi at the regulator. The pattern doesn't get wider from 50 psi to 60 psi, so spraying above 50 psi doesn't improve atomization. It just wastes finish material due to excessive bounce-back. Fifty psi, or just a little less, is therefore the optimum air pressure to use with this gun and finish material at these temperature conditions.

Both methods of optimizing the air pressure to a spray gun can be done with just a regulator, which is attached to smaller, portable compressors and is mounted on the wall with larger, stationary compressors. This picture shows air and moisture filters along with the wall-mounted regulator.

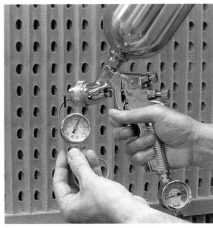

Optimizing can also be done using a pressure gauge attached to the air-inlet nipple at the bottom of the gun's handle, but no advantage is gained over simply using the regulator. To determine if you are complying with the HVLP standard of not exceeding 10 psi at the air cap, you will need a special air cap and attached air pressure gauge.

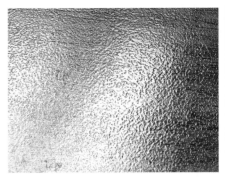

When the dots at the edge of a spray burst are large, you get an especially bad case of orange peel as shown here. Orange peel is so named because of the resemblance to the texture in the peel of an orange.

with the HVLP requirement of 10 psi or less, is made at the air cap. Unlike the more generic gauges that attach to the air inlet, gauges for the air cap are specific for each gun and can cost several hundred dollars.

You don't need any of these gauges, however, and you don't need to rely on manufacturers' suggestions. You can figure out the optimum air pressure for your gun and for the finish you're spraying with just the regulator and a simple test. (Smaller, portable compressors have a regulator attached. Larger, stationary compressors don't. These compressors are meant to hook up to piping and you have to install a regulator at the point where you want your air hose to attach.)

The Test

To find the optimum air pressure, begin by opening all the controls on your gun to their maximum and turning the air pressure at the regulator down to well below where you think it should be – for example, to 20 psi.

With the regulator set to about 20 psi, spray a short burst onto brown paper or cardboard. (The finish shows up better on a brown surface than on white paper.) You'll get a relatively small, center-heavy pattern with noticeably large dots around the edges.

Increase the air pressure by 10 psi and spray another burst. The pattern will be a little wider and the dots a little smaller.

Continue increasing the air pressure in increments of 10 psi and spraying short bursts. Each time you increase the pressure the pattern will get wider and the dots at the edges of the pattern will get smaller.

It's important to hold the gun at the same

distance from the target for each burst. The easy way to do this is to open your hand fully, placing the tip of your little finger against the target and the tip of your thumb against the air cap on the gun. Then spray each burst at this distance, which is about 8".

When you reach a pressure that doesn't widen the pattern from the previous and doesn't make the dots smaller, you've gone too far. You have achieved the best atomization, but you're now wasting material because more than necessary is bouncing back off the target.

So reduce the air pressure to the previous setting, or maybe a little further – to just before the pattern starts shrinking and the dots start becoming larger.

This is the optimum setting for the viscosity of the material you are spraying in the current temperature conditions. Here's the mantra you can repeat to remind yourself of how this works: "When the pattern is right, the pressure is right."

As long as the viscosity and temperature conditions remain the same, there's no reason to do the test again. Simply set the air pressure at the regulator the same each time you spray.

If you change to a different finish material, or if you thin it differently, or if the temperature changes (for example, if you keep your shop cooler at night, the finish will be thicker first thing in the morning), you'll need to perform the test again to find the optimum pressure.

But you shouldn't need to start over from a too-low pressure. You will learn quickly how to make simple adjustments, increasing the pressure a little when it is cold and

decreasing the pressure a little when you have added more thinner.

If you should want a wider fan pattern for spraying large surfaces, you'll need to get a larger fluid nozzle and needle. Then go through the optimization procedure again to set the air pressure.

Once you have established the optimum pressure for the equipment you're using, you can narrow the fan width a good bit using the fan-width control knob without losing significant efficiency.

Remember that this test doesn't work with turbine-air supplied guns because you don't have the same control of air pressure. For the most part, the only adjustment you can make using a turbine gun is adding more or less thinner.

Spray Gun Maintenance

Avoid problems and lengthen the life of your tool with two simple acts.

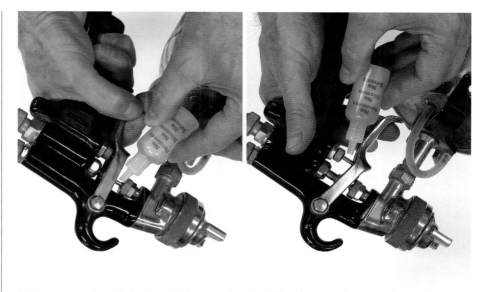

It's important to keep the fluid-needle "packing" oiled and flexible so it seals around the needle to prevent leaking. The packing is held in place by the packing nut, which is just in front of the trigger. Lubricate the packing without removing the nut by applying oil to the needle (left). If your spray gun has an exposed air-valve needle behind the trigger (right), you should keep it oiled also. Use oil that is free of silicone and petroleum distillate.

As with any tool, a properly working spray gun is a joy to use. On the other hand, one that isn't working well can go unused or even end up in the trash if you don't know how to resolve the problems.

You can avoid most problems by keeping your spray gun well maintained. There are three levels of maintenance: lubricate the moving parts; clean the gun; rebuild the gun.

I cover lubricating and cleaning below. Rebuilding can be accomplished in two ways. You can do it yourself with a kit of springs, washers and packings that you buy from the manufacturer, or you can have someone rebuild the gun for you.

If your spray gun is sold at an auto-body supply store, you can usually buy the kit there, and most of these stores know someone who will rebuild your gun for you. Also, some manufacturers of turbine guns supply kits and a rebuilding service, but not all.

The need to rebuild a spray gun should be about as rare as the need to rebuild a router, unless you let paint or finish cure in the gun. You can avoid the need for rebuilding for a very long time, and maybe forever, if you follow these simple lubricating and cleaning procedures.

Lubricating a Spray Gun

There are two parts on a spray gun that should be lubricated often: the fluid-needle packing, which is similar to a gasket and located just in front of the gun's trigger, and the air valve just behind the trigger. You can also lubricate the pin that the trigger swings on and the screw threads at the back of the gun. But I don't find either of these critical.

Use a type of oil that doesn't contain silicone or petroleum distillate (thinner). Mineral oil is a good choice. Auto-body supply stores and many spray-gun manufacturers sell a handy oil-containing squeeze bottle with the correct oil.

If you use the spray gun on a daily basis, you should perform the lubrication at the end of each day. Otherwise, you can do it at the end of each project, before you put the gun away.

Cleaning a Spray Gun

If you spray only shellac or lacquer, it's rare that you should have to disassemble the spray gun and clean it. The thinner makes the gun self-cleaning because alcohol or lacquer thinner dissolves any finish that might have hardened and caused blockage.

However, spraying any other finish or any paint can lead to blockage if you don't clean the gun adequately after each use. With some finishes you can do this adequately by spraying solvent through the gun. But with water-based finishes, I find I have to disassemble the gun and clean the parts after every use. You may find you have to do this with other finishes also.

Some manufacturers sell cleaning kits containing brushes, picks and needles of proper sizes for their guns. An all-purpose kit with cleaning tools that fit all spray guns is sold by Spray Gun Solutions (www.spraygunsolutions.com).

For a cleaning solvent, I'm using lacquer thinner. This, or acetone, is the most effective, commonly available, solvent to use. I'm using a Binks #7 spray gun for demonstration. It's an old-fashioned high-pressure gun, but its parts photograph well. Every spray gun is a little different. Use the following as a guide for cleaning your gun.

1 *Remove the air cap, fluid nozzle, fluid needle and plastic air tube and soak them in lacquer thinner. After soaking you may be able to clean these parts adequately using compressed air. Otherwise, perform the steps detailed on the next page.*

2 Scrub the air cap inside and out using various brushes. Be very careful if you use a toothpick because it may break off and become lodged, which will create greater problems. You can use an old toothbrush for most surfaces.

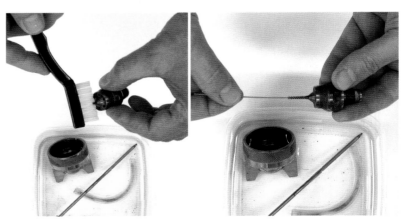

3 If necessary, clean the atomization holes using a needle of some sort. For example, the needle on a small brass safety pin works well. Don't damage these holes by using a metal that is harder than the metal in the cap or larger than the holes themselves, or you may end up having to replace the part.

4 Follow the same cleaning procedures on the fluid nozzle that you used on the air cap.

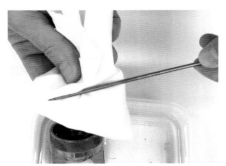

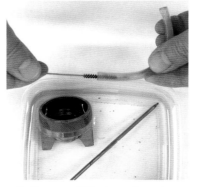

5 Wipe the fluid needle with solvent and a cloth to remove any finish or paint stuck to it. Don't use an abrasive such as steel wool on the tip or you will damage it.

6 Remove all blockages from the air tube.

7 Use a round bristle brush to scrub the inside of the fluid tube.

8 Use a brush, metal pick or toothpick to remove any blockage from the air inlet hole on the top of the spray-gun cup. The dimensions of this hole aren't critical like on the air cap and fluid nozzle.

9 Finally, use a round bristle brush to scrub the fluid chamber and fluid inlet. Then reassemble the gun.

Common Spray Gun Problems

Don't be a drip – learn how to keep your equipment in fine working order.

A spray gun is a precisely made tool with moving parts, so many things can go wrong. You need to be able to identify and fix the most common problems.

In the last chapter I showed you how to maintain and clean a spray gun. Keeping parts oiled and the spray gun free of gummy or solidified finish is critical for achieving good results. Problems can still occur, however, even with a clean spray gun.

The most common problems are unevenness in the spray pattern, pulsating spray and a gun that drips. Following is a discussion of how you can identify and correct each of these problems.

Spray Pattern That's Heavy at the Ends or in the Middle

Spray normally exits a spray gun in an oval pattern, often called a "fan" because it resembles the shape of an unfolded hand fan. To get an even coating on the wood, the fan pattern should be even from end to end.

Uneven spray patterns that are heavy at both ends or heavy in the middle and light at the ends are common problems, especially if you use a compressor (instead of a turbine) to supply the air. The uneven pattern is caused by the air pressure you are using not being appropriate for the viscosity of the liquid you're spraying.

Too much air pressure will push the liquid to the ends of the spray pattern. Too little air pressure will leave the liquid bunched in the center of the spray pattern.

With this explanation, the correction is obvious. If the fan pattern is heavy at the ends, decrease the air pressure or increase the viscosity of the finish (add less thinner). If the fan pattern is bunched in the middle, increase the air pressure (if you are using a compressor) or add thinner to decrease the viscosity of the finish.

If you are using a turbine to supply air to your spray gun, you have to thin the finish to correct a center-heavy fan pattern because you can't increase the air pressure.

To test your spray pattern, spray a short burst of finish onto paper, cardboard or scrap wood. The goal is to create an elongated and evenly shaped oval pattern.

Spray Pattern Heavy at One End

If the spray pattern is heavy only at one end, there is an obstruction in the air cap or fluid nozzle, or one of these parts is damaged.

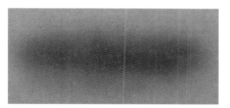

To get an even coating using a spray gun, the spray pattern should be an elongated oval that is even from end to end.

If the spray pattern is heavy on the ends and light in the middle (called a "split" pattern), there is too much air pressure for the viscosity of the liquid. Reduce the pressure or add less thinner.

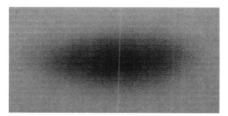

If the spray pattern is bunched up in the center, even with the spray-gun controls wide open, there isn't enough air pressure for the viscosity of the liquid. Increase the air pressure (if your air is supplied by a compressor) or thin the liquid.

If the spray pattern is heavy at one end, there is an obstruction in the fluid nozzle or air cap, or one of these parts is damaged. Clean the gun. If this doesn't solve the problem, the damaged part must be replaced.

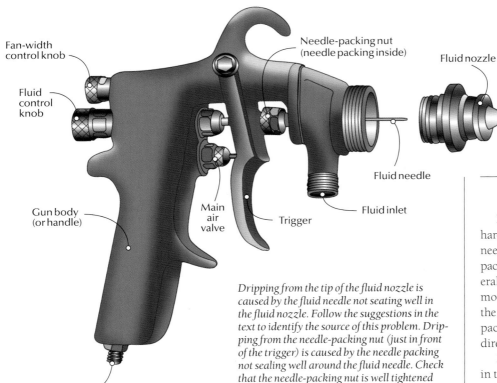

Fan-width control knob

Fluid control knob

Gun body (or handle)

Main air valve

Trigger

Needle-packing nut (needle packing inside)

Fluid nozzle

Air cap

Horn

Fluid needle

Fluid inlet

Air inlet

Dripping from the tip of the fluid nozzle is caused by the fluid needle not seating well in the fluid nozzle. Follow the suggestions in the text to identify the source of this problem. Dripping from the needle-packing nut (just in front of the trigger) is caused by the needle packing not sealing well around the fluid needle. Check that the needle-packing nut is well tightened and that the needle packing is lubricated.

To determine which part has the problem, spray a short burst of finish onto paper, cardboard or scrap wood. Then rotate the air cap one-half turn and spray another burst. If the disrupted pattern stays the same, the problem is in the fluid nozzle. If the pattern reverses, the problem is in the air cap.

Try cleaning the part that is causing the problem. If this doesn't work, the part is probably damaged (usually the tip of the fluid nozzle), and you will have to replace it.

Pulsating Spray

A pulsating or fluttering spray is usually caused by blockage in the spray-gun cup's air-inlet hole. When finish is being drained from the cup as you spray, the volume has to be replaced by air. If the air-inlet hole is blocked, the replacement air can enter only through the fluid passageway and this results in a pulsating spray. (It's similar to the "gluck, gluck" when you pour paint thinner rapidly from a full can.)

The solution is obvious. Clean the air-inlet hole on the cup.

Pulsating can also be caused by air getting into the fluid passageway and mixing with the finish. There are three ways this can happen.

> The most common is tipping a gun with a low liquid level in the cup too far as you spray. Be sure that the angle of the bend in the tube running into the cup is forward, and add more stain or finish if necessary.

> The cause can also be a needle packing (the gasket that surrounds the fluid needle just in front of the trigger) that is dry or too loosely compressed by the needle-packing nut, or an untightened or damaged fluid nozzle. Check the tightness of the needle-packing nut and fluid nozzle, and if this doesn't solve the problem, oil or replace the needle packing or replace a damaged fluid nozzle.

> An obstruction in the fluid passageway may also allow air to enter the fluid stream. Try "backflushing" the passageway by pressing your finger over the center hole of the air cap while spraying a short burst. If this doesn't remove the obstruction, take the gun apart and do a thorough cleaning.

Dripping from the Front of the Gun

The cause of fluid (stain or finish) leaking from the tip of the fluid nozzle at the front of the spray gun is the fluid needle not seating well in the fluid nozzle. There are a number of possible causes. Here are the most common in rough order of their frequency.

> The packing that surrounds the fluid needle may be squeezed so tightly by the needle-packing nut that it prevents the needle from moving freely. Loosen the nut a little.

> The needle packing may have dried and hardened to the point that it doesn't allow the needle to close tightly. Lubricate the needle packing with a non-silicone oil such as mineral oil. Apply the oil to the fluid needle and move it back and forth several times with the trigger, or remove the needle and needle-packing nut and apply several drops of oil directly to the packing.

> There may be dirt, paint or finish stuck in the tip of the fluid nozzle that prevents the fluid needle from seating fully. Clean the fluid nozzle.

> The tip of the fluid nozzle or the tip of the fluid needle may be badly worn or damaged, which prevents proper seating. Replace the damaged part.

> The spring that pushes the fluid needle closed may have weakened or broken. This spring is located just inside the screw-knob on the back of the gun that controls the fluid needle. Replace the spring.

> The fluid needle may be too small or too large for the fluid nozzle, which prevents proper seating. Change parts so the two seat well. Fluid needles and nozzles are sold as sets meant to work together. You can buy them from the manufacturer of your spray gun.

Dripping from the Packing Nut

If the needle packing isn't sealing well around the fluid needle, fluid will pass through and drip from the needle-packing nut. There are two possible causes.

> The needle-packing nut may not be screwed on tightly enough to press the needle packing into contact with the needle. Try screwing this nut tighter (but not so tight that it interferes with the easy movement of the needle).

> The needle packing may be worn or dry. First, try lubricating the packing with a non-silicone oil such as mineral oil. If this doesn't work, replace the packing with a new one, which you can get from your spray-gun supplier or from an auto-body supply store.

Aerosol Spray Finishing

For small or specialty jobs, spray-can finishing is a good choice.

Aerosols make possible the packaging of various finishing products in convenient, easy-to-use containers. The packaging raises the price of these products compared to using them in a spray gun, but the convenience of aerosols is so great that it's rare to find a professional finish shop without a shelf full of them.

Many amateurs also use aerosols as an inexpensive substitute to buying a spray gun – inexpensive, at least, as long as the amount of finishing being done is not too great. Aerosols are ideal for small projects.

Most popular finishes are packaged in aerosols in sheens ranging from gloss to flat. These include polyurethane, shellac, water-based finish, lacquer and pre-catalyzed lacquer. (Pre-catalyzed lacquer is a fast-drying finish like lacquer, but it's considerably more durable so it's often used to finish kitchen cabinets and office furniture.) Other useful products, such as sanding sealers, toners and blush removers, also are packaged in aerosols.

The finishes in aerosols are the same as those you spray through spray guns except they are thinned much more to fit easily through the small hole in the nozzle. You normally would have to spray at least twice the number of coats to get the same film build you would achieve with a spray gun.

Local paint stores and home centers rarely stock many aerosols, but you can find a large choice at many online finish suppliers.

How to Spray Aerosols

Aerosols have the same application advantages spray guns have when compared to brushes: speed and better appearance. It's faster to spray a finish than it is to brush it, and spraying produces a more level surface than does brushing, which leaves fairly pronounced brush marks.

Spraying with an aerosol is almost identical to using a spray gun. The most important

For spraying large surfaces you can purchase an accessory trigger unit for your aerosol cans. These units are inexpensive (about $5), effective and available at most home centers.

rule is to arrange the object and lighting so you can always see a reflection in the area you're spraying. This way, you'll see if you're spraying properly – a fully wet coat that's not so wet it puddles or runs. With the help of reflected light, you can adjust the distance you hold the aerosol from your work and the speed you move it to achieve a good result. Practice on scrap wood or cardboard until you feel comfortable.

To help avoid puddles and runs, begin your spraying a few inches off the surface and continue spraying past the opposite edge. Keep the aerosol moving at all times, and avoid spurting by keeping your finger from partially covering the hole in the nozzle.

If you're spraying a large flat surface such as a tabletop, ensure an even thickness by spraying your first pass 50 percent off the front edge and 50 percent on. Then overlap this pass entirely with the second and

continue overlapping each additional pass by 50 percent.

Finally, make your last pass on the back edge 50 percent off the edge and 50 percent overlapping the next-to-last pass. This way, every part of the surface will have received a double application.

To further ensure an even thickness, perform the same routine again, this time by working perpendicular to the first passes. Every part of the surface will then have received four applications of finish.

Toning with Aerosols

Toning is under-appreciated, especially among those who have never sprayed. It involves applying color to a surface by adding a pigment or dye colorant to the finish itself and spraying it. (Brushing a toner can create uneven coloring or very noticeable brush marking). Too much pigment will

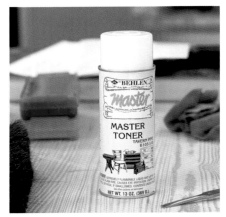

An aerosol toner (a common brand is shown above) provides an effective way to match a finish color.

muddy the wood like a thin coat of paint, but dye will add coloring and be almost totally transparent.

Toning can be used to adjust the coloring of an entire object after a sealer or finish has been applied, or it can be used to adjust the coloring of just part of an object. Examples include blending sapwood to heartwood or a light wood species to a darker species. Another example is creating highlighting in some areas, such as the centers of panels, by spraying toner on the area around them. Most higher-quality factory furniture has been toned.

Removing Water Rings

One of the most useful functions of an aerosol is as a "blush" remover. A blush is the milky-white coloring that sometimes occurs when spraying lacquer in high humidity. It's also the milky whiteness of a water ring, and it's much easier to use an aerosol with the right solvent to remove the ring on-site than it is to take a table to your shop and use a spray gun.

Water rings are caused by moisture getting into a finish and creating voids that refract light and prevent it from passing through. The voids are usually near the surface, so abrading the finish with fine steel wool or rottenstone and a lubricant usually removes them. But this disrupts the sheen causing the rubbed area to appear different.

A less disrupting method is to mist the damaged area with the very slow evaporating lacquer solvent, "butyl Cellosolve," which is contained in aerosol blush removers. Remember that you're dissolving the finish, so don't spray too much or touch the sprayed area before it's thoroughly dry.

Aerosol Breakdown

Whatever liquid an aerosol might contain, the cans themselves are pretty much the same – a nozzle (made up of a valve and an actuator), a diptube and a gas to propel the liquid through the hole in the nozzle.

Before 1978, chlorofluorocarbons (CFCs) were used to propel the liquid, but these have been eliminated in all but a few exempt items due to their negative effect on the upper ozone layer. Most of today's aerosols contain liquefied petroleum gases (LPGs) such as propane, iso-butane and n-butane.

The nozzle on most aerosols has a simple cylindrical-shaped actuator that you push down to activate a cone-shaped spray pattern. But some others can be adjusted to spray a vertical or horizontal fan pattern like a spray gun. The fan can be adjusted from vertical to horizontal by using pliers to rotate a small rectangular disk. These aerosols lay down a more even finish than the cylinder type.

With both types, you need to shake the can before using. If the can contains any solid material, such as pigment or flatting agent, it will contain a ball that you'll hear knocking against the sides as you shake. This ball helps put the solids into suspension. If you don't hear this ball knocking around, continue shaking until you do, then shake for another 10-20 seconds.

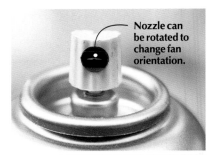

Nozzle can be rotated to change fan orientation.

Not all aerosol nozzles are the same. Some (top) spray an oval fan pattern. Others (below) spray only a cone-shaped pattern. If you have a choice, choose the oval-pattern nozzle.

When finished spraying, clean the diptube and valve so the finish doesn't dry and clog them. Do this by turning the can upside down and spraying until no more liquid comes out.

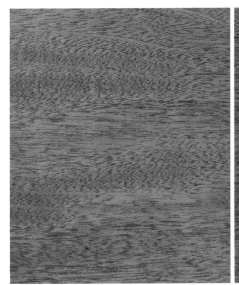

This photo shows how I used a green toner on the right side to "kill" some of the red in the red-dyed mahogany. The added green makes the color more brown.

Exhausting Overspray in the Home Shop

If you want to spray finishes indoors, you need an exhaust system. This simple homemade setup makes it possible and affordable.

Spray guns, especially the High-Volume Low-Pressure (HVLP) type with turbine-supplied air, have become fairly popular with amateur woodworkers. Like all spray systems, turbine HVLP guns transfer the finish from the can to the wood faster than brushing and produce a more level surface (no brush marks).

Also like all spray systems, turbine HVLP guns create overspray, though considerably less than high-pressure guns. This overspray should be exhausted to remove explosive vapors, for health reasons and to keep the dried particles of finish from settling back on the finished work and other objects in your shop. Rarely is this need for exhaust, or ways of accomplishing it, mentioned in ads for spray equipment or in articles about turbine HVLP spray guns or spraying.

Commercial Spray Booths

Professionally equipped shops and factories use commercially made spray booths to exhaust overspray. Essentially, a spray booth is a box that's open at one end with an exhaust fan at the other and filters in between to catch overspray. Commercial spray booths have the following features:

❯ Steel construction for fire safety.

❯ Filters to catch and hold overspray before it is drawn into the fan.

❯ A chamber for collecting the air to be exhausted after it has passed through the filters. This exhaust chamber makes it possible for air to be drawn uniformly through a much larger square footage of filters than just the simple smaller diameter of the fan.

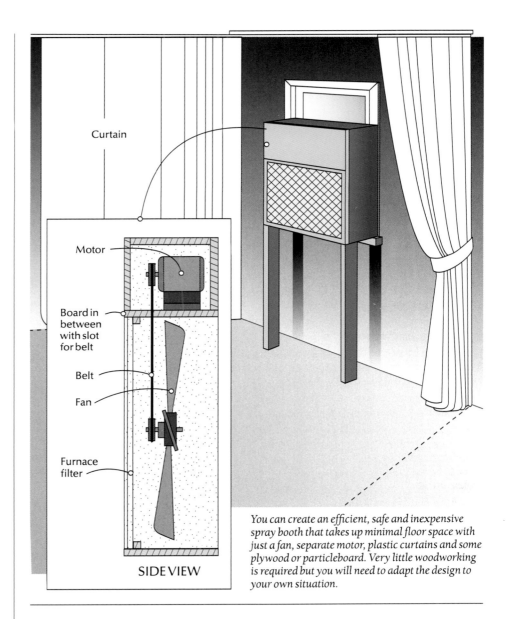

Curtain

Motor

Board in between with slot for belt

Belt

Fan

Furnace filter

SIDE VIEW

You can create an efficient, safe and inexpensive spray booth that takes up minimal floor space with just a fan, separate motor, plastic curtains and some plywood or particleboard. Very little woodworking is required but you will need to adapt the design to your own situation.

❯ A large enough fan to create an air flow of 100 feet-or-more per minute, which is enough to pull "bounce-back" overspray away from the object being sprayed. The fan and motor are also "explosion proof" to eliminate the possibility of sparks causing a fire or explosion it they come in contact with solvent vapors. (Be aware that a buildup of vapors can be ignited by a pilot light in your furnace, your water heater or from another source in your home, also.)

❯ Side walls and a ceiling to create a work chamber or "tunnel" for directing the flow of air over the work being sprayed and through the spray booth's filters.

❯ Ceiling and sometimes side lighting so the operator can see a reflection off the surface he or she is spraying. (Working with a reflected light source is the only way an operator can know if the finish is being applied wet and without orange peel, runs, sags or other problems.)

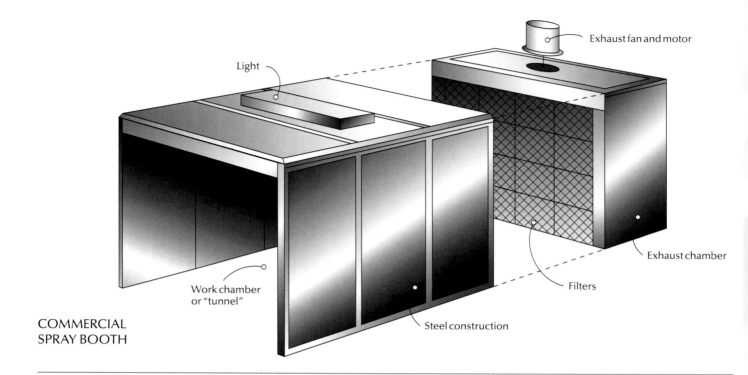

Light

Exhaust fan and motor

Work chamber
or "tunnel"

Exhaust chamber

Filters

COMMERCIAL
SPRAY BOOTH

Steel construction

Commercial spray booths are an essential tool for production shops, but these booths are too large, too expensive ($3,000 to $5,000 minimum) and require too much make-up air (heated air to replace the air being exhausted) for almost all home shops. If you are using a spray gun on an infrequent basis at home and have to work inside to avoid cold, wind, bugs, falling leaves and so on, you should consider building your own modified spray booth.

Making Your Own

With a note of caution that doing any type of spraying in your house, with or without a spray booth, could affect your homeowner's insurance, here's how to build a safe, inexpensive spray booth that will be adequate in the volume of air and overspray exhausted and take up very little space.

The spray booth consists of a fan with a separate motor connected by a fan belt, one or more furnace filters and plastic curtains.

The purpose of the separate motor is to avoid solvent vapors being drawn over a center-mounted motor in a typical box fan. The furnace filters trap overspray so it can't build up on the fan. The plastic curtains create a tunnel so air is drawn more efficiently over your work and through the fan.

Your choice of fan is determined by the amount of air, measured in cubic feet per minute (cfm), you want to move and is a trade-off between better exhaust of overspray and reducing the need to supply heated

make-up air on cold days. In other words, the more air your fan moves, the better the exhaust but the more windows you'll need to open at the opposite end of your shop and the faster the heat in your shop will be lost. Generally, the larger fan and the more sharply angled its blades, the more air it is capable of moving.

To mount the fan, construct a box approximately 1' deep from plywood or particleboard. Both ends of the box must be open. The dimensions of the four sides should be adequate to hold the fan at one end and furnace filters, which should be efficient enough to trap all overspray particles before they reach the fan, at the other.

Cut a slot on the top of the box (or on the side or bottom if you mount the motor there) large enough for the fan belt to pass through and mount a motor adequate in horsepower to drive the fan on the outside of the box. A ¼- to ½-hp motor (1,725 rpm) would be typical. To protect the motor from contact with solvent vapors, enclose it in a tightly constructed box with the only opening being for the fan belt to pass through. With this design you can avoid the expense of an explosion-proof motor.

Place the box with the enclosed fan just in front of a window, possibly resting on a stand, and seal the spaces between the box and window opening. Then hang plastic curtains from the ceiling on either side of the fan running out about 8' from the window

wall. If the window is near a side wall, you could use it as one side of your booth instead of a curtain. You want the curtains to be wide enough apart so you can stand inside, or just outside, the tunnel when spraying.

The best curtains to use are heavy, fire-resistant, "Industrial Curtain Partitions" with supplied ceiling tracking available from auto-body supply stores, Grainger's or Goff's Curtain Walls (www.goffscurtainwalls.com). You can use any type of plastic sheeting; the downside is that if it's lightweight, it might be sucked in a little by the exhaust fan.

Mount the curtains to tracking on the ceiling so they can be pushed back when you aren't spraying and pulled open when you are. This way, you lose almost no space in your workshop.

You may still need to wear an organic-vapor respirator if your exhaust isn't pulling all the vapors and overspray out of your work area fast enough.

For lighting, recess a four-tube, four-foot fluorescent fixture between the joists in the ceiling as close as possible to the window. Insert glass plates between the light and ceiling to shield them from overspray and vapors. For the best color balance, use full-spectrum fluorescent bulbs.

To avoid a fire hazard with your spray booth, it's essential that you keep it clean. Sweep the floor after each job and clean or replace the filter. If finish starts to cake on the curtains or fan box, clean or replace them.

8

Stains
& Staining

The Basics of Coloring Wood

The keys to overcoming the greatest challenge in wood finishing.

Coloring wood usually presents the biggest challenge in the wood finishing process because more can go wrong. By organizing and defining the major differences in the woods, the various types of products used to color wood and the application methods, you can see the big picture and get a better idea of all the choices you have and the "tools" at your disposal. You will improve your chances for a successful result.

The Wood

Any color can be matched, but not any wood. You have to pay attention to how the wood or woods you're finishing compare to the sample you're trying to match.

There are four large categories of woods: softwoods such as pine and fir; tight-grained hardwoods such as maple, birch and cherry; medium-grained hardwoods such as walnut and mahogany; and coarse-grained hardwoods such as oak and ash.

Within each of these categories, you can pretty successfully match any two woods using some combination of bleach and stain. But trying to match woods of two different categories has its limitations because of the large differences in grain and figure. You should take these limitations into account when you're choosing the wood for your project.

Types of Stain

The basic way to change a wood's color is to apply stain. In choosing a stain, you need to take into account the four ways in which they differ besides the obvious variances in color.

> *Type of colorant.* There are two types of colorant used in stains: pigment and dye. Pigment is finely ground natural or synthetic earth that is suspended in a liquid. Dye is a chemical that dissolves in a liquid. Everything that settles to the bottom of a container is pigment, and all the color that

The same stain was applied to the lower side of each of these woods – from left to right: oak, pine, mahogany, maple. Yet each still looks like the wood it is. There are limitations in what you can accomplish in trying to make one wood look like another.

remains in the liquid after the pigment has settled is dye.

Pigment is better at highlighting grain if the excess is wiped off, and at obscuring, or "muddying," the wood if the excess is left in any thickness on the surface. Dye is better at changing the color of wood without muddying it – especially dense woods such as birch and maple.

Some commercial stains contain only dye, some contain only pigment, and some contain both. Because all dyes fade in strong UV light, choose stains with pigment for objects that will be subjected to sunlight and fluorescent light.

Dye stains are available dissolved in just a solvent (no binder), and these are the most useful for getting light woods dark without obscuring the wood and for matching color. The two large categories of solvent dye stains are water-soluble and non-grain-raising (NGR). NGR dyes are also called metalized or metal-complex dyes.

> *Amount of colorant.* Stains differ in the ratio of colorant (pigment and/or dye) to liquid (binder and/or solvent). The higher the ratio of colorant in the first coat of stain you apply, the darker the stain will make

the wood. All commercial stains vary in the ratio of colorant they contain, but rarely is any indication given on the container. You will have to learn the differences by experience.

You do have some control, however. You can add pigment or dye to the stain to increase the ratio of colorant, or you can decrease the ratio by adding thinner.

> *Type of binder.* Most commercial stains contain a binder, which glues the pigment or dye to the wood. The common binders are oil, varnish, lacquer and water-based finish. The biggest difference among binders is drying time – oil and varnish dry slowly, while lacquer and water-based dry rapidly. Also noteworthy is water-based stain's characteristic of raising wood grain.

Some dye stains, usually identified as "non-grain-raising" (or NGR), "water-soluble," "alcohol-soluble" or "oil-soluble" don't contain a binder.

If a stain contains a binder, every coat after the first remains on top of the wood; it doesn't go into the wood. Pigment in these stains obscures the wood if some is left on the surface. Dye in these stains is fairly transparent. Dye without a binder continues to add

Color Intensity

All types of stain can vary in color intensity depending on the ratio of colorant (pigment, dye or chemical) to liquid (oil, varnish, solvent, thinner, etc.). The higher the ratio of colorant to liquid, the darker the stain colors the wood. You can change the ratio in any stain by adding pigment, dye or thinner.

Sometimes you hear that you can make wood darker by leaving a stain on the surface longer before wiping off the excess. The explanation given is that the stain penetrates deeper. This is only partially true. What also happens is that more thinner evaporates increasing the ratio of colorant to liquid.

The color intensity of a stain is determined by the ratio of colorant to liquid. A full-strength commercial oil stain darkens wood more (left) than the same stain thinned 50 percent with mineral spirits (right).

MOST IMPORTANT PROPERTY	WHEN TO USE	COMMENT
› Dries slowly so provides plenty of time to wipe off excess	› Under any finish except water-based › You don't need a special property of another stain	› Allow overnight drying before coating over with a finish
› Dries hard so doesn't need a topcoat when coating over a stained and finished surface	› On small surfaces › You want to leave excess to build › When coating over an already stained and finished surface	› If wiping off excess, work rapidly or have a second person help
› Reduces exposure to solvents	› Under a water-based finish › To avoid exposure to solvents › You want easy water clean up	› If wiping off excess, work rapidly or have a second person help
› Eliminates blotching on softwoods such as pine	› Staining pine or similar softwood	› Compared to a liquid stain, gel stain reduces depth on many hardwoods
› Dries very rapidly	› For very fast drying › To make a toner with lacquer	› You have to wipe off the excess within a minute or two, so it helps to work with a second person
› Colors more uniformly and intensely than pigment	› For very fast drying › For deeper and more even coloring than can be achieved with pigment › To make a toner with lacquer.	› Spray the stain evenly and leave it, or work with a second person if wiping off excess
› Colors more uniformly and intensely than pigment	› For deeper and more even coloring than can be achieved with pigment › To avoid exposure to solvents	› Brushing a water-based finish over the dye may dissolve and smear it; avoid this by applying a barrier coat of thinned shellac or varnish (a "washcoat") in between

Making Sense of Dyes

Don't allow the packaging to cause you confusion.

When I opened my furniture making and restoration shop in 1976, there were two types of dye in wide use. I made great use of both, but for different situations.

These two types are still the most widely available and useful today, but packaging has introduced some confusion so a discussion using brand names is warranted. Before launching into comparisons, however, I need to explain what I mean by "dye," because packaging makes the understanding of this term confusing also.

Understanding Dye

There are two common colorants used to color wood: dye and pigment. The difference is simple. Dye is a colored chemical that dissolves in a liquid. Pigment is a solid substance (sometimes earth) ground into very small particles that suspend in a liquid. Dye is like coffee or tea; the color stays in solution. It doesn't settle. Pigment is the colorant in paint; it settles and has to be stirred into suspension before using.

When you apply a solution of dye to wood, the color penetrates along with the

The two types of dye discussed in this chapter, in three types of packaging, are (left to right) concentrated liquid NGR, acetone-thinned liquid NGR and four containers of water-soluble powders.

liquid. Very dense woods such as maple and the dense areas of oak can be colored as dark as you want without muddying the wood.

When you apply a suspended pigment to wood, the pigment stays on the surface. Wipe off the excess stain and some pigment remains lodged in recesses created by the grain of the wood (think of the coarse grain

of oak and how dark it gets) and sanding scratches. The coarser the sanding scratches the more pigment lodges and the darker the result.

Confusion about dye in stains is caused by the different ways it is packaged. Dye can be used together with just a solvent or it can be used, usually in combination with pigment, together with a solvent and a binder, as is typical in the cans of stain you buy at home centers.

The binder is a finish used to glue the pigment to the wood so the particles can't be wiped off after the solvent evaporates. All oil, varnish and water-based stains contain a binder. Oil stains contain oil; varnish stains contain varnish; water-based stains contain water-based finish.

The stains at home centers usually contain both pigment and dye. Some contain only pigment. A few contain only dye. But they all work the same because of the included binder and provide limited flexibility for controlling color.

You can thin the stain with the appropriate thinner (mineral spirits for oil and varnish stain, and water for water-based stain) to make the color lighter, or you can apply an extra coat or two after the stain has dried

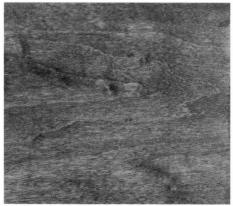

A dye stain is dye dissolved in a liquid. When applied to wood, the dye penetrates along with the liquid (left). An oil, varnish or water-based stain is dye and/or pigment in a solvent and binder. The binder limits the versatility of the stain, keeping most of the colorant on the surface of the wood. So the wood doesn't get as dark when you wipe off the excess stain (right).

to make the color darker. But because each coat builds on top of the previous, each additional coat muddies the wood a little and can introduce a weakness in the film that might separate if knocked.

In contrast, dye in a solvent with no binder doesn't build. Each additional coat simply dissolves into the previous coat making it darker and creating the same effect as if you had used a more intense dye color in the first place. Dyes in a solvent with no binder can create much deeper and richer colors in wood than dyes or pigments packaged with a binder.

Stains that contain only dye and a solvent (no binder) are called dyes or dye stains.

Dye has one big downside compared to pigment. Dye fades in sunlight and fluorescent light. So you shouldn't use a stain that contains dye outside, and you should think carefully before using the stain on objects that will be placed near windows or in offices.

You can mix all brands of dye that thin with the same solvent. So as long as the dye is dissolved in water, for example, you don't have to stay with one brand.

Applying Dyes

Apply a dye stain the same as oil, varnish and water-based stains. Apply a wet coat using any tool (rag, brush, paint roller, spray gun) and wipe off the excess, or most of the excess, before the stain dries. As long as you have prepared the wood well – that is, sanded out all the machine marks – and as long as the wood isn't naturally prone to blotching, you will always get an even coloring.

Clearly, the evaporation rate of the solvent in the dye is critical for determining the time you have to remove the excess. Water-soluble dyes provide the most time. All other dyes are difficult to remove quickly enough.

Fortunately, dye stains are more forgiving than oil, varnish or water-based stains. A wet coat of dye tends to spread out and level better so streaks show less. With practice, you can usually wipe, brush, roll or spray a dye onto wood and it will spread well enough to produce an even coloring without wiping off the excess.

You can always get a second person to wipe right after you apply if you want to get the excess removed from a fast-drying dye.

Types of Dye

There are four types of dye – but you would rarely use two of them: powdered dyes that dissolve in alcohol and powdered dyes that dissolve in petroleum-distillate solvent

These are typical oil, varnish and water-based stains. They are widely available and easy to use, but they can't produce the rich, intense colors that a dye stain can.

To dissolve water-soluble dye powders, begin by measuring out the amount of dye and water you want to use. Suppliers recommend ratios for achieving their standard colors, which are reproduced in their catalogues or on their web sites. But you can use any ratio to produce whatever color intensity you want.

Combine the water and dye powder in a non-metal container, adding the dye to the water. Then stir until the dye is totally dissolved. If there is any possibility of clumps of dye powder remaining, strain the solution. If you want to make an intense color, it's better to use hot water because you can get more dye to dissolve. I've never had a problem using tap water, but distilled water is usually recommended.

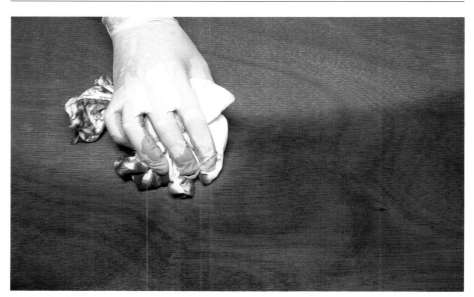

Apply a dye the same as an oil, varnish or water-based stain. Apply a wet coat of the dye to the entire surface using any application tool, then wipe off all or most of the excess before the dye dries.

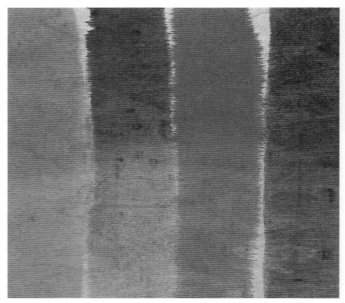

Water raises the grain of wood, making it feel rough and look dull (right side of this panel). There are three ways to deal with raised grain: let it happen with the water-soluble dye, then carefully sand the wood smooth with #400-grit sandpaper before applying the sealer coat; "bury" the raised grain with the sealer coat, then sand smooth; pre-wet the wood with water, let the wood dry, sand it smooth, then apply the stain.

Though "metalized" dyes used in NGR stains are more fade resistant than water-soluble dyes, they still fade rather quickly in sunlight. The lower half of this board was exposed to sunlight for six months through two panes of glass in a west-facing window. From left to right: TransTint concentrated NGR, Lockwood water-soluble, Arti water-soluble and acetone-thinned NGR. Clearly, you wouldn't want to use any of them in sunlight exposure.

(called "oil-soluble dyes"). Alcohol-soluble dyes are used primarily by people doing touch-up on furniture, and oil-soluble dyes are used primarily by manufacturers who add them to oil-based stains.

The two types of dye you will almost always use are powders that dissolve in water and dye already in liquid form. In fact, this is the easiest way to separate and identify them: water-soluble powders and liquids.

Water-soluble powdered dyes have the longest history for use on wood. These dyes (often called aniline dyes because the first dyes were made from aniline) were developed in the late 19th century for use in coloring textiles. By the end of the century, they were used in factories to color wood.

In the mid-20th century, ways were found to modify (by "metalizing") the dyes so they are more fade-resistant. The emphasis is on "more" because these dyes still fade far more rapidly than pigment.

Metalized, or "metal-complex," dyes are almost always packaged in liquid form because they are usually dissolved in a solvent that isn't widely available – glycol ether. The dissolved dye can then be thinned with water, alcohol or lacquer thinner (not mineral spirits or other petroleum distillates).

These liquid dyes are widely available to the professional finishing trade as "non-grain-raising" (NGR) stains. If you shop at woodworking stores or from catalogs, you may be familiar with this stain as Solarlux from the finish supplier Behlen.

NGR dyes sold to the professional trade are thinned quite substantially with acetone (they used to be thinned with methanol). They are ready to spray or add directly to any finish that thins with water, alcohol or lacquer thinner.

Throughout my woodworking and restoration career I've found these two types of dye (water-soluble and NGR) extremely useful. I've used the water-soluble dye powders to stain wood because these dyes provide enough "open time" for removing the excess and getting an even coloring, and they are easier to manipulate on the wood and available in many more useful wood-tone colors than NGR dyes.

I've added liquid NGR dyes to shellac and lacquer to make toners for tweaking the color on the wood when my staining didn't give me exactly what I wanted. Good wood finishers and refinishers find toners extremely useful for matching colors.

The Confusion

Non-grain-raising (NGR) dyes are now available to woodworkers in concentrated form – that is, with the glycol-ether dissolving solvent but without the acetone thinner. These dyes are very versatile because they can be thinned with water and used the same as a water-soluble powder dye, or they can be added to water-based finish, shellac or any finish that thins with lacquer thinner, to make a toner.

The packaging can cause confusion, however. These concentrates are exactly the same as the widely available NGR stains. In other words, thin a concentrate with acetone and you have Behlen Solarlux. So there are still just two very useful types of dye to choose from – even though you might find three packaging options at the store.

Choosing Among Options

If you are making a toner using shellac or any finish that thins with lacquer thinner, the NGR type, whether concentrated or thinned with acetone, is the only one you can use. Personally, I find myself using the acetone-thinned NGR because a toner almost always has to be thinned a great deal anyway to maintain control. Otherwise, you risk building the color on the wood too fast and getting it too dark.

If you are making a toner with water-based finish, you can use the concentrated or the acetone-thinned NGR, or the water-soluble powder. The NGRs are easier to use because you don't have to do the dissolving. Only if you want one of the colors available in powder form should you choose that type.

For staining wood by hand (not spraying), I find the water-soluble powders, especially those from W. D. Lockwood, far more useful than either of the NGRs for two reasons. First, the powder dyes are much easier to lighten right on the wood if you get the color too dark. Second, the dyes from Lockwood are available in a much larger choice of colors, including a great many that reproduce very accurately those colors we associate with traditional furniture. (See "W.D. Lockwood & the History of Wood Dyes.")

I find the ability to easily lighten or change the color after the dye has dried invaluable when trying to match the wood color to something else – for example, a "paint chip," an existing piece of furniture or an already finished object when replacing a part. Chang-ing the color means applying another color that, when combined with the original, gives you what you want. Doing this darkens the original color, however, so you often have to lighten it first, or lighten the result.

The downside of using a powder dye, of course, is that you have to go through the extra step of dissolving it in water. Both types of NGR dye are ready to use. (Keep in mind that though "NGR" is the acronym for "non-grain-raising," this dye raises the grain of wood if it is thinned with water.)

Also, if you are brushing water-based finish over a water-soluble dye that redissolves easily in water, you have to apply a barrier coat of another finish (shellac, varnish or lacquer) or you will drag the color and cause streaking.

For more information about the dyes available in most woodworking stores and catalogues, go to the web sites of the two principal suppliers at www.wdlockwood.com and www.homesteadfinishing.com.

Manufacturers rarely tell you what colorants they use in their oil, varnish or water-based stains. To determine this, let the stain sit undisturbed on a shelf for a week or more. Then insert a stirring stick into the can. If the stick becomes colored near the surface, the stain contains dye. If you have to go to the bottom of the container to pick up a colorant, the stain contains pigment. If both, as in this example, the stain contains both dye and pigment.

I stained this maple board with a Lockwood water-soluble dye. After letting the stain dry, I applied a second coat to the left side and wiped the right side with a wet cloth. Two applications deepen the color significantly without muddying the wood. Wiping with water removes a significant amount of color, lightening the wood. I find the Lockwood brand of dyes the most versatile because they are the easiest to lighten.

W. D. Lockwood & the History Of Wood Dyes

Dyes were developed in the late 19th century for use in the textile industry, but it didn't take long for furniture manufacturers to realize they could use the dyes also.

Early American and British reproduction furniture was very popular at that time. But the colors of the new wood didn't match the colors of 100- or 200-year-old oxidized wood. The easiest and most transparent way to make the new wood the color of the old was with dye.

W. D. Lockwood was started in 1895 in New York City by a chemist, a practicing wood finisher and a business entrepreneur, none of whom were named W. D. Lockwood. The company has always been located in lower Manhattan and may have been the first to adapt the textile dyes for use on wood.

Lockwood's business model was (and still is) to buy dye powders from the large dye manufacturers such as BASF and blend them to the color specifications of furniture manufacturers, many of whom were making reproduction furniture.

Hundreds of wonderful wood-tone formulas dating back to 1895 are contained in Lockwood's files, with about 85 water-soluble examples available to wood finishers. Examples of the colors include: Tudor Oak, Flemish Brown, Jacobean, Antique Cherry, Sheridan Mahogany and Phyfe Red.

Lockwood also has many alcohol- and oil-soluble colors blended to imitate traditional wood tones. None are "metalized" NGR dyes.

Many woodworking catalogues and some stores stock Lockwood dyes. One company, Woodworker's Supply, labels their Lockwood dyes "Moser" dyes.

Wipe, Don't Brush

Wiping is an efficient way to apply stain.

Stain can be applied to wood in many ways, but except for spraying and dipping, wiping is the most efficient method.

Wiping is fast, almost as fast as spraying (without the downside of having to clean the spray gun). Wiping is also every bit as effective as brushing in all situations except possibly getting the stain into recesses such as inside corners, fluting, deep carvings and the like.

Don't get me wrong. I'm not against brushing stains. I just don't see why anyone would do it, especially on large surfaces, and even more especially, when using any stain other than a slow drying oil-based stain. All other stains, including water-based, lacquer and all the dye stains, dry too rapidly to allow time to both brush on and get wiped off of large surfaces before the stain begins drying.

The Basics

The basic rule for getting good results with any stain is to apply a wet coat and wipe off the excess before it dries.

You can use any tool – rag, brush, paint pad, roller or spray gun – to apply the stain. You can even dip the object into stain or pour the stain onto the wood and spread it around. It's only important that you wipe off all the excess before the stain dries.

If you let the stain begin to dry in spots before wiping off, you will get a type of blotching that is different from the blotching caused by uneven densities in woods such as pine, cherry and birch. You'll get a blotching caused by thick dry spots of stain next to clean areas where the still-wet stain wipes off easily.

If you're brushing one of the fast drying stains, not only might you cause blotching when you wipe off the excess, you may get lap marks caused by brushing more stain over stain that has dried.

Brushing is the slowest method of applying stain. So not only might you get blotching or lap marks, you're also wasting time.

It's more efficient to wipe stain than to

The most efficient method of applying stain is to wipe it on using a soaking-wet cloth. Notice on this stereo cabinet, which was made without a back, that I'm not having any problem getting the stain into inside corners.

brush it, and you're less likely to have color problems.

The Exception

There is one exception, however. Brushing can be more efficient for getting stain into inside corners and other recessed areas.

To use a cloth (or even a sponge) successfully requires getting it very wet. I've noticed that many woodworkers resist, for some reason, getting their cloth wet enough so the stain flows into recessed areas. If this is your

An oil-based stain dries slowly, which allows plenty of time to get the excess removed with a clean cloth before the stain dries. Had I been using a faster drying water-based, lacquer or dye stain on such a large object, I would have had a second person following closely behind my application wiping off. It's not important to apply or wipe off with the grain as long as you wipe off all the excess. But on critical surfaces such as tabletops I typically make my last wiping-off strokes go with the grain just in case. The grain will disguise any streaks I may leave.

problem, you can solve it by having a cheap throwaway brush handy to quickly work the stain into the hard-to-get-to places.

But a brush is unnecessary. You can get stain everywhere with a cloth as long as it is soaking wet. In my years of refinishing old furniture, most of which required staining, I don't remember ever using a brush to apply a stain. And I rarely used a spray gun because of the time involved in cleaning the gun.

I almost always used, and continue to use, a very wet cloth.

Fast Drying Stains

Most woodworkers use oil-based stains, which dry so slowly it's rare to have wipe-off problems. But some use water-based stains, some use dye stains and many professionals use lacquer stains.

Water-based stains (all stains that list water for clean-up) dry hard as quickly as the water evaporates. This can happen very rapidly in hot temperatures.

Dye stains (for example, Lockwood, Moser, TransTint and Solar-Lux) dry as quickly as the dye solvent, usually water, alcohol or acetone, evaporates. Again, they dry much faster in warm temperatures.

Professionals typically apply lacquer stains onto large surfaces such as kitchen cabinets by having one or two employees following right behind the application person wiping off the excess stain with large cloths.

You can do the same, of course, by getting a friend to follow after you apply.

But you still wouldn't brush on the stain. Attempting to brush one of these fast drying stains onto a large surface is a sure ticket for uneven coloring.

Modern VOC laws have led some stain manufacturers to replace solvent with oil, sometimes linseed oil, which can spontaneously combust. To be safe, always drape oil-stain-soaked rags over a trash can or other object to dry out and harden before disposing them.

Brushing a stain thick, as has been promoted in a television ad, and not wiping off the excess, leads to a poor bond.

The way to test for good adhesion is to score the stain and finish (on scrap) with a razor blade in a cross-hatch pattern with the cuts about 1/16" apart. Then press masking tape over the cuts and lift it quickly. If the cut lines remain fairly clean, the bond is good. If the tiny squares lift with the tape as they do here on this stain that was brushed and not wiped off, the bond is very poor.

(If you find yourself with some dried patches of stain, quickly apply more stain, maybe to smaller areas at a time, and work faster to get the excess removed. The additional stain will dissolve what is there.)

Why People Brush

I can think of only two reasons woodworkers brush rather than wipe stain onto their projects: cleanliness and the Minwax television ad.

It's cleaner to brush than to wipe with a cloth that drips onto the floor and even onto your clothes if you aren't careful. But drips can be cleaned up, and you can wear old

clothes or an apron for protection.

Cleanliness is not an excuse for brushing stain.

Cleanliness can't be the only reason for brushing, however. For many years I've taught hands-on finishing and restoration classes and watched with amazement as virtually everyone in the class pulled out a brush (usually a foam brush) for applying their stain. Why aren't they using a cloth?

A surprising number have explained that they thought a brush was the best tool because they saw one used on a television ad, which has run off-and-on for years (and hopefully will be taken off the air by the time you read this). This ad shows someone slowly brushing a stain onto a panel, each stroke lined up perfectly side-by-side with the previous, and no trailing off as the brush runs out of stain.

Looks easy – but it's almost impossible to do. You can't keep brush strokes lined up so perfectly and you can't control the release of the liquid stain so exactly over any significant length. Plus, a thickly applied stain (no wiping off is shown) will usually crack and result in peeling if struck by a blunt object.

To be fair, Minwax does present the option of wiping on the stain in the instructions on its cans – but the accompanying illustration still shows brushing.

All this aside, the basic question remains: Why brush when it's so much faster to wipe?

Lacquer, water-based stains and dye stains dry rapidly. So they could lead to this type of blotching if some of the stain dries before you have time to get it all wiped off.

If you don't get your cloth wet enough with stain, you'll have trouble getting the stain into recesses. You can always use a brush to help do this.

Battling Blotching

Using wood conditioner and gel stain to reduce blotching.

The instructions on the cans of Minwax and Olympic Wood Conditioners say to apply a stain "within two hours" of applying the wood conditioner. Varathane's web site, www.woodanswers.com, says to apply the stain quickly "before the conditioner dries," but Varathane says on the can to wipe off the excess and then "allow the conditioner to penetrate for 30 minutes before staining." Talk about contradiction! The instruction that works best is to wait overnight.

The worst single thing that can happen in wood finishing is blotching – that is, uneven stain coloration caused by uneven densities in the wood. Blotching is the only problem that can't be fixed, even by stripping and starting over. You have to sand or plane off as much as $1/32"$ of wood to get below the dark areas.

In woods such as pine, spruce, fir, aspen and alder, blotching is almost always quite ugly. In woods such as cherry, birch and soft maple, blotching is usually ugly but can be attractive. In woods such as walnut, curly maple, bird's eye maple and most burls, blotching is usually very attractive. Woods such as oak, ash and mahogany don't tend to blotch.

Of all these woods, pine, which is the first wood used by most beginning woodworkers, blotches worst. So I'm going to use pine for my illustrations here. But almost everything that applies to reducing blotching in pine applies equally to the other woods.

There are two widely available products that reduce or eliminate blotching: wood conditioner and gel stain. Wood conditioner is marketed to solve the blotching problem, but the directions on most cans don't lead to acceptable results. Gel stain is not promoted to solve the blotching problem so most people don't understand its value, but in many cases gel stain is the best product to use. Let's look at each of these products in some depth.

Wood Conditioner

Wood conditioner is a very simple product. Most brands are one part alkyd or polyurethane varnish thinned with approximately two parts mineral spirits (paint thinner). You can easily make your own.

(Water-based wood conditioners also exist, but I don't see a need for them because water-based stains don't cause the same degree of blotching oil-based stains do. The water-based wood conditioners cause more problems than they solve because of grain raising. If you want to use a water-soluble dye and you're applying a solvent-based finish over it, you can use a varnish-based wood conditioner without any problem.)

The effect of thinning the varnish finish is to reduce the "solids" – that is, the ratio of finish to thinner – enough so the wood doesn't get totally sealed. When a stain is then applied, it still colors the wood near the surface but is prevented from going deep in those areas that will blotch.

The equivalent product used by most professionals spraying lacquer is called a washcoat. It is most often lacquer thinned to about the same solids content as wood conditioner and sprayed on the wood before a stain is applied. Wood conditioner is thus equivalent to what is used in the best furniture factories – with one big exception. Lacquer dries within 15 minutes while varnish requires overnight.

It's here that the directions on the cans of wood conditioner cause so many woodworkers to experience failure when using this product.

The directions on the cans call for the stain to be applied within two hours of applying the wood conditioner. Because two hours is much too little time for varnish to cure, the stain just mixes with the still-liquid wood conditioner and still penetrates deeper in

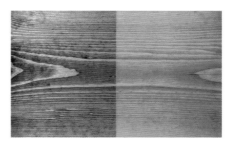

Professionals used thinned lacquer as a washcoat instead of wood conditioner. Lacquer dries very rapidly so it is thoroughly dry before a stain is applied. The result is that a lacquer washcoat is very effective at reducing blotching (as shown at right).

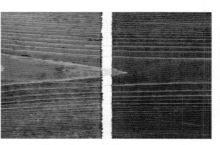

Liquid oil-based stain (left) causes considerably worse blotching than liquid water-based stain (right) because water-based stain doesn't penetrate as deeply. So there is less need to use a water-based wood conditioner under a water-based stain.

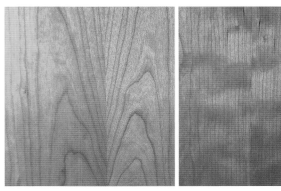

The left side of this cherry panel was washcoated, then a common cherry stain was applied to both sides (there is no stain on the middle stripe). Notice that the washcoat reduced the intensity of the blotching a little but didn't totally eliminate it. The washcoat also prevented the stain from coloring the wood as much.

Cherry doesn't always blotch. It depends on each specific board. Both of these panels were finished with a clear finish – no stain. The left panel didn't blotch and the right blotched severely.

some of which we like and some we don't. Cherry machines very nicely and has an especially pleasant aroma, but it blotches.

At least it usually blotches. Just as with pine and birch, which are also notorious for blotching, the blotching in cherry and whether it looks nice or not depends on the particular board. Some boards blotch in a particularly ugly way. Some blotch in a beautiful way – often referred to as curly or mottled. And some don't blotch at all.

Unfortunately, no wood supplier grades cherry (or any other wood for that matter) by it's blotching characteristics (though veneers are graded for curly and mottled). Wood suppliers grade wood for the number and size of its knots.

So you have to figure out for yourself how the cherry you are using will finish. This is much easier to do with surfaced cherry than with rough lumber.

With both situations, the easiest way to see how a finish will look on the wood is to wet the wood. Wetting gives almost the same appearance as a finish does, the difference being that the wetting evaporates and a finish turns to a solid making the coloring permanent.

You can use any liquid, but non-grain-raising liquids such as mineral spirits, alcohol and lacquer thinner are usually best, especially on surfaced wood.

Aging & Darkening

Besides blotching, another quality of cherry is the tendency of its heartwood to darken as it ages. The darkening is brought about by exposure to oxygen and light. Light accelerates the process, especially UV light, such as sunlight and fluorescent.

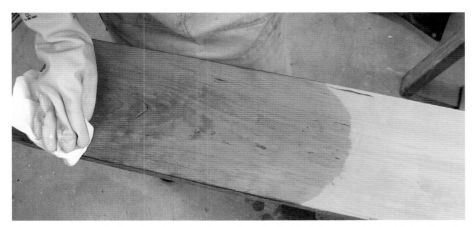

The easy way to test for blotching is to wipe the surface of unfinished cherry with a liquid. Any liquid will work, but solvents such as alcohol, mineral spirits and lacquer thinner are best because they don't raise the grain like water does. It's much easier to see if a board will blotch when the test is done on surfaced cherry than on raw, unsurfaced cherry.

Cherry darkens as it ages due to exposure to oxygen and light. This 60-year-old chest has taken on the rich rust-red color typical of old cherry. Notice that the darkening has served to mute and disguise the darker blotching somewhat as the lighter colors have darkened to blend.

As cherry darkens, the blotching becomes muted – that is, the lighter non-blotchy areas darken to the color of the darker blotchy areas. So time does a pretty good job of disguising blotching in cherry. This is the reason I've always believed that the best way to finish cherry, if your goal is to make it look like old cherry, is to let it get there naturally.

You can always accelerate the darkening a little by placing the ready-to-finish or already finished wood in the sunlight for a few days. This will darken the heartwood a little, but it will still take years to reach the rust red of old cherry.

If you want to achieve the rust-red color immediately, and are using non-blotchy cherry or are willing to live with the blotching, the most accurate way to do so is to stain the wood with a cherry dye stain. The most accurate color I've found is W.D. Lockwood's "antique cherry" water-soluble dye stain. But keep in mind that the wood will still darken

under the stain, giving you a result you (or your customers or descendants) may not be so pleased with after several decades.

How Factories Do It

If you've ever looked at factory-finished cherry furniture, you've surely noticed that it doesn't look like old cherry. It's usually considerably darker, sometimes so dark and opaque it's even difficult to see that the wood is cherry. But it's not very blotchy.

Cherry furniture manufacturers solve the blotching problem by putting most of the color on top of the wood rather than in it. Instead of using stains, they get the color with glazes and toners. Glazes are thickened stain applied in between coats of finish. Toners are the finish itself with the color (usually dye) added. Toners are always sprayed.

The end result is reduced blotching because it is covered over. Though there's no reason you couldn't finish cherry in this

manner yourself, the look attained is not what most woodworkers want.

Conclusion

Here's the bottom line on cherry: Most boards blotch when stained, and also when finished without a stain. There's no way to avoid this, other than finding boards (or veneer) that don't have the tendency.

Over time the blotching is muted as the heartwood darkens naturally to a rust-red color. If you choose, you can get to this color immediately by staining with a cherry-colored dye stain. But in time the wood will darken further underneath the dye.

You can also add color and disguise the blotching with glazes and toners, but you can't achieve the rich, transparent rust-red look of old cherry this way.

The only way to get the old cherry look is to finish with just a clear finish, any solvent-based clear finish, and let the wood age naturally.

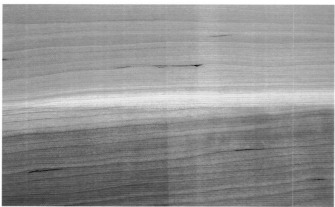

Because the darkening of cherry is accelerated by light, you can place your sanded parts in sunlight for a couple days (as I did with the left half of this panel) and achieve some degree of darkening to begin the process. The bottom half has a clear finish applied. The middle stripe is where some of the UV passed through the masking tape.

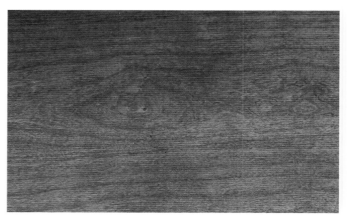

Furniture factories disguise blotching by using glazes and toners to put most or all of the color in the finish rather than in the wood. This creates a different appearance than naturally aged cherry.

If you are using relatively non-blotchy wood or are willing to live with the blotching, you can achieve a color very close to aged cherry immediately by using a cherry dye stain (left). Lockwood "Natural Antique Cherry" water-soluble dye (also sold as Moser "Natural Antique Cherry") provides the most accurate coloring in my experience. These dyes are available by mail order from many suppliers. But keep in mind that the color of the wood under the dye will still darken and result in a much darker coloring than you may want after a number of years.

Finishing Walnut

Unlock the awesome beauty of this classic cabinet wood with simple finishing techniques.

Walnut is a classic wood that's easy to make look good with just about any type of finish.

Though American black walnut has lost some of the popularity it had a decade or two ago, it remains one of the easiest of all woods to finish, primarily because almost every possible stain, finish or other decorative material looks good on it – even the non-film-building finishes, wax and oil.

All wood stains, whether pigment or dye, look good on walnut, and most tend to make the wood, which has a naturally cold caste, look warmer. The pores of walnut are relatively tight for an open-grained wood, and they look good kept "open" with very thin finishes and also filled to a mirror-flat appearance. Two-part bleach can be used to make walnut nearly white (it can then be stained to whatever color you want), and black dye stain can be used very effectively to "ebonize" it.

The only finishing product I can think of that doesn't always look good on walnut is water-based finish, which tends to make the wood look flat and washed out. But even this can be overcome by applying a stain first. The rich colors are then brought out by the finish.

Choosing a Finish

The three primary qualities you look for in a finish are ease-of-application, durability and color. Considerations of application ease and durability are the same for walnut as they are for all finishes.

Oil and wax are the easiest finishes to apply because you wipe off all the excess. So there aren't any runs, brush marks or orange peel, and dust isn't a problem. Oil-based varnish and polyurethane are the most difficult finishes to make look nice because they dry so slowly that runs have time to develop and dust has lots of time to become embedded. All other finishes fall in between.

Oil and wax are also the least durable finishes because they never get hard. Shellac, lacquer and water-based finish are next, and oil-based varnish and polyurethane are the most durable common finishes. Catalyzed lacquer is also very durable, but it is used primarily in professional shops and factories.

Color is the finish quality that has specific meaning for walnut. Some finishes darken wood more than others, and other finishes add a yellow (actually more of an orange) coloring to wood. In my opinion, walnut looks best with this warmer orange tone.

Clear wax is the only finish that doesn't darken wood. Oil finishes tend to penetrate and darken wood more than faster drying finishes such as lacquer. Along with orange (amber) shellac, varnish and polyurethane, oil finishes also add more yellowing than do other finishes.

Water-based finishes darken wood but they don't add yellowing. Blonde or clear shellac, nitrocellulose lacquer and catalyzed lacquer add some degree of yellowing, but not as much as varnish and polyurethane.

You can clearly see that there are real choices to be made with finishes, but all look good on walnut depending on your priorities.

Choosing a Stain

All stains look good on walnut, too. Though walnut blotches a little, it does so in a way that most people find attractive. So blotching, the ugliest effect that can occur in staining, isn't a problem with walnut.

The question is whether to stain at all, and there is a widespread feeling in the woodworking community that wood, especially a high-quality wood such as walnut, should not be stained. Maybe it's all right in factories where boards are glued up randomly, but woodworkers can pick and choose boards and arrange them to achieve maximum beauty. Why would anyone want to stain walnut?

I have two answers: one general to the broader question of staining and the other specific to walnut itself.

Amateur wood finishers in the United States suffer greatly because finish manufacturers are so sparse (and often inaccurate) with the information they provide on their cans, and woodworking magazines and books haven't filled the void – publishing much too much information that is contradictory and therefore confusing. As a result, most woodworkers don't feel comfortable with stains, finding them the cause of too many problems.

Walnut resembles ebony when dyed black (left), and it can be bleached almost white (right).

Varnish applied to the left side of this walnut board adds a warmer coloring than does water-based finish applied to the right side.

Implied, here is that woodworkers would not be so adamant against staining if they had control of the process.

Specific to walnut, it has a colder natural coloring than most woods and almost always looks warmer with a stain, even if it's nothing more than an off-the-shelf "walnut" stain.

Dealing with Sapwood

If walnut has a problem, it is the sharp color contrast between heartwood and sapwood – and stains can be used effectively to blend these colors. The easiest method is to apply a walnut dye stain to the entire surface. But a more effective method is to apply a "sap stain" to the sapwood before applying a wiping stain. These methods can also be used, of course, to blend white woods like maple and poplar to walnut.

Sap stains aren't widely available, but it's easy to make the stain yourself. Just add a little black dye stain to walnut dye stain (any type will work) so it becomes "off black." The amount you add will vary depending on the strengths of the particular dyes you're using, but think in terms of 10 to 20 percent black to begin with and adjust from there. Practice on scrap wood to get the feel.

It's best to apply the sap stain by spraying so you don't leave a sharp line at the intersection of sapwood and heartwood, but you can use a brush or cloth if you "feather" the stain onto the heartwood. A little sap stain getting on the heartwood isn't a problem as long as the stain is feathered out because it will be disguised by the next step.

When the sap stain is dry, apply an oil-based, walnut wiping stain, which won't cause problems with any dye stain, to the entire surface. Finally, when this stain is dry, apply the topcoat finish of your choice.

American black walnut is considered the king of woods for its beauty and working qualities, and it should receive the same acclaim for its finishing characteristics.

The walnut stain applied to the right side of this walnut board adds warmth to the normally cold coloring of walnut.

The dye stain applied to the right side of this walnut board is fairly effective at blending the sharp contrast between sapwood and heartwood.

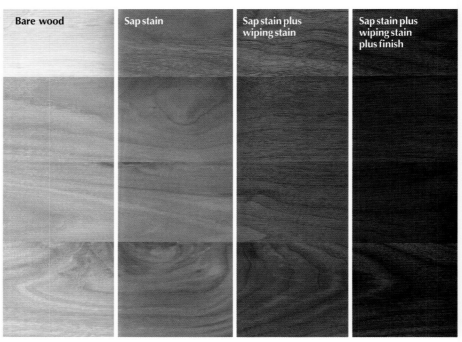

A more effective method of blending sapwood with heartwood is to apply a sap stain (first colored column from the left), then apply a walnut wiping stain and finally apply a finish.

9

Advanced Decoration

Glazes & Glazing Techniques

One of the oft-forgotten tools in finishing is glazing. Here's how to get started with this handy technique.

Glazing is the act of applying, then manipulating, color over a sealed surface. The color can come in many forms, including common stain, oil color, Japan color, universal-tinting color, or a specially made product called "glaze." A glaze is simply a stain that is thick so it stays where you put it, even on a vertical surface. Gel stain, for example, makes a good glaze.

Note that it's the position of the colorant in the order of finishing steps – over at least one coat of finish, but under a topcoat – that defines glazing. You don't have to use a glaze to be glazing. On the other hand, even if you are using a glaze, you are staining, not glazing, if you apply it directly to bare wood.

Though it's easy to do, glazing is still a sophisticated decorating technique because of the many effects you can create. These include adding depth to three-dimensional surfaces such as raised panels and mouldings, faking the wear and dirt accumulation associated with age, adding definition to painted surfaces, adjusting color after the actual finishing has begun, and creating faux (fake) grain or other decorative patterns.

Besides its ease, glazing is also one of the most forgiving steps in finishing. You can actually practice on the wood you're finishing, and if you don't like the effect you get, you can remove the glaze and start over without damaging any of the finish.

Though the actual application of glaze is not difficult, there is skill involved in knowing the look you want to create (having an artistic sense), and in maintaining consistency when glazing multiple objects, such as all the doors on a set of cabinets.

Glazing Products

There are two types of glaze: oil-based and water-based. Oil-based glaze gives a deeper,

By applying glaze between coats of finish you can add the appearance of age to furniture. Here, I applied and left glaze in the recesses on the right side of a ball-and-claw foot to illustrate.

richer appearance and is easier to control because of the longer working time. You can remove oil-based glaze for up to an hour or more by wiping with paint thinner or naphtha, neither of which will damage any underlying paint or finish.

Water-based glaze is more difficult to work with because it dries so fast. But it has much less solvent smell, so it is less irritating to be around. Once you've applied a water-based glaze, you have only a few minutes to remove it using water before it dries too hard.

Oil-based glaze is best for cabinets and furniture when the finish is lacquer, varnish, or shellac, and you're applying the glaze in a shop with good ventilation. Water-based glaze is best for faux finishing on large surfaces such as panels and walls in buildings where there is very little air movement, and on furniture and woodwork when you're topcoating with a water-based finish. To use a water-based finish successfully over an oil-based glaze, you have to let the glaze cure

completely, which could take a week or more depending on the temperature conditions.

Brands of glaze vary in thickness and drying time, but all brands produce good results. Some manufacturers provide glazes in a range of colors. Others provide only a clear glaze base to which you or the paint store add the pigment. Dark browns and whites (for pickling) are the colors most often used on furniture and cabinets.

If you need to thin a glaze to lighten its color, it's usually best to thin it with clear glaze base instead of common thinner so you don't lose the run-resistant quality. If you need to adjust the color of a glaze, you can do so easily by adding pigment ground in oil or Japan (which means varnish) to oil-based glaze, and pigment ground in glycol solvent or acrylic to water-based glaze.

Applying Glaze

You can use any finish, sanding sealer, or paint under the glaze. You can sand this first coat if you want. But sand lightly with fine sandpaper so you don't sand through, or the glaze will become a stain and color the wood. Sanding or using steel wool has the benefit of roughening the surface so the glaze can bond better to it.

You can stain the wood under the sealed surface, leave the wood unstained, or fill the pores of the wood. But in all cases, you should apply the glaze close enough to the wood so you can still apply one or more topcoats of finish to protect the glaze from being rubbed or scratched off without getting the overall finish build too thick.

Because there's no build with oil finishes or wax, you can't glaze successfully between coats of these finishes. You must use one of the film-building finishes.

To apply glaze, wipe, brush or spray an even coat onto the surface. Then manipulate the glaze with the following methods.

❯ Wipe off the unwanted glaze while it's still wet. In most cases, this means wiping the glaze off raised surface areas and leaving it in recesses on carvings, turnings, mouldings, and raised panels. But it can also mean wiping off flat surfaces in a way that imitates grain or other decorative effects.

❯ Wipe off the unwanted glaze right after the thinner has flashed off and the glaze has become dull. This is the same as wiping off while still wet, but the glaze is usually a little easier to control at this point.

❯ Using fine steel wool, abrade off the unwanted glaze after it has dried. There is a risk that you might abrade through to the wood, but it's nice to know that you can always use steel wool to remove glaze if you

don't get enough off with a cloth before the glaze gets too hard.

❯ Using an almost-dry brush, spread the glaze out thin to achieve the appearance you want. All this amounts to is continuing to remove glaze with a brush you keep fairly dry by wiping with a clean cloth until you achieve the effect you want.

❯ Adjust the color of the object you're finishing by brushing glaze out thinly and evenly over the surface. As long as you keep the glaze thin, you won't muddy the wood much. This is an excellent technique for creating a more perfect color match.

❯ Using tools such as rags, sponges, brushes, grainers and toothbrushes (to create a spatter effect), create a decorative faux pattern. Here, the techniques and colored patterns you can achieve are endless. Many books explain these techniques. Most are focused, however, on decorating walls rather than woodwork.

❯ Instead of manipulating glaze you've already applied, use a "dry" brush to apply the glaze to raised areas of carvings or turnings, or to flat surfaces to create the appearance of dirt accumulation. Begin with a totally dry brush and swirl it in some thick oil or Japan color you've applied to paper, cardboard or wood so that some of the color is transferred to the bristles without making them wet. Then brush lightly.

Glazing Problems

Most glazing problems occur because you've applied the glaze too thick or not allowed it to cure enough before applying the topcoat

Glaze is particularly effective at creating an antique appearance when brushed out thin over a painted surface. Continue brushing out and removing excess glaze until you get the look you want.

of finish. The two are related because a thick layer of glaze takes significantly longer to cure.

Too thick a layer of glaze (most common in crevices and recesses) weakens the bond of the finish to the wood because the glaze layer itself is not strong. The finish applied on top of the glaze could separate if knocked or abraded and this would pull some of the glaze with it and leave some attached to the surface underneath. This problem is even more likely to occur if the glaze hasn't thoroughly cured.

Not allowing the glaze to thoroughly cure can also lead to the topcoat wrinkling or cracking. If this happens, you'll have to strip the finish and start over.

You can use glaze to accentuate the three-dimensional construction of raised-panel cabinet doors. This door was stained and sealed before the glaze was applied and wiped off from the raised areas. Then the door was topcoated.

As long as you keep the glaze very thin, you can use it to adjust a color after you've sealed the wood without causing significant muddying. Here, I've added glaze to the left side of this cherry board to redden the color.

Filling Pores for an Elegant Look

Two methods to create a mirror-flat surface.

Very few woodworkers or refinishers fill the pores of wood anymore. The process is not well understood and it's perceived to be difficult. So if the wood has large open pores, the pitting is usually allowed to show.

This open pored, "natural wood" look has even become quite popular and is often promoted in the woodworking literature.

But for some, the natural wood look creates a less-than-elegant appearance. This is surely the view of companies that mass-produce high-end furniture and most people who buy this furniture. For the last 150 years, in fact, most better-quality, factory-produced furniture has had its pores filled to create a "mirror-flat" appearance.

Better-quality furniture in the past was made largely from mahogany, walnut or quarter- or rift-sawn oak. It's these and other woods with similar pore structures that look better with their pores filled (in contrast to plain-sawn oak, for example, which is difficult to get flat because of the wide segments of deep grain).

If you use these woods to make furniture or you restore old furniture, and you want the wood to look its most elegant, you need to know how to fill pores.

Two Methods

There are two ways to fill pores in wood to produce a mirror-flat finish. One is to apply many coats of a film-building finish such as lacquer, shellac, varnish or water-based finish and sand them back (a little after each coat, or a lot after all the coats) until the pitting caused by the pores comes level. The other is to fill the pores almost level with grain filler (also called "paste wood filler" or "pore filler") then complete the filling by sanding the finish level.

The first method is fairly effective with alkyd and polyurethane varnish, and with water-based finish, because these finishes build rapidly. It's often less work to leave out the filling step with these finishes.

The difference on a wood such as this mahogany between an unfilled surface (left side) and a filled surface (right side) is striking. The pores on the unfilled side break up the light creating a raw look. The filled side looks richer, deeper and more elegant.

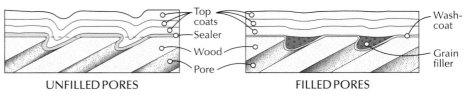

UNFILLED PORES
Topcoats follow the contours of this unfilled wood surface.

FILLED PORES
You can use grain filler to fill pores almost level. But to get the surface perfectly mirror-flat, you still have to sand a little.

But with lacquer and shellac, it's definitely more work using only the finish to fill the pores. It is also wasteful of finish material and sandpaper, and the finish shrinks back into the pores more over time than if grain filler is used.

Keep in mind that until recently, with the introduction of water-based and high-performance two-part finishes, the furniture industry and most shops have always used either shellac (until the 1920s) or lacquer (since). So most discussion of filling pores has always been connected with these finishes.

If you use shellac or lacquer on a wood with a pore structure resembling mahogany, you should consider using grain filler. If you use varnish or water-based finish, you could experiment with both methods to see which you like best – or simply not mess with grain filler at all.

Filling with Finish

There's nothing complicated about filling pores with just the finish. It's simply a matter of applying enough coats so you don't sand through when sanding them level. You won't know how many coats is enough without trying first on scrap because woods vary and people vary in how thick they apply each coat. Four-to-six coats of varnish or water-based finish should be enough, but more will be necessary with shellac and lacquer.

For instructions on sanding and rubbing a finish to the sheen you want, please refer to "Rub to Create a Great Finish," which is the next chapter in this book.

Here are three sample boards before filler is applied to the grain. They are (from left) unstained and unsealed wood, unstained and washcoated wood and stained and washcoated wood. It's usually best to stain and washcoat the wood before applying the filler. Notice the thinness of the washcoat on the right two panels.

A walnut-colored grain filler stains and fills the unsealed wood at left but fills and colors only the pores of the washcoated wood in the middle and the stained and washcoated wood at right.

With both alkyd varnish and lacquer, dedicated sanding sealers are available which are much easier to sand than the finish itself. Sanding sealers contain a soap-like lubricant that causes the finish to powder rather than clog sandpaper, so it's easier to bring the pore pitting level with sanding sealer than with varnish or lacquer.

But sanding sealer causes bonding problems if applied thick, so you shouldn't apply more than one or two coats. A trick you can use, if you decide you want to fill the pores with sanding sealer, is to apply a full coat of the varnish or lacquer first, then apply several coats of sanding sealer on top.

Sand the sanding sealer using non-stearated sandpaper until you reach a little resistance, which tells you that you have reached the varnish or lacquer. Then stop sanding so you don't sand through. Using this technique will eliminate the build of sanding sealer that could cause problems.

Water-based finish and polyurethane varnish sand fairly easily, so no sanding sealer is necessary – or even available.

Grain Filler

I've heard of people using all sorts of products to fill grain, including wood putty, plaster-of-paris and joint compound. I can understand how these could be made to work, but they provide very little working time. At least with shellac, lacquer and varnish, oil-based grain fillers are a lot easier to use.

These fillers are made thick with a high percentage of solid material (usually silica) added to some oil, which acts as the binder, and a little thinner.

A few brands offer grain filler in colors, but most fillers are available only in "natural"

To fill the pores of wood and keep it looking as natural as possible (left), without any color in the grain, use just the finish and sand it level after many coats. To speed the sanding of alkyd varnish and lacquer, apply a coat of the finish, then several coats of varnish or lacquer sanding sealer. Then sand off the sanding sealer, as I'm doing here (right), until you reach the resistance of the varnish or lacquer. You are filling the pores with the sanding sealer.

To thin oil-based grain filler to make it easy to brush or spray, use mineral spirits to add more time for large surfaces or naphtha to speed up the drying on small surfaces. You can also mix the two thinners to get something in between. Thin to a brushable consistency.

to which you have to add a colorant. Adding color is critical with oil-based fillers because they don't "take" stain well after they have dried.

You can add any colorant to oil-based grain fillers, including Japan, oil and universal colorants. Use universal colorants with water-based fillers. These are the same colorants paint stores use to tint latex paint. Don't use a dye colorant because it could fade and leave the pores lighter than the surrounding wood.

You can also add stain to the filler to get the color you want, but this is not usually the best practice because it locks you into the evaporation rate of the thinners in the stain,

which may not be what you want. Also, the stain may contain dye, which could fade.

Usually, a walnut color is best, but there are situations where you might want another color, such as white for a pickled effect.

In most cases it's best to thin the grain filler to make it easier to spread or spray. Use mineral spirits or naphtha (for faster evaporation) with oil-based fillers and water with water-based fillers. You can apply grain filler successfully at any consistency. I like to thin it about half to an easily brushable consistency.

All commercial brands of grain filler I've tried, which is most, work well, the critical difference being drying time. It's best

to adjust your work rhythm to the drying time of the product you're using, but you can also add a little boiled linseed oil (to slow the drying) or some Japan drier (to speed the drying).

It's not easy to change the rapid drying of water-based fillers. Temperature and humidity will be critical.

Sealing First

Instructions have created confusion about whether or not to seal the wood before applying the grain filler. Unquestionably, the best practice is to seal first. But before discussing why, I want to discuss "seal."

A sealer coat is a first coat of finish. It can

The most efficient method of applying grain filler is to brush or spray it to get an even thickness that hazes uniformly over the surface as the thinner evaporates. A thinned grain filler soaks into the pores on its own. If you apply the filler thick with a cloth, you should press it into the pores as you wipe.

When the grain filler hazes, it's ready to be removed. Removing the filler before it hazes will result in more shrinkage in the pores as the remaining thinner evaporates.

One method of removing the excess grain filler is to wipe with a cotton cloth across the grain so you pull less filler back out of the pores. If you time it just right, the filler will still be soft and moist enough to remove easily with the cloth. Finish by wiping lightly with the grain to remove streaks.

If the grain filler has hardened too much to be removed easily with a cotton cloth, use burlap instead. Burlap is coarser but not so coarse that it scratches the wood. On turnings, carvings and inside corners, use a stiff brush or sharpened dowel to remove the excess filler.

be any finish, but it's usually the same as you're using for the topcoats.

If this sealer coat is applied heavy, it will round over the pores and more of the filler will be pulled out when you wipe off the excess. So it's best to thin this first coat to create what is called a "washcoat." A washcoat is about 10 percent solids content, which translates to varnish thinned with about two parts mineral spirits (the same as "wood conditioner"), lacquer thinned with about 1½ parts lacquer thinner and shellac thinned to about a ³/₄-pound cut.

Water-based finishes don't work well when thinned with a lot of water, so use a commercial water-based washcoat or wood conditioner instead of doing the thinning yourself. Or apply the water-based grain filler directly to the wood as I describe below.

A washcoat will leave enough film build to block the color in the filler from getting through to the wood while leaving the top edges of the pores sharp enough so more of the filler will remain in the pores. It's not necessary to sand this washcoat, and in fact you shouldn't because you might sand through.

The best practice, therefore, especially with oil-based grain filler, is to stain the wood, apply a washcoat, then apply the grain filler. Here are the reasons.

❯ You'll get better contrast between the pores and the wood, which will create more depth.

❯ The surface will be slicker so it will be easier to wipe off the excess filler.

❯ The washcoat will create a cushion so you're less likely to sand through stain if you have to sand off some streaks of filler later.

❯ A washcoat makes it possible to apply filler to small areas at a time without getting lap marks, which are darker colored streaks caused by overlapping.

❯ If you don't get all the filler removed before it begins to harden, you can remove it with solvent (mineral spirits or naphtha for oil-based and water for water-based) without also removing some of the stain.

On the other hand, you can skip the stain and washcoat and use a colored grain filler to stain the wood and fill the grain in one step. There is nothing wrong with doing this.

With water-based grain filler a case can be made for applying the filler directly to unstained wood. Then scrape or wipe off as much of the excess as you can and sand off any remaining after it dries. Use colored grain filler as a combination stain and filler. Or use natural, then apply a stain after you have wiped and sanded off all the excess. Most brands of water-based grain filler take stain fairly well.

I've applied water-based grain filler both ways—over a washcoated surface and directly to the wood. I like the first method best, but I sometimes use the second with colored filler. The second doesn't produce the depth the first does, and neither method using water-based grain filler produces the depth the oil-based system does.

Other Considerations

Because you can't wait until all the thinner has evaporated from an oil-based grain filler, or it will be too hard to remove, there will always be some shrinkage. So you will always get a more level filling with two applications, the second after the first has dried overnight.

If you are spraying lacquer over an oil-based grain filler, spray the first coat or two very light, even to the point of just "dusting" the finish by holding the gun farther from the surface and moving it faster. Try to avoid wetting the surface excessively. A wet coat will cause the filler to swell and push up out of the pores. Sanding to level the surface then removes some of the filler and leaves the pores partially open.

You could also apply a coat of shellac between the filler and the lacquer coats. The alcohol in the shellac will not cause the swelling and the shellac will slow the penetration of the lacquer thinner that is causing the problem.

Unlike the other finishes, the thinner in each fresh coat of lacquer opens up the pores a little even if you have sanded the surface perfectly level. If you want a perfectly mirror-flat surface, you'll have to sand the last coat level and rub it to the sheen you want. Very little sanding will be necessary.

The biggest fear is usually that the filler will set up hard before you get it all wiped off. You need to get used to the drying rate of the product you're using, of course, and you can washcoat the wood first, then fill smaller areas at a time. But if the grain filler still gets too hard to wipe off, even with burlap, remove all or most of the excess quickly by wiping with mineral spirits or naphtha for oil-based filler or water for water-based filler, then fill again — working faster or in smaller areas at a time.

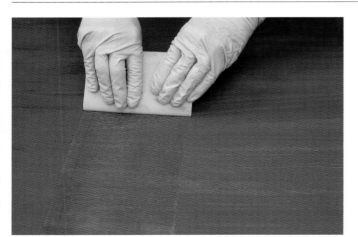

An efficient method of removing the excess grain filler is to scrape it off with a plastic spreader. Then follow with a cotton cloth or burlap. Whichever method you use, finish by wiping lightly with the grain to remove streaks.

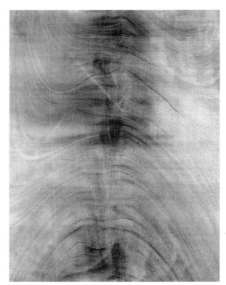

It's nearly impossible to get all water-based grain filler wiped off of wood (such as this crotch mahogany) when no washcoat is applied. You'll have to sand it off, trying to avoid sanding so deep you open up some of the pores.

Rubbing for a 'Perfect' Finish

Don't be satisfied with a rough finish. Here's how to finish the job right.

To create the smoothest oil finish possible, sand the second and each subsequent coat while it is still wet with finish (before wiping off) using #600-grit (P1200-grit) sandpaper.

After spending countless hours building a project, you naturally want the finish to be perfect. To achieve this you need to understand the one thing that separates an OK finish from a great one. A great finish feels smooth!

Think about it. What do you do when checking out someone else's finish, whether in a store or at a friend's home or shop? You run your hand over the finish. If it feels rough, you disapprove (though you might not say anything). If it feels smooth, you think, "Boy, I wish I could do this."

A Great Finish is a Smooth Finish

Of course, there are also other factors, including thorough wood preparation to remove machine marks, dents and tear-out, and achieving an even coloring. But when it comes down to it, the one factor that separates a great finish from an average finish is smoothness.

You achieve a smooth finish by rubbing it. This is the only way. You can't get a perfectly smooth finish straight off a rag, brush or spray gun.

In most cases, there's no advantage to rubbing surfaces that aren't seen in a reflected light and aren't touched. To make these surfaces (table legs, for example) the same sheen as the surfaces you're rubbing, apply a finish that produces that sheen naturally – gloss, semi-gloss, satin or flat.

There are two significantly different types of finish: penetrating and film-building. A penetrating finish is one that doesn't harden, so all the excess has to be wiped off after each coat. Oil finishes are penetrating finishes. Oil finishes include boiled linseed oil, tung oil, and a mixture of varnish and one or both of these oils.

All finishes that harden are film-building finishes. They can be built to a greater thickness on the wood by leaving each coat wet on the surface to dry. The procedure for rubbing is different for oil and film building finishes; I'll discuss both.

Oil Finishes

You can create a fairly smooth oil finish by sanding between coats using very-fine-grit sandpaper (#320 grit or finer). Be sure to allow each coat to fully cure, which means leaving overnight in a warm room. Some oil finishes, such as Watco Danish Oil and Deft Danish Oil, instruct to apply coats within an hour or two; following these directions won't produce good results.

To create an ultimately smooth oil finish, sand each coat while it's still wet on the surface using very fine grit sandpaper. Then wipe off the excess and allow what's left to cure overnight. Sanding while wet with oil makes use of the oil as a lubricant, which is what produces the exceptionally smooth results. Here's the procedure.

❯ Sand the wood to remove machine marks and other flaws.

❯ Wipe or brush on a wet coat of oil and keep the surface wet for several minutes, rewetting any areas that become dull because the finish has soaked in.

❯ Wipe off all the excess. Be sure to hang your wet rags to dry, or drape them singly over the edge of a trash can, so they can't build up heat and spontaneously combust.

❯ Allow the finish to dry overnight in a warm room.

❯ Wipe or brush on a second coat of oil and sand the surface while it's still wet in the direction of the grain using #600-grit wet/dry sandpaper. Sand over all areas with three or four back-and-forth strokes. There's no gain sanding more than this. European standard "P-grade" sandpaper is rapidly replacing the American standard. Above #220 grit, P-grade numbers move up much faster than non-P-grade. Sandpaper of #600 grit is approximately equivalent to P1,200 grit; #400 grit is about P800.

❯ Wipe off the excess oil and allow the surface to dry overnight.

❯ Apply a third coat of oil and again sand wet. Remove the excess and allow overnight drying. This is usually all you need to do to achieve an ultimately smooth finish, but you can repeat the procedure with a fourth coat, and with as many additional coats as you want.

One caveat. Sanding an oil finish wet (or even sanding dry between coats) is risky if you have stained the wood. You might sand through some of the color, especially at edges. Sand lightly and carefully.

A second caveat. Nothing is gained by using a flat block to back your sandpaper with either of these methods. Using just your hand is fine. The grit sandpaper you're using is too fine to cause noticeable damage to the flatness of the surface.

Film-building Finishes

Film-building finishes include varnish, lacquer, shellac, water-based finish and two-part catalyzed finishes. Both varnish and water-based finish have a version called "polyurethane." This is the regular finish (alkyd or acrylic) with some polyurethane resin added. Catalyzed finish is also available in one part called "pre-catalyzed lacquer."

Except for varnish, each of these finishes hardens within a couple of hours in a warm room so several coats can be applied in a day. Varnish, on the other hand, requires overnight drying between coats.

The Sealer Coat

The first coat you apply of any of these finishes is called the "sealer" coat. It stops up the pores and seals the wood. It also leaves the wood feeling rough, so you should always sand the sealer coat smooth. (Though you could skip this sanding and still achieve total smoothness at the end by sanding just the last coat, it's easier to sand the sealer coat because it's thin and has thus hardened quickly.)

Varnish (not including polyurethane varnish) and lacquer are more difficult to sand than other finishes because they tend to gum up the sandpaper. So manufacturers provide a special product called "sand-

ing sealer" to use as a first coat under these finishes. Sanding sealer is varnish or lacquer with a soap-like lubricant included. Sanding sealer powders when sanded.

If you are finishing a large project such as a set of cabinets with varnish or lacquer, it will be worthwhile to use a sanding sealer for your first coat. But if your project is small, requiring little sanding, it's better to avoid using sanding sealer because it weakens the overall protection of the finish. The included soap weakens the moisture barrier and makes this layer softer than the finish itself.

Instead of using sanding sealer to gain easy sanding, you can thin the finish itself about half with the appropriate thinner (mineral spirits for varnish or lacquer thinner for lacquer). The thinner layer hardens faster so it is easier to sand sooner.

If you are finishing a wood with resinous knots (such as pine), or you are refinishing

A varnish or lacquer sanding sealer has soap-like lubricants included, which make the finish powder when sanded. Sanding sealer reduces protection for the wood, however.

It's always best to sand between coats of a film-building finish to remove dust nibs. Use stearated sandpaper to reduce clogging.

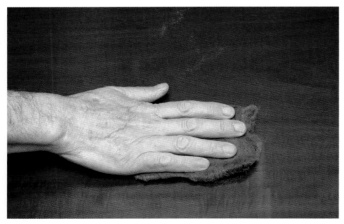

You can create a fairly smooth finish with an even sheen by rubbing with #0000 steel wool. Be sure to rub in the direction of the grain.

Instead of using steel wool dry, wet the surface with soap and water or mineral oil and then rub. Rubbing wet produces better results, but you run the risk of rubbing through and not seeing it happen. You will make the rub-through much worse.

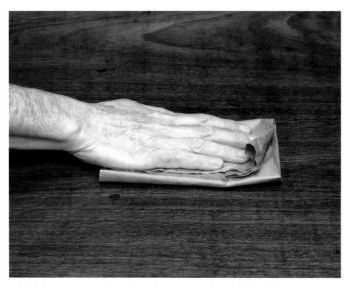

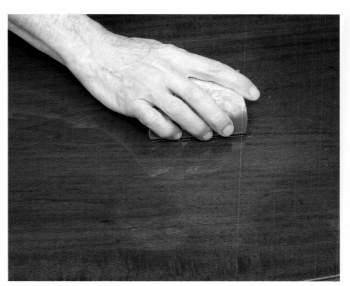

A folded brown-paper bag from the supermarket is fairly effective at leveling dust nibs so the finish feels smoother. As long as the finish is fully cured, the paper won't scratch it.

If you want to create the most perfect results when using a film building finish, you have to level it using fine wet/dry sandpaper, a backing block and a lubricant.

wood with silicone contamination (it causes the finish to roll up in ridges) or animal-urine or smoke odors, use shellac as the sealer coat. Shellac blocks off these problems (but it is not easier to sand). There's no reason to use shellac otherwise.

No matter what you use for the sealer coat, sand it after it dries using a grit sandpaper that creates smoothness efficiently without causing larger than necessary scratches – most often a grit between #220 and #400 (P220 and P800).

Sanding Between Coats

It's always best to sand lightly between every coat of finish to remove dust nibs. This is done easily using very-fine-grit sandpaper: #320 or #400 grit (P400 or P800). Using a "stearated," or dry-lubricated, sandpaper is best because it clogs least. This sandpaper contains the same soap-like ingredient as sanding sealer.

Sand just enough so you can no longer feel the dust nibs. There's no reason to sand out brush marks or orange peel (caused by spraying) at this point.

Rubbing the Finish

When you have applied all the coats you want, usually three or more including the sealer coat, it's time to make the surface feel smooth. If the dust nibs aren't bad, you can usually improve the feel significantly by simply rubbing lightly with a folded brown-paper bag.

As long as you have allowed the finish to

harden well (so you can no longer smell any odor when you press your nose against it), the bag will level the nibs without damaging or changing the sheen of the finish.

To create a more perfect and attractive surface, rub it with #0000 steel wool or a gray Scotch-Brite pad. Rub in the direction of the grain. Rub the three or four inches nearest the ends using short strokes (so you are less likely to rub over the edges and cut through). Then rub the entire length, being careful to stop just short of the edges.

On small surfaces, you can stand at the end of the piece and rub away from you and then back toward you, but on larger surfaces, you should stand at the side and rub side to side. When you do this, be conscious to not rub in an arc, which is the natural way your hand and arm want to move. Instead, think in terms of making a reverse arc, like a shallow concave, so the actual stroke is straight.

You can use a lubricant with the abrasive pad to soften the scratches you're putting in the finish, but you risk making rub-throughs worse, because if you do cut through (most likely on the edges), you won't see it when it first happens and stop. I recommend against using a lubricant until you've practiced a few times.

Any liquid or paste will work well for the lubricant. The more oily or pasty (mineral oil or paste wax) the lubricant, the slower your cutting action and the less obvious the scratches. The more watery the lubricant (water, soap-and-water, or mineral spirits), the faster you'll cut and the more the scratches

will show. (Products with names such as "Wool Wax" or "Wool Lube," which are sold as rubbing lubricants, are simply soap in paste from – like Murphy's paste soap.)

Rubbing with an abrasive pad, with or without a lubricant, improves the feel and appearance, but it doesn't remove the flaws; it just rounds them over and disguises them with fine scratches. To achieve the ultimate rubbed finish you have to level the finish first, then rub it.

Leveling & Rubbing

Leveling a finish is a mechanical exercise employing the same exact procedure as sanding wood, with two differences: you use finer grits of sandpaper and you use a lubricant with the sandpaper to prevent clogging. Here is the procedure.

Using a flat cork or rubber sanding block to back your sandpaper, sand the surface until it is perfectly flat. Use a grit sandpaper that cuts through the flaws efficiently without creating larger-than-necessary scratches that then have to be sanded out.

If you don't have any idea what grit to start with, begin with #600 grit (P1,200), sand a little, remove the lubricant and see what progress you've made. If you haven't completely flattened the surface with 10 or 15 strokes over the same area, drop back to a coarser grit and continue dropping back until you find a grit that flattens the surface quickly.

Use wet/dry sandpaper (black in color) and a lubricant of mineral oil, mineral spir-

You can create an even satin sheen on a leveled surface by rubbing it with pumice and a mineral-oil or mineral-spirits lubricant. Use a felt or sponge pad.

To achieve a soft-appearing gloss on a leveled surface, first sand up to about #2,000 grit, then rub with rottenstone and a mineral-oil or mineral-spirits lubricant. Use a felt or sponge pad.

its, or a mixture of the two. The oilier the lubricant the slower the cutting and the less likely the sandpaper will clog. (I find that sandpaper clogs more quickly with a water or soap-and-water lubricant, but you can use one of these also.)

On unfilled, open-pored woods you will probably need to apply more than three coats so you don't sand through. Because finishes differ in solids content and thus build, and because everyone applies finishes differently, you should experiment on scrap wood to learn the number of coats necessary so you don't sand through. Think in terms of four to seven for shellac and lacquer.

A finish has no grain so you don't need to sand with the grain. In fact, you can sand in circles, which I find easier, and you can sand cross-grain near the ends (to keep from sanding through the finish at the edges).

Each time you advance to a finer grit sandpaper, change directions (circles, with the grain, across the grain) until you reach your finest grit which should go with the grain. By removing the sanding sludge with naphtha or mineral spirits, you will be able to see clearly when you have removed all the scratches from each previous grit sandpaper (a big advantage over sanding wood).

You will see your progress better if you use gloss finish rather than satin. After sanding a little, scrape off the sludge from parts of the surface using a plastic spreader. If you see shiny troughs or spots, the surface isn't level. When the surface is an even satin sheen overall, it is level and you can move to a finer-grit sandpaper to remove the coarser scratches.

Once the surface is level, sand or rub it with finer and finer grit abrasives until you achieve the sheen you want. Begin by sanding up to #600 or #1,000 grit (P1,200 or finer), continuing to back your sandpaper with a flat block or a felt or sponge pad. Then rub with #0000 steel wool, or with pumice (finely ground lava) and a mineral-oil lubricant using a felt or cloth pad.

Following pumice with rottenstone (finely ground limestone) is too big of a jump in grit, so if you want a higher gloss, sand up to #2,000 grit (P2,000 or higher). Then rub with rottenstone and a mineral-oil lubricant using a felt or cloth pad. Or use any other abrasive rubbing compound.

A Final Word

I find that woodworkers are often afraid of sanding a finish on a newly made wood project for fear of sanding through. This is sort of like the fear of sanding veneer the first time. You have to do it to learn that it takes a lot of sanding to actually sand through. So with rubbing a finish, I suggest you first practice on a scrap piece of veneered plywood to gain confidence. Apply a number of coats of finish and sand them after they harden to get a feel for how much sanding it takes to sand through.

You will be able to see your progress leveling a finish better if you use gloss finish. When you remove the rubbing sludge, glossy spots show the places you haven't sanded enough.

10

Finishing Myths

9 Myths of Finishing

Some are marketing ploys, others are just plain bewildering.

I doubt any craft is more burdened with myth than wood finishing. We all suffer from misinformation about the finishing products we use, what they are, what they do and how to use them.

On the other hand, the existence of so many myths demands that they regularly be debunked. So even though many of the myths I've included here are also covered elsewhere, it doesn't hurt to review.

Myth 1: **Tung oil is one of the best finishes you can use.**
Tung oil is difficult to use and is far less protective and durable than the finish that's actually in most of the cans labeled "tung oil."

It all started on TV infomercials in the early 1970s when Homer Formby promoted tung oil as a great finish, then put varnish thinned with paint thinner in the containers he sold. People had success with his product because varnish, even thinned varnish, really is a great finish.

But the promotion launched one of the most pervasive deceptions in the finishing industry – that cans labeled tung oil really contain tung oil. Many manufacturers have now joined Formby and market their own thinned varnish, which they label or promote as "tung oil." (FYI: Real tung oil is usually labeled 100 percent tung oil, never contains petroleum distillate, takes two or three days to dry with the excess removed and doesn't get hard.)

Myth 2: **Oil & oil/varnish blends such as Watco are good finishes because they protect the wood from the inside.**
Hey, when you're trying to sell a finish that dries too soft to be built up for good protection, you've got to come up with something. So why not claim that what can't be done on the surface can be done where it can't be

Myth 7: Bubbles in your finish aren't caused by shaking the can. They're the result of turbulence created as you move your brush. You can usually fix the problem by brushing back over the finish.

seen – in the wood? Now that's some pretty clever marketing.

But it's not true. While oils do penetrate the wood deeper than fast-drying, film-building finishes, all oils and oil/varnish mixtures are notorious for water spotting – rapidly developing areas of dullness caused by water penetrating and raising the grain. If you use one of these finishes, you'd be wise to wet the wood and sand off the raised grain

before applying the finish. This way the water spotting will be much less noticeable.

Myth 3: **The only finishes safe for cutting boards, salad bowls & baby objects are oils with no metallic driers.**
If this were true, how would you account for products called "salad-bowl finishes" that are marketed and promoted as food-safe?

These finishes are varnish that must contain metallic driers or they would take weeks to cure. (And if you've used a salad-bowl finish, you know it dries rapidly.)

In fact, salad-bowl finishes do contain metallic driers, but this isn't a problem. The FDA approves the use of metallic driers in coatings that will come in contact with food. They do require, though, that the finish be allowed to fully cure before use, and this is what you should be looking for. All finishes – and I mean all finishes – are safe for contact with food or babies once the finish has fully cured.

I mean, you'd hear about it on the news if they weren't safe! Why this myth persists, I simply don't understand.

Myth 4: A pigment stain (applied to the left side of the board) doesn't obscure the grain, it highlights it.

Myth 4: Pigment stain obscures or muddies the wood's grain.

Come on! I know you've used a stain that contains pigment because almost all the stains sold in paint stores and home centers do. So you know they don't obscure wood when the excess is wiped off; they actually intensify the wood's characteristics.

Sure, if you leave any stain on too thick, it will obscure the wood, but no one is advocating doing something like this.

Myth 5: You need to use a sealer under a finish to promote finish adhesion.

If this were true, why are you specifically told to not use a sealer under polyurethane? Why do you rarely find a sealer for water-based finish and never for shellac? Does it make any sense that varnish and lacquer require sealers for bonding and other finishes don't?

Here's the explanation: The first coat of any finish bonds perfectly well, whether it's applied full strength or thinned. Special products are used for the first coat when there's a problem to be dealt with. Sanding sealers are used under varnish and lacquer to make sanding the first coat easier. Shellac is used as the first coat when there's a problem in the wood that needs "sealing off" – such as pine resin, silicone or odor from animal urine or smoke.

Myth 6: Shellac is the best sealer.

This is the case only if there's a problem (as explained above), and you rarely have a problem with newly built projects. Wouldn't the high-end furniture industry use a shellac sealer if it really performed better? Furniture manufacturers spend huge amounts of money on their finishes, and they don't use shellac. Why would they skimp on sealing or bonding if shellac really did these better?

Myth 7: You can prevent air bubbles by not shaking or stirring a finish.

Try it (if you haven't already). Take a can of varnish, polyurethane or water-based finish. Remove the lid very carefully so as not to disturb the finish. Insert your brush and spread the finish onto a surface. Voila! Bubbles.

It's not shaking or stirring that causes bubbles, it's the turbulence created by moving a brush over the surface. You can't avoid bubbles during application. Your goal should be to keep them from drying in the finish.

Do this by lightly brushing back over the finish (called "tipping off") to break the bubbles, or thin the finish a little so the bubbles have more time to pop out on their own before the finish skins over.

Myth 8: Silicone in furniture polishes damages finishes.

For more than half a century, the most popular furniture polishes have contained silicone because this substance (actually a synthetic oil) provides better scratch resistance and adds depth and richness. Is it possible that the majority of all consumers were destroying their furniture all this time without anyone ever noticing? Not likely.

In fact, silicone is totally inert, and it doesn't damage anything.

What silicone does do when it gets into the wood is cause craters or "fish eyes" in new finishes applied during refinishing,

Myth 8: Silicone in furniture polish does not damage your finish. The only problem silicone can cause are craters or "fish eyes" when the wood is refinished. This will take more effort to overcome.

and this problem requires extra time to prevent. So refinishers and conservators hate silicone, and they are the ones responsible for spreading this myth.

Myth 9: Oil-based varnishes last only a couple years in the can because the metallic driers deactivate.

Not all myths are old. This one began only a few years ago in a prominent woodworking magazine and has already been repeated. It's probably the most amazing myth of all because almost everyone has a can or two of varnish (or oil paint, for that matter) that is more than two years old and it cures just fine. How far removed from real-world finishing does a person have to be to come up with this myth?

I don't know that varnish ever goes bad – except, of course, when it skins over and cures in the can because of exposure to oxygen.

7 Myths of Polyurethane

Oft-repeated 'rules' that are, quite simply, wrong.

All levels of finishing are burdened with myths, but the types of finishes used by amateurs and sold in home centers and woodworking stores suffer the most. Myths about polyurethane are a good example of the problem.

What is Polyurethane?

Oil-based polyurethane is simply a type of varnish. It's common alkyd varnish made with some polyurethane resin added. Alkyd is the resin used in almost all varnishes and oil-based paints. The polyurethane resin adds scratch, heat, solvent and water resistance to the alkyd varnish.

Pure polyurethanes (with no alkyd resin) are always two-part products. They cure in several ways: With the addition of moisture (an example being Gorilla Glue), with heat (many common plastics), or they are packaged as two separate components, which cure after they are mixed (similar to the way two-component epoxy adhesives work).

The two-component polyurethanes are becoming more common in the furniture industry because they perform well and have a very high solids content, meaning less solvent to escape into the atmosphere.

One-component, "uralkyd," polyurethane has become so dominant in the woodworking and home-consumer world that it's now becoming somewhat difficult to even find old-fashioned alkyd varnish.

Confusion has been added in the last decade or two with the introduction of water-based finishes, some of which combine polyurethane with acrylic resins. These finishes are sometimes labeled "polyurethane," with no obvious reference to their being an entirely different class of finish, one that performs less well than oil-based polyurethane and has very different application characteristics.

This isn't to say you shouldn't use water-based polyurethane. Just be aware that it is an entirely different finish – a water-based finish. This chapter deals solely with oil-based polyurethane.

Myth 1: It's not necessary to brush across the grain, as I'm demonstrating here, to work the finish into the wood. The finish penetrates perfectly well by capillary action no matter how it is applied.

The Myths

Myths are much more prevalent in finishing than in woodworking because finishes are chemistry, and you can't always "see" differences in chemistry. For example, polyurethane and lacquer look the same, both in a can and on the wood, even though they have very different characteristics.

In contrast, woodworking is physics. You can see that a band saw is a band saw and not a table saw (even though both have a table) and that a mortise-and-tenon joint is not a dovetail.

So authors and manufacturers have much more opportunity to provide inaccurate information, intentionally or not, about finishes than about woodworking tools and procedures. And consumers are more vulnerable to misinformation – that is, "myths" – about finishing than about woodworking.

Once a myth gets into print, it's common for it to be repeated endlessly until it becomes "fact," simply because everyone says it. Here are some of the most common myths concerning polyurethane (and varnishes in general).

Myth 1: **Brush across the grain first to work the finish into the wood.**
All finishes soak perfectly adequately into the wood no matter how they are applied. They do this by capillary action, the same physical phenomenon that allows water and nutrients to rise from the ground to the top of a tree.

If it were necessary to brush across the grain first, or diagonal to it (as I've also seen advocated) to get the finish to penetrate into the wood, how would a sprayed finish penetrate?

are in the sun or shade. When the cupping stresses become great enough, the boards check and split.

There must be an explanation for warping other than the ring pattern of the wood or whether the wood is finished on both sides. And there is. It has to do with the greater amount of moisture that comes in contact with the top of a tabletop or the top of a deck.

Compression Shrinkage

Over a period of many years a tabletop can be wiped thousands of times with a damp cloth. As the finish ages, it becomes more porous and lets moisture through, so the wetness gets into the wood. Likewise on a deck, more moisture enters the top surface than the bottom, because rain wets the top more than the bottom.

When moisture enters wood, it causes the wood to swell. The top surfaces of the tabletop and deck thus try to expand. But the wood's thickness remains stable and prevents this. As a result, the cells at the top surface are compressed from their original cylindrical shape to an oval shape. When the wood eventually dries out again, the cells don't return fully to their cylindrical shape. The top surface thus shrinks, pulling the board concave.

Each time the top is wetted and dries out, it shrinks a little more. This phenomenon is called "compression shrinkage" (or "compression set"), and it explains warpage and eventual splitting when neither the ring pattern of the wood, nor a finish applied to one or both sides does.

A built-up film finish in good shape resists water penetration pretty well, but a deteriorated finish doesn't. So refinishing whenever a finish ceases to serve its protective function extends the useful life of the object. This is the problem with the "do not refinish" message being conveyed by the popular television series, "Antiques Roadshow." If people heed this message, a lot of furniture will be destroyed over the long term. Thoughtful refinishing can extend antiques' lives.

Straightening Warps

Understanding warping caused by compression shrinkage helps us find a method for straightening warps. Recreate on the bottom the same conditions that caused the cupping on the top. You could do this by wetting the bottom and letting it dry out many times until the wood flattens out, but there is a faster way.

As wood dries out, it shrinks about twice as much around its rings than perpendicular to its rings. (Wood doesn't shrink appreciably in its length.) As a result, plain-sawn boards cup on the sap side (think of the shrinkage as causing the rings to partially straighten out), and quartersawn boards shrink without warping.

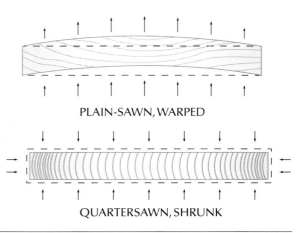

PLAIN-SAWN, WARPED

QUARTERSAWN, SHRUNK

Place the warped board upside down and hold it firmly in clamps so it can't expand. Then repeatedly wet the upper bowed side by covering it with a wet cloth. At the same time, place some weight on this side to encourage compression shrinkage. Once thoroughly wet, remove the wet cloth and let the wood dry, with the weight still in place. You can encourage the flattening even more by introducing steam using wet cloths and a hot iron.

You have to be very careful when doing this not to put so much pressure on the wood with clamps or weight that you cause it to split, or that you soak the wood so much that you cause glue bonds to separate. If there are already severe splits in the wood, this fix probably won't work.

As few as one or two cycles of wetting and

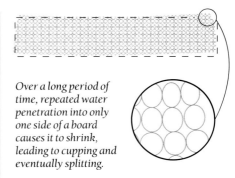

Over a long period of time, repeated water penetration into only one side of a board causes it to shrink, leading to cupping and eventually splitting.

drying should result in some improvement. Usually it takes quite a few cycles to bring a severe warp reasonably flat again.

However many wettings it takes, the real benefit of this type of repair is that it does no damage because you're always working on the bottom, unfinished side.

When straightening a board, place it in clamps so the cupped side is face down. Place a wet cloth on the bowed side. Weights encourage compression shrinkage.

11

Finish
Problems

5 Common Finishing Problems

Bleeding, blushing, blotching, orange peel and fish eye.

The basics of wood finishing are really quite simple: You use one of three tools – a rag, brush or spray gun – to transfer a liquid stain or finish from a can to the wood. Finishing becomes more complex when problems occur.

Here are five common problems, together with how to avoid them and how to deal with them when they happen.

Bleeding

Bleeding refers to an oil finish oozing out of pores after being applied and wiped off. It is more likely to occur on large-pored woods such as oak or mahogany than on tight-grained woods. And it is more common with thinned commercial blends of oil and varnish (Watco Danish Oil, for example) than with pure oils such as boiled linseed oil or tung oil.

Bleeding is also more likely to occur on hot days, especially if you move the wood into warmer temperatures or sunlight before the finish has completely cured.

If you allow the bleeding to dry and harden, it will form glossy scabs that can't be removed without also removing (by abrading or stripping) the finish around each. Sometimes, however, you can disguise the scabs adequately by rubbing the surface with #0000 steel wool, then apply another coat to even the sheen.

To prevent the scabs from forming, keep a close eye on your project and wipe over the surface with a dry cloth every half hour or so until the bleeding stops.

Once the wood is sealed, meaning the first coat has cured, there shouldn't be any more bleeding. So bleeding is usually limited to the first coat.

Blushing

Blushing is a milky whiteness that occurs in fast-drying shellac and lacquer finishes in humid weather. It's caused by moisture in the air condensing onto the finish as the solvents evaporate and cool the surface. The moisture then evaporates leaving air voids that refract light rather than let it pass through.

Blushing doesn't occur in varnish because it dries so slowly, or in water-based finish.

To avoid blushing you have to slow the drying of the finish. Do this by adding lacquer retarder to the lacquer or shellac.

(Brushing lacquer has already been retarded enough so that blushing is very rare.)

Adding retarder slows the drying of the finish, so don't add more than needed. You will have to experiment to find this amount because retarders use different solvent formulas and humidity can vary.

Blushing will sometimes clear up on its own. Otherwise, spray some retarder onto lacquer, or alcohol onto shellac on a drier day. Or let the finish harden and sand or rub it with a fine-grit abrasive paper, pad or steel wool. The blushing occurs right at the surface of the finish, so it doesn't take much abrading to remove it.

Blotching

Blotching is uneven stain coloring usually associated with uneven densities in the wood. Blotching can also be caused by not getting all the excess stain wiped off before it begins to dry.

This would be very rare with an oil stain because the drying is so slow, but it is common with water-based stains and lacquer stains. (Lacquer stains are fast-drying stains used by professional finishers who usually spray the stain and have a second person following closely behind wiping off.)

Once the blotching occurs, quickly apply more stain, or the thinner for the stain (water

The shiny spots on this oak panel show where an oil/varnish blend has oozed out of the pores and dried on the surface. To keep this from happening, check your project every half hour or so after you apply the finish and wipe off any bleeding before it dries.

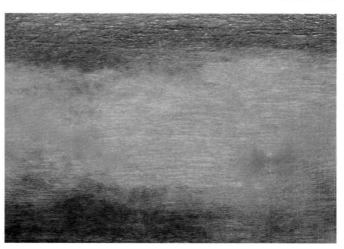

The milky white area in the center of this panel is called "blushing" and occurs often during the application of shellac or lacquer on humid days. To keep it from happening, slow the drying of the finish by adding a little lacquer retarder to it.

or lacquer thinner), to soften the hardened stain so you can wipe it off. If you use the thinner for the stain, you will lighten the color on the wood, and you may have to restain it.

To avoid the blotchy drying, work in smaller areas at a time, work faster or get a second person to wipe off.

Orange Peel

Orange peel is the spraying equivalent of brush marks left when brushing. It can occur with any finish and is usually caused by spraying too thick a liquid with too little air pressure. When stated this way, the solution is obvious: thin the liquid or increase the air pressure.

If you're using a spray gun with air supplied by a turbine rather than a compressor, you won't be able to increase the air pressure. You'll have to thin the liquid.

Another cause of orange peel is holding the spray gun too far from the work surface or moving the gun so quickly that you don't deposit a fully wet coat. Holding the gun too close can blow the finish into ridges and also cause orange peel. The best way to determine the proper distance and speed is to watch what's happening in a reflected light.

By positioning yourself so you can see a reflection on the surface, you will see when the finish is going on too thin or thick and you can make the necessary adjustment.

Other than stripping, the only way to remove orange peel after it has occurred is to sand it out. Once you have leveled the

A common spraying problem is orange peel, caused by spraying too thick a liquid with too little air pressure, or moving the spray gun too fast or holding it too far from, or too close to, the work surface. To reduce orange peel, thin the finish, increase the air pressure, and watch in a reflected light to get the speed and distance correct for the best results.

surface, you can either rub it to the sheen (gloss, satin or flat) you want using abrasives, or spray another coat being sure to make the necessary adjustment so you don't get orange peel again.

Fish Eye

Fish eye, which is also referred to as "cratering" or "crawling," is caused by a surface tension (slickness) difference between the finish and oil that has gotten into the wood. The oil that causes the greatest problem is silicone oil, contained in many furniture polishes, lubricants and skin-care products.

You're unlikely to experience fish eye when finishing new wood, but it's common when refinishing old wood and occurs most often when applying lacquer or varnish. To prevent fish eye, use one or more of the following procedures (for really bad cases of contamination you may need to use two or even all three).

❯ Wash the bare wood thoroughly with mineral spirits or naphtha, or with household ammonia and water or a strong oil-removing detergent such as TSP.

❯ "Seal in" the silicone oil by applying a first coat of shellac. It will flow over the oil in the pores and form a barrier so you can apply another finish on top.

❯ Add a fish-eye eliminator, which is silicone oil sold under various trade names (the most common is "Smoothie") to the finish. This lowers the surface tension of the finish enough so it flows over the oil already in the wood. When adding this product to varnish or polyurethane, thin it first in a little mineral spirits or naphtha, then add it.

Once fish eye has occurred, it's usually best to wash off the finish with the appropriate solvent and start over, taking one or more of the precautions discussed above. Decide quickly, as "washing off" is easy if done right away, before the finish has totally set up.

Alternatively, you can sand out the craters and add silicone oil to your next coats. Once you've added silicone oil to any coat, you have to continue adding it to each additional coat or it will fish eye.

The darker spots on this oak panel are areas where the stain dried before it was wiped off. To keep this from happening with fast drying water-based and lacquer stains, work faster or on smaller areas at a time, or get a second person to wipe off quickly after you apply the stain.

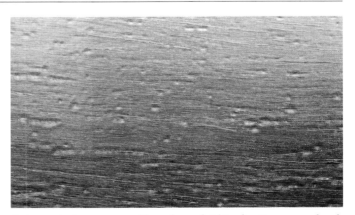

An increasingly common problem when refinishing furniture or woodwork is fish eye, or craters, which is usually caused by silicone-containing furniture polish having gotten through cracks in the finish and into the wood. Because it has already happened you have to deal with it. Do so by washing the stripped wood thoroughly, sealing the wood with a coat of shellac, and/or adding fish-eye eliminator (silicone oil) to the finish to lower its surface tension so it flows out level.

Slow Drying

Why stains and finishes sometimes dry slowly.

A friend called with a problem. He had applied an ebony oil stain to oak and after the stain had dried for two days the polyurethane he then brushed picked up some of the color and smeared it around the surface.

Was there a problem with the stain, or did he do something wrong?

Well, I could think of several possible problems with the stain. First, a very dark stain requires more pigment. So maybe the manufacturer just hadn't added enough binder (oil or varnish) to encase all the pigment well. Second, some manufacturers are replacing solvent with slow-drying oils to comply with California VOC rules, then selling this product to the entire country to avoid having to make two lines. Oils dry more slowly.

But my first thought was the weather. Though it had been mild lately, with highs in the 60s and lows in the 40s and 50s, that's still too cool for normal drying. Most stains and finishes need at least 65-70 F temperatures for eight hours or more to dry at a normal rate. (Exceptions are water-based stains and finishes, which are affected more by humidity than temperature; and lacquers, which can be made to dry normally in cold weather by adding acetone or fast evaporating lacquer thinners available from auto-body supply stores.)

So I asked about the shop temperature while the stain was drying. My friend assured me he had heat, but on further questioning he revealed that he turned it off at night.

After trying the stain myself in my warm shop, I concluded the problem was lack of adequate heat. This is usually the cause of stains and finishes drying slowly, and it is the first thing you should think of when faced with a drying problem.

If you can't avoid a cold shop you could bring the project inside your house after each coat, or you could keep the finish warm with a heat lamp or even a blow dryer for small objects. Alternatively, you're just going to have to give each coat longer to dry.

If your varnish brush is picking up some of the stain color as shown here, the most likely cause is cool temperatures in your shop. I let this oil stain dry 24 hours in a shop at about 55 F, clearly not long enough at this temperature.

Temperature isn't the only cause of slow drying. Others include:

› Applying oil or varnish onto oily woods

› Not wiping off all excess oil finish

› Using shellac that is too old.

Oily Woods

Most exotic woods, such as teak, rosewood, cocobolo and ebony, contain natural resins that feel and act like oil. These resins retard the drying of oils and varnishes (and also oil stains).

This is counter-intuitive – so much so that it's common to see instructions in woodworking magazines calling specifically for the use of oil or varnish on oily woods because these finishes are "compatible." The opposite is the case. Oils and varnishes are the only finishes that don't dry well.

The explanation is this: The non-drying oily resins on the wood's surface mix into the wet oil or varnish finish and keep the finish molecules apart so they don't bump into each other and crosslink. The resins act like paint thinner that doesn't evaporate.

Once you have applied an oil or varnish to an oily wood and discovered the finish isn't

drying, there are only two good fixes: apply heat to the surface to excite the molecules so they are more likely to bump into each other and crosslink, or strip the finish and start over. It's usually quite easy to strip (actually just wash off) an oil or varnish that hasn't dried using naphtha or lacquer thinner. Sometimes mineral spirits is strong enough.

To prevent a drying problem before it happens (or after you have stripped a non-drying finish), remove the oil from the surface of the wood or seal the wood with shellac.

To remove the oil wipe the wood with one of several solvents: mineral spirits, naphtha, alcohol, acetone or lacquer thinner. Mineral spirits and naphtha are the least effective, but they don't lift and smear the color of the wood. Each of the other solvents could remove some of the color along with the oily resin.

So if you have joined two or more woods, as in a cutting board or segmented bowl, try mineral spirits or naphtha first. Check that the colors don't smear on scrap wood before using one of the other solvents.

Whichever solvent you use, wet the wood well with one rag then dry the wood with another rag so you remove the oil, not just smear it around. Apply the finish right after the solvent evaporates so there's not time for the oily resin in the wood to rise back to the surface.

Alternatively, you can seal the wood with another finish before applying the oil or varnish. Shellac is the most effective at blocking off the oil.

Oil Finish

The common instruction for applying oil and oil/varnish-blend finishes is to wet the surface well then wipe off the excess after the finish has had a few minutes to soak in. This instruction is vague because different interpretations can be given to "wipe off the excess."

What is meant is ALL of the excess. The surface should not be left damp to the touch. Oil doesn't dry well, so leaving even a very thin film of damp finish (anything that wets your fingers or feels sticky) will result in a sticky surface for a long time.

If you have a situation where you didn't remove enough of the oil and it's now too sticky to remove with a dry cloth, follow the instructions above for dealing with an oil or varnish that won't dry on an oily wood.

Shellac

Shellac deteriorates much more rapidly than other finishes. The deterioration leads to slower drying and reduced water resistance.

In solid flake form, bleached or "blonde" shellac deteriorates much faster than non-bleached, sometimes within a year or two (non-bleached remains good for many years). The variables are the methods used to bleach the shellac and the temperature in which the shellac is stored, with higher temperatures leading to faster deterioration.

You can slow the deterioration by storing the shellac in a refrigerator.

Once the shellac is dissolved in alcohol, all types of shellac deteriorate, again with this occurring faster the higher the temperatures in which the shellac is stored. You should use the shellac within a year of its having been dissolved in alcohol if you are using it as a finish and not just as a sealer under another finish.

For any critical project, such as a tabletop, you should dissolve your own flakes and use the shellac as quickly as possible – within several weeks or months.

Other finishes also deteriorate, of course, but the deterioration doesn't lead to significantly slower drying. Pre-catalyzed lacquer loses some of its durability after a few years (the time varies with different manufacturers), and water-based finishes sometimes curdle after a number of years. I've never seen varnish or lacquer deteriorate as long as air is kept out of the can, no matter how old.

The oily resin in some woods slows the drying of oil and varnish finishes, so you should remove this resin before applying either finish. Acetone is the most effective solvent for removal, but it can lift some of the color and smear it over other woods if you are using several hardwood species together, as I'm doing here. Mineral spirits and naphtha won't do this, but they are less effective at removing the oily resin.

You should always wipe off all oil finish from the wood after each coat. If you leave the wood a little damp, as I've done here, the finish won't dry well. It will remain sticky for days, or longer.

Bleached shellac loses its ability to dissolve after a few years. If the shellac looks like this, even after overnight in alcohol, it is no good and should be thrown away. The "blocked" flakes to the left of the jar are a good indication that the shellac may not dissolve.

Dissolved shellac deteriorates as it ages so that it dries slower and loses its water resistance. This is the reason you should use shellac as freshly dissolved in alcohol as possible. Here, my finger still leaves a mark in the shellac after overnight drying. The shellac was five years old.

12

Repairing
Finishes

Repairing Color Damage

If the scratch isn't deep, the fix isn't difficult.

Even if you aren't a professional woodworker, you must get called on now and then to look at finish damage on cabinets or furniture belonging to friends and neighbors. Your woodworking skills are appreciated in our mass-production society, and your friends and neighbors may not recognize that repairing a finish is not the same as making something out of wood. But it would be nice if you could help them out anyway.

The most common damage to a finish is missing color in minor nicks or scratches. Here's an explanation of what to look for and how to go about repairing it. (I'm not going to discuss how to fill deep scratches or gouges; that involves a different and more complicated procedure.)

The Four Types of Damage

There are four categories of damage, each requiring a different repair procedure.

❯ Enough color remains in the wood, either from the natural color of the wood itself or from some remaining stain, so that all you have to do is apply a clear finish to the damage to blend it in.

❯ Not enough color remains in the wood, so you have to add some color to repair it.

❯ The wood is still sealed, and this prevents added coloring from penetrating. You have to apply a colored finish on top.

❯ The fibers of the wood are so damaged, that any liquid you apply makes the color too dark. You have to use a neutral-colored paste wax, water-based finish or a very fast-drying finish.

Determine the Problem

Because the fix for each of these situations is different, you need to test in advance to learn what is most likely to work. Here's the easy test. Apply some clear liquid to the damage and see what happens. Does the liquid bring out the color already there to make the mark disappear? Does the liquid darken the damage, but not enough? Does the liquid do

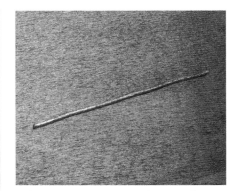

Before you can repair a scratch you need to diagnose the problem.

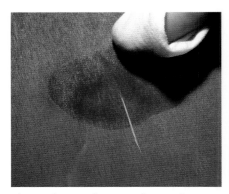

The simple test to determine the procedure to repair a scratch that shows white is to dab some liquid onto it.

nothing? Or does the liquid make the damaged area too dark?

The best liquid to use is mineral spirits (paint thinner) because it will simultaneously show the color and remove any wax that might be partially sealing the wood. But mineral spirits isn't always handy, and you don't want to have to run home to get some. So here's the easy trick, the method I almost always use to provide the clue.

Take some liquid from your mouth and dab it onto the damaged area using your finger. You could call this "The Spit Test," but doing so might not endear you to your onlookers. "Liquid from my mouth" is how I describe it.

Whatever the liquid, and whatever the application tool, the liquid will tell you the situation within a couple of seconds. The color in the damaged area will blend, it will darken but not enough, it won't change, or it will become too dark.

Here is how to proceed once you know what you're up against.

If the Liquid Restores the Color

All you need to do is apply a clear finish. Your choices are oil (boiled linseed oil, Danish oil or antique oil), shellac or varnish. The differences are as follows.

Oil will penetrate deeper because it cures slowly, so it will make the wood darker than the other two finishes. Moreover, the color will continue to darken some as the oil ages. If the color produced by the test liquid is just a little light, oil might be the best choice.

If a liquid is all you need to restore the color in a scratch, wipe the surface with an oil finish.

Shellac dries very rapidly, so it doesn't penetrate as deeply or darken the wood as much. Clear shellac is probably what you should use, not amber, and you may want to apply the shellac with a fine artist's brush depending on the size of the damage.

Varnish darkens more than shellac but less than oil, and it also darkens a little as it ages. An artist's brush is also useful for applying varnish to small areas.

If the Liquid Doesn't Darken Enough

You need to apply a stain, and as long as you use an oil-based wiping stain or a water-soluble dye stain, you can simply wipe the stain over the damage, then wipe off all the excess. With this method you won't leave any mark on the surrounding finish.

Choose between the two types of stain

Photos by Al Parrish; special thanks to Keith Mealy of Guardsman FurniturePro for assistance

trick is to dampen the cloth just enough so it leaves the appearance of a comet's tail of evaporating alcohol trailing as you wipe. (You can practice by wiping across a more resistant surface such as polyurethane or plastic laminate.)

If you get the cloth too wet, the alcohol may soften the finish too much and dull the sheen or smear the finish. This is especially likely if the finish is shellac (used on most furniture finished before the 1930s), but this technique is most effective on shellac.

› Spray a light mist from an aerosol "blush" eliminator over the water damage. The solvent is butyl Cellosolve, which will dissolve lacquer and restore the transparency. Be very careful to avoid too wet a spray or it could damage the finish.

These aerosols are sold to professionals. You might find one at a distributor that caters to the professional trade, or you could spray a mist of lacquer retarder if you have a spray gun and can get it to the furniture or the furniture to it.

› Cut through the damage by rubbing with a mild abrasive such as toothpaste, or with rottenstone (a very fine abrasive powder available at most paint stores) mixed with a light oil. Fine #0000 steel wool lubricated with a light oil, such as mineral oil, is more effective because it cuts faster, but steel wool will leave noticeable scratches in the surface. Use steel wool only as a last resort.

Rub the damaged area until the water damage is gone, being careful not to rub through the finish. Then, if the sheen is different from the surrounding area, even it by rubbing the entire surface with an abrasive that produces the sheen you want.

› French polish over the damaged area using padding lacquer, another product sold to professionals. The lacquer-thinner solvent in the padding lacquer will soften the finish (the same as if it were wiped or sprayed on separately) and often clear up the damage. It may be necessary to continue polishing the entire surface to get an even sheen.

This technique works fairly well on surfaces in good condition, but it is risky on crazed or deteriorated surfaces. If the watermark doesn't come out entirely with your initial application, you will seal in the remaining milky whiteness and make removing it more difficult.

If you have no experience removing milky-white watermarks, I recommend you try wiping with an alcohol-dampened cloth or rubbing with an abrasive. Both techniques are usually effective and the risk of serious damage is less.

Dark Watermarks

The easiest and least damaging way to remove dark watermarks is to bleach them out of the wood with oxalic-acid wood bleach. This chemical is available in crystal form at pharmacies and at many paint and hardware stores. Don't confuse this bleach with household bleach, which removes dye, or with two-part bleach, which takes the natural color out of the wood.

Dissolve some oxalic-acid crystals at a ratio of one ounce to one quart of warm water or, to make it easier, just make a saturated solution by adding the crystals to hot water until no more will dissolve.

A glass jar makes a good container, but leave some air space at the top for gases to collect if you store the solution. Never use a metal container, because it rusts.

Brush a wet coat of the solution over the entire surface, not just over the stains, to keep the color even. If you are working on mahogany or cherry, which usually darken as they age, the oxalic acid may lighten the wood back to its original color.

Let the oxalic acid dry, then wash the crystals off the wood with a hose or well-soaked sponge or cloth. Don't brush the crystals into the air because they will cause you to choke if you breathe them in.

Usually, one application will remove the black marks, but you can always try a second if the first doesn't work. Often, a light tan mark will remain after the black has been removed. It can be removed easily with a light sanding.

CAUTION: Oxalic acid is toxic, capable of causing severe skin and respiratory problems. Wear gloves and goggles when using it, and don't generate airborne dust.

Oil Finishes

Dark watermarks occur easily in oil finishes because they're too thin to be effective against water penetration. Milky-white watermarks are very rare, however. The lighter watermarks you sometimes see in oil finishes are almost always caused by random light reflection from raised grain telegraphing through the thin oil.

To repair light, raised-grain watermarks in oil finishes, level the raised grain with sandpaper or steel wool and apply more oil finish. Abrade the damaged area as little as possible to avoid lightening the color of the wood.

To remove dark water stains, you'll usually have to remove the finish first. Then dissolve some oxalic acid crystals to a saturated solution in hot water.

Brush on the oxalic acid solution over the entire surface. The dark marks will begin to fade immediately, though it will take a little longer for them to disappear entirely.

When the wood dries, the crystals will reappear. Wash them off with a hose or wet rag or sponge. Never brush the crystals off the surface because they are toxic to breathe.

Fixing Finish with French Polish

Sometimes it's a good technique for repairing damaged finishes.

In the woodworking community, French polishing is usually thought of as a technique for finishing new wood. But in the repair community, French polishing is commonly used to renew worn or damaged finish surfaces, especially tabletops.

Following is a typical example of what can be done using this technique on a high-end 1950s mahogany dining tabletop. I did the repair in the client's home.

The owners had caused an alcohol-filled heating apparatus under a large chafing dish to explode, spattering alcohol across half of the tabletop. The alcohol cratered out hundreds of depressions approximately the thickness of a normal sheet of paper. The owners loved the color (patina) of the wood and didn't want it stripped and refinished.

The finish was a very sophisticated, multi-step finish involving numerous coloring steps as shown in the illustration below, and the color had of course aged and mellowed. It would have been very difficult to match the other pieces in the dining set anyway, and also very expensive. So the owner's wishes notwithstanding, the best procedure was still to try to repair the finish.

When diagnosing damage of this sort, it's critical to determine if there are color prob-

This is a photo of the dining table after I French polished it on site to repair the damage.

lems. For example, did the damage go so deep that it removed some of the glaze or toner in the finish or some of the stain in the wood? For one or two spots, it wouldn't be a problem coloring them in, but for the hundreds on this table, restoring the color would have been out of the question. It would have taken much too long, and it would have been much too difficult to disguise so many.

So I did a simple test. Using #600-grit sandpaper, I sanded back a small area of finish to see if I could sand to below the damage without affecting the color. I could. The damage was confined to the topcoats of clear finish. The first step, therefore, would be to sand out all the damage.

There were two possibilities for the next step. One would be to rub the surface with finer and finer grit abrasives until the desired sheen was reached. The other would be to apply more finish.

Rubbing increases the risk of abrading into color and requires protecting all the surfaces in the room if electrical tools are used. Rubbing is also less successful if the finish is old and somewhat deteriorated, as this one was. It can be impossible to bring up an even shine.

The way most tabletops are restored when working onsite is by applying more finish. Almost any finish can be used, but there are the following caveats.

> Working onsite makes spraying difficult. It can be done, however, using a turbine

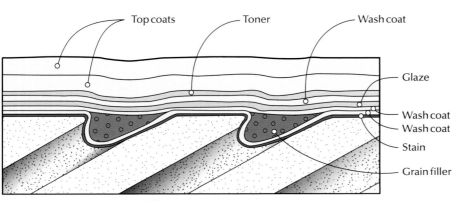

A complex finish requires many different layers.

HVLP and hanging plastic sheeting to protect everything in the room. Although challenging, spraying has the advantage of producing an almost perfectly flat surface.

➤ The lacquer thinner in lacquer finishes has the potential of blistering any finish, even old lacquer. Begin by spraying light "mist" coats. Lacquer thinner also has a strong odor, and this has to be taken into account when working in an owner's home.

➤ Water-based finish can be sprayed without the risk of blistering and without the strong odors. Many refinishers use this finish, coating over desks at night and on weekends in offices.

➤ Varnish or polyurethane can be used, but there is a long drying time and strong odor that has to be considered, and the finish should be leveled and rubbed out afterward. To avoid the leveling step, the finish could be thinned at least 25 percent and wiped on, or a gel varnish could be used. Both still dry slowly and collect dust.

➤ Shellac can be applied successfully over any finish, and the French polishing method of applying shellac is perfectly suited to this type situation. This is the finish and the technique (as shown below) I commonly use when working onsite.

7-Step Guide to Repairing a Finish with French Polish

1 Here is a close-up of the damage, which was spread over half the tabletop. The damage looks worse than it was, because it was confined to the clear topcoats. It didn't penetrate into the color layers in the finish.

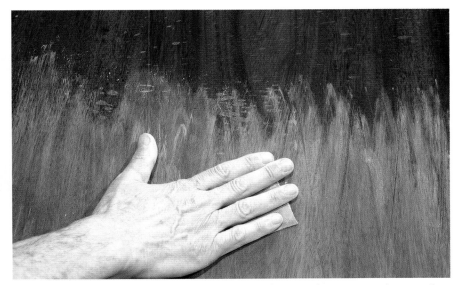

2 The first step was to sand the surface to below the damage. There are several ways to do this: by hand or by machine, and with dry sandpaper or with a lubricant.

I always begin sanding by hand because there's too much risk of sanding through using a sanding machine. If I were to sand into the color layers and remove some of the color, the problem would be almost impossible to fix. This is also the reason I start out sanding dry. Wetting the surface to lubricate the sandpaper masks sand-throughs so they aren't visible until too late. When I begin to feel comfortable with the thickness of the topcoats, I add a lubricant.

The choice of grit is a judgment call. Always choose the finest-grit sandpaper that will still cut through the damage efficiently. Coarser grits leave scratches that then need to be sanded out. Here, I began with #600-grit sandpaper. With shallower damage, I'd use a finer grit.

3 Grits above #400 are black, wet/dry sandpaper. Without a lubricant, this sandpaper clogs easily, so you need to change often to fresh sandpaper. Clogging causes larger-than-necessary scratches in the surface, which can be difficult to remove.

The downside of sanding dry is that you can go through a lot of sandpaper, and wet/dry sandpaper is fairly expensive. This is the reason to start using a lubricant as soon as you feel comfortable doing so. The lubricant I almost always use is mineral spirits – I choose the "odorless" type when working in someone's home. Sometimes, I add some mineral oil to lengthen the working time. I avoid using water because it may cause problems with an old finish, and it isn't as effective at preventing clogging.

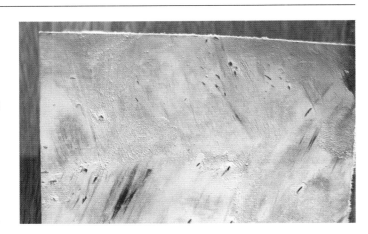

Continued on page 152

7-Step Guide to Repairing a Finish with French Polish – *continued*

4 The first step in French polishing is to make a pad – a ball of absorbent cloth wrapped tightly within another cloth to create a smooth bottom surface. Typically, I use cheesecloth for the inner ball and an old, well-worn, handkerchief for the outer cloth. I fold the cheesecloth into a tight square, wrap the handkerchief around it and twist tight.

With the polishing pad made, I pour on some shellac. A plastic squeeze bottle works great. I make the cloth damp, not wet, and tap the pad hard against my other hand to disperse the shellac.

I use two-pound-cut, blonde shellac I've dissolved myself from flakes. Using freshly made shellac produces the fastest drying, hardest and most water-resistant finish.

5 I begin wiping the shellac onto the surface. At first, I'm just trying to get some build (you could even brush or spray the shellac). I usually just wipe the pad across the surface in straight strokes with the grain.

After covering the surface (or in this case one section at a time), I add some mineral oil to the bottom of the pad to lubricate it so it doesn't "drag" the shellac already on the surface. I find it easiest to remove the cap from the bottle of mineral oil and pour a little oil into it. Then I dip my finger into the oil and spread it onto the pad whenever I feel I need to add more, usually each time after adding more shellac.

Once I start adding oil, I begin padding in circles or figure eights. But there's nothing wrong with continuing to pad in straight strokes with the grain.

Here's the first trick to French polishing (whether on new wood or on an old finish). Have one squeeze bottle with shellac and one with straight denatured alcohol. Once you've applied enough shellac to the surface to cover the sanding scratches, begin thinning the shellac progressively with the alcohol until you're just rubbing with alcohol. The goal is to eliminate all the marks left by the cloth.

Thin the shellac right on the pad. Pour on a little shellac. Then pour on a little alcohol. Tap the pad against your other hand to disperse the liquid, then apply one or two finger dabs of mineral oil to the bottom of the pad and tap it again. After you've been rubbing an area for a while, you won't need as much oil. There will be enough already on the surface.

Here's the second trick: As soon as you start adding oil to the pad, you want to see a vapor trail following the pad as you rub. The vapor trail is caused by the alcohol evaporating through the oil. This tells you that you have the right mixture.

You won't see this vapor trail if your pad is too wet or too dry. You will see just wetness or streaking. As you start padding, the vapor trail can be up to a foot long. It should tighten as the pad dries until it trails by only an inch or two. Then refresh the pad with more shellac, alcohol and maybe oil.

Any time you cause a problem in the finish (rag tracks too pronounced, a mark because you stopped moving the pad, whatever), you can always sand it out and keep going. Use the finest grit sandpaper that will remove the problem, usually #600 or #1,000 grit.

6 Here is a small section of the tabletop showing some of the damage (left) and the damage sanded out (right).

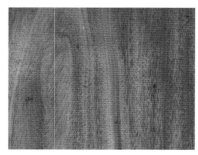

7 Here is the same section of the tabletop after having sanded out all the damage and French polished. The repaired table is shown at the beginning of this chapter.

13

Stripping Paints & Varnishes

Paint & Varnish Removers

Learn the differences between the five types of strippers on the market.

From the left, the four types of solvent strippers plus refinsher are methylene chloride (MC); a combination of methylene chloride and acetone, toluene and methanol (MC/ATM); acetone, toluene and methanol (ATM) with wax added to make it a stripper and ATM "refinisher" without wax; and n-methyl pyrrolidone (NMP).

No step in refinishing is as messy and unpleasant as stripping off old paint or finish. Though stripping can't be made clean and enjoyable, it does help to know something about the stripping products available so you can choose intelligently among them.

Fortunately, in the case of strippers (unlike other finishing products), the primary ingredients are almost always listed on the container, so it's possible to make sense of the products by separating them into types.

There are three types of strippers that are solvents and one type that is lye. You can also buy a stripper that combines two of the solvents, so there are actually five types of strippers on the market today:

> Methylene chloride (MC)
> Acetone, toluene and methanol (ATM)
> N-methyl pyrrolidone (NMP)
> A combination of methylene chloride plus acetone, toluene and methanol (MC/ATM)
> Lye

MC, ATM, and MC/ATM are available in various thicknesses, ranging from liquid to semi-paste. The thickness makes a difference in how well the stripper clings to vertical surfaces, but not in strength or effectiveness.

NMP is always fairly thick.

Lye is available in powder form, which you have to mix with water, and in paste form, which is ready for use.

Methylene Chloride (MC)

The strongest and fastest-acting of the four solvent types is methylene chloride. You can identify this stripper in two easy ways: "non-flammable" is highlighted on the front of the can, and the can is noticeably heavier than other solvent strippers.

Methylene chloride is very effective at removing all types of coatings, and even though it is moderately expensive, it has been the primary solvent used in strippers for the last four decades. In the mid-1980s, the Environmental Protection Agency listed MC as a probable human carcinogen, though the evidence for such a listing remains highly controversial.

Some manufacturers add acids or alkalies to their MC strippers to increase their strength, but these additives are seldom listed on the container. All manufacturers add wax, which rises to the surface and retards the evaporation of the MC.

The wax residue must be washed off before finishing the wood or the finish may not dry or bond well. Manufacturers misleadingly call this washing step "neutralizing."

Acetone, Toluene, Methanol (ATM)

This is the cheapest solvent stripper and is essentially nothing more than lacquer thinner. It's effective at removing shellac and lacquer, but is slow on all other coatings.

When manufacturers add wax to slow evaporation, they call the remover a "stripper." When they don't add wax, they call it a "refinisher." To use refinisher, you must work on very small sections at a time due to the fast evaporation of the solvents.

Other members of the three solvent families – ketones, petroleum distillates, and alcohols – are sometimes added to or substituted for acetone, toluene and methanol to change evaporation rates, but the stripper is still in the ATM category. All of the solvents used in this category are extremely flammable, and mention of this is made on the can.

MC/ATM

By combining MC and ATM in varying proportions, manufacturers produce a stripper that is in between in both effectiveness and cost. Combination strippers list a number of solvents, including methylene chloride, and also warn of flammability. These strippers are effective on all but the most stubborn coatings.

N-Methyl Pyrrolidone (NMP)

The possibility that MC could cause cancer and the high flammability of ATM and MC/ATM strippers opened the market to an alternative solvent stripper – n-methyl pyrrolidone. This solvent is expensive and evaporates very slowly, so no wax is added. It is also non-flammable, biodegradable (which is often promoted) and is claimed to be less toxic than MC and ATM.

To reduce the expense of NMP stripper, all manufacturers I'm familiar with add less expensive ingredients, which also reduce the strength. These ingredients are usually di-basic esters (dimethyl glutarate, dimethyl adipate or aluminum silicate), which can also be listed as soybean esters and the stripper sold as a "soy" stripper (but it's NMP that's the active ingredient).

Slow evaporation translates into reduced effectiveness (consider that these strippers are packaged in plastic containers), but an NMP stripper will still remove all but the most stubborn coatings given enough time – overnight or longer in many cases.

The claim of biodegradability as a plus is a little disingenuous because the faster MC and ATM solvents evaporate so fast there's nothing left to biodegrade.

Concerning safety, it's not that NMP is less toxic, but that it evaporates so slowly the air in a room has time to replace itself several times over before toxic concentrations are reached.

The reasons NMP strippers haven't caught on better are their expense and the misleading claims on most containers saying the product works considerably faster than it actually does. Claiming too much for a product may get a customer to buy it once, but rarely a second time.

For what it's worth, however, NMP strippers are my favorite anytime I'm not in a hurry, because if you leave these strippers in contact with the coating long enough (sometimes several days), they will penetrate to the wood and you can remove all the coats of paint or finish at once and with little effort. This is in contrast with the struggle often associated with the fast-evaporating MC and ATM strippers, keeping them wet and active, especially on hot days.

Lye

Though it's rarely used, lye (sodium hydroxide) is both cheaper and more effective than the solvents discussed above. The problem with lye is that it will burn you severely if it gets on your skin, it can cause significant damage to the wood by making it soft and punky, and it may separate veneer, darken the wood and cause finishing problems. Lye is a very questionable remover for furniture.

You can buy lye in powder form at paint stores and sometimes at supermarkets, and mix it with water, about $^1/4$ pound of lye to one gallon of warm water. Pour the lye into the water, not the other way around or it may boil over and burn you, and use a steel container such as a coffee can, not aluminum, plastic or glass. The heat that is created by the chemical reaction of the lye and water will heat the container, so don't hold it while mixing.

You can also buy lye in powder or paste form packaged with a cloth that you can apply over the lye to aid in the removal of paint or finish.

Conclusion

For difficult coatings such as paint, polyurethane and catalyzed (two-part) finishes, you should use a strong MC or lye stripper. For weaker shellac, lacquer, water-based and oil finishes, any of the strippers will work well, given enough time.

Paint & Varnish Removers: Strongest to Weakest

STRIPPER TYPE	HOW TO IDENTIFY	DESCRIPTION	POTENTIAL PROBLEMS	COMMENTS
Lye	Contents list sodium hydroxide or caustic soda. Available as powder or paste. Warns of severe burns if it comes in contact with your skin.	The most effective stripper.	Damages wood. Darkens many woods and can cause finish problems.	Very dangerous to use because it causes severe burns to skin and eyes. Keep clean water close by for washing.
Methylene chloride (MC)	Contents lists methylene chloride. Non-flammable is highlighted. The can is noticeably heavier than other strippers.	The strongest and fastest-acting solvent stripper.	Contains wax which must be removed before applying a finish.	Fumes are a health hazard. Work outside or in a room with cross ventilation.
Methylene chloride/Acetone, Toluene, Methanol (MC/ATM)	Contents list methylene chloride, methanol, and some combination of acetone, methyl ethyl ketone, toluene and xylene.	The weakest and cheapest methylene-chloride stripper.	Contains wax which must be removed before applying a finish.	Fumes are a health hazard. Fumes and liquid solvent are a fire hazard.
Acetone, Toluene, Methanol (ATM) "Stripper"	Contents list some combination of acetone, MEK, toluene, xylene and methanol.	Almost as effective as MC/ATM but without methylene chloride.	Contains wax which must be removed before applying a finish.	Fumes are a health hazard. Fumes and liquid solvent are a fire hazard.
Acetone, Toluene, Methanol (ATM) "Refinisher"	Contents list some combination of acetone, MEK, toluene, xylene and methanol.	Very inefficient as a stripper because no wax is included to slow evaporation.	Too slow on everything except shellac and lacquer.	Fumes are a health hazard. Fumes and liquid solvent are a fire hazard.
N-methyl pyrrolidone (NMP)	Contents list n-methyl pyrrolidone and at least one or two additional ingredients.	Effective on most finishes, but much slower and more expensive than methylene-chloride strippers.	Trying to rush it.	Fairly safe to use because of slow evaporation rate and non-flammability.

Stripping Finishes from Wood

Learn the right techniques for using furniture strippers and how to avoid the most common problems people have when using them.

Stripping paint or finish is a chore, but it can be made less so if you know what you are doing. Here are the steps for using paint strippers and for dealing with the most common stripping problems.

1. Work outdoors in the shade or in a room where you have arranged cross-ventilation provided by fans – air in from one window and out another. Don't work near an open flame or source of sparks if you're using a flammable stripper.

2. Remove hardware and difficult-to-reach wood parts that can be easily disassembled. Soak hardware that requires stripping in a coffee can filled with stripper.

3. Wear eye protection and chemical-resistant gloves (butyl or neoprene), and a long-sleeved shirt if you're using lye.

4. Spread newspapers on the ground or floor to catch the waste.

5. Shake the container of stripper, then cover it with a cloth and open the cap slowly to allow the pressure inside to escape. Pour the stripper into a large can, such as a coffee can.

6. Brush the stripper onto the wood using an old or inexpensive paintbrush. Avoid unnecessary brushing; you want to lay on a thick coat, but also minimize solvent evaporation. (Be aware that some synthetic bristles will dissolve in methylene-chloride-based strippers.)

7. Allow the stripper time to work. Test the paint or finish occasionally with a putty knife to see if you can lift it from the wood. Apply more stripper as the original dries out. All strippers will lift many layers at once if the surface is kept wet so the stripper has time to penetrate.

8. Remove the dissolved, blistered or soft-

Working outside in the shade or inside with cross-ventilation, spread the stripper thickly onto the surface using an old or inexpensive brush.

ened paint or finish using one or more of the following methods.

❯ Use paper towels to soak up and wipe off dissolved finish.

❯ Use wood shavings from a jointer or planer to soak up dissolved finish. Then brush off the shavings with a stiff-bristle brush.

❯ Scrape the "gunk" off flat surfaces into a can or cardboard box with a plastic spreader or a wide, dull putty knife. Keep the putty knife clean and smooth, and round its corners with a file so it doesn't scratch the wood.

❯ Break blistered or softened film loose from mouldings, turnings and carvings with #1 steel wool or a Scotch-Brite pad.

❯ Pull a coarse string or hemp rope around the recesses of turnings to work out blistered paint or finish.

❯ Pick the softened paint or finish out of cracks and recesses with sharpened sticks

or dowels, which won't damage the wood as metal picks will.

9. Wash the wood with paint thinner, naphtha, alcohol or lacquer thinner to remove wax residue left from strippers containing wax. You may also wash with a strong detergent and water, or simply with water if the stripper is "water-washable," which means it already contains the detergent.

10. Let the solvent evaporate out of the stripping sludge, then dispose of it in the trash unless local laws forbid this. (The dried sludge is what was on the furniture before you stripped it, so it is no more polluting than tossing the entire painted or finished object into the trash.)

Common Problems

If you've ever done any stripping, you know it's seldom as easy as step-by-step instructions

When the finish or paint is dissolved, blistered or loosened from the wood, scrape it into a box or can using a wide putty knife or plastic spreader.

With all strippers except lye and NMP, wash the surface with a solvent to remove the wax residue. In this case the stripped finish was shellac, so I'm using denatured alcohol to aid in removing any remaining shellac.

suggest. Here are some of the most common stripping problems and their solutions.

❯ The Stripper Doesn't Work

If the stripper you're using doesn't dissolve, blister, or break the bond of the paint or finish film from the wood, either you need to allow more time for the stripper to work or use a stronger stripper.

First allow more time. Strippers work much slower in temperatures below 65 Fahrenheit. Keep the surface wet by applying additional coats of stripper or covering the surface with plastic wrap to prevent evaporation.

If you still have problems, try a stronger stripper. The only paint or finish that can't be removed with a solvent-based stripper is milk paint. It was used in the 18th century and in rural areas of the U.S. in the 19th century. You can remove it with lye.

Some modern coatings are very difficult to strip. Rough them up with coarse sandpaper to increase the surface area, then try again with a strong methylene-chloride stripper.

❯ You Can't Get Paint out of The Pores

Paint is softened by the stripper but doesn't come out of the pores until some mechanical force is applied to it. Stripping shops often use a pressure washer. You can use that (with a water-washable stripper) or a soft brass-wire brush, which won't damage hardwoods.

Apply more stripper to the surface, then scrub in the direction of the grain. Remove

Here is the stripped tabletop after the residue solvent had dried out of the wood.

If you want to know what type of finish you're stripping, dab some denatured alcohol and lacquer thinner onto the wood. If the alcohol causes the finish to get sticky and smear, it is shellac. If lacquer thinner causes the finish to get sticky and smear, it is lacquer. If neither solvent damages the finish, it is a reactive, cross-linking finish. Here, the finish is clearly shellac.

the gunk with rags or paper towels. Repeat until the wood is clean.

❯ You Can't Get Stain Out

There are several types of stain, and whether a stripper removes the stain depends on how that particular stain is affected by the stripper. If the stripper doesn't remove the stain, use household bleach to remove dye stains, or scrub the wood with a brass-wire brush together with more stripper to remove pigment stains.

You don't have to remove stain, however, if you intend to restain darker than the color of the stripped wood. Simply restain right over the remaining color.

You can tell that all the finish is off when there aren't any remaining shiny places on the wood or in the pores when the wood is dry. You can also test by sanding lightly with fine-grit sandpaper after the wood is dry. If the sandpaper clogs, the finish hasn't been entirely removed.

❯ The Stripper Streaks & Darkens The Wood

Lye and any stripper containing an alkali may darken wood. The darkening often shows up as streaks resembling brush marks. To bleach out the dark stains, make a saturated solution of oxalic-acid crystals, available at pharmacies and many paint stores.

Brush the solution over the entire surface, not just over the stains. Let the oxalic acid dry back into crystal form. Then wash the crystals off the wood with a hose or well-soaked sponge or cloth. The crystals will cause an uncontrollable coughing if you brush them into the air and breathe them.

Oxalic acid will also remove black water rings and rust stains. It has little effect on the natural color of the wood.

❯ Sandpaper Clogs After Stripping

Clogged sandpaper indicates that some finish remains on the wood, or that the stripper hasn't completely evaporated. As long as all the finish has been removed, sanding isn't necessary if the wood is smooth. Sanding will remove the wood's patina (the appearance of age brought about by light and use).

❯ Wood Won't Stain Evenly

You may not have removed all the old finish. If this is the case, you'll have to resume stripping until all the finish is removed. Uneven stain penetration can also be caused by uneven density or swirly grain in the wood itself.

❯ The New Finish Won't Dry, Or It Peels After It Has Cured

Both of these problems are caused by wax left on the wood by the stripper. All strippers

Knowing that the finish is shellac, I can use alcohol-soaked rags to dissolve the finish and avoid having to work with the more toxic strippers. Also, there won't be any wax that has to be removed afterwards.

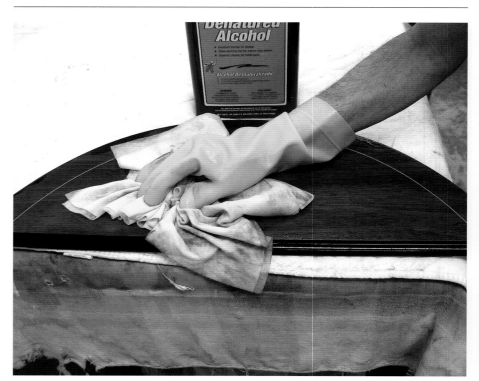

When the finish is dissolved, simply wipe it off with the alcohol-soaked cloth.

based on methylene chloride and acetone, toluene and methanol (ATM) contain wax. The wood must be washed thoroughly (not neutralized as most directions suggest) with a detergent or solvent for wax. Flood the surface, then wipe with a dry cloth, turning it frequently so you lift the wax from the wood rather than just move it around.

14

Finishing Odds & Ends

Choosing an Exterior Coating

Five different types of protection exist. Here's a guide to choosing the best one for your project.

The need to protect wood outdoors is much greater than the need to protect it indoors because of exposure to sunlight and rain. These cause wood to gray, split, warp and rot; and moist conditions make the growth of mildew possible.

You can use paint, stain, clear finish, water repellant and preservative to prevent or retard damage to exterior wood. But first, it's helpful to understand the causes of the damage.

Exterior Damage

Sunlight contains strong ultraviolet light, which is very destructive over time. UV light destroys the lignin that glues the cellulose wood cells together, and rain then washes the lignin away. Because the lignin contains the extractives that give wood its distinctive coloring, the wood turns silvery gray on the surface when the lignin is gone.

Sunlight also heats the surface of the wood and draws out moisture, causing shrinkage. This leads to splitting and warping, and these are made worse by rain when it comes in contact with only one side of the wood – as on decks, tabletops and exterior doors. The water makes the surface cells swell, but the thickness of the wood prevents the surface from expanding. The cells are forced to compress to oval shapes, and they hold these shapes even when dry.

This phenomenon is called "compression shrinkage" or "compression set." Compression shrinkage causes wood to warp and split as the exposed side continues to shrink a little more each time it goes through the wetting and drying cycle.

Rain is partially responsible for rotting and the growth of mildew, because both require moisture to occur. Rain is also indirectly responsible for a visually similar damage – insect infestation – because insects require moisture to thrive.

This front door faces west with no trees or other obstructions to block afternoon sunlight. You can see that the door is in good shape at the top where the deep recess in the framing protects it. But the condition worsens progressively from there down because of contact with both sunlight and rain. An overhang would offer the best protection, but this would change the design and the architect's intent. To preserve the design, the best solution is to coat the door with a marine varnish high in UV-absorber content, and sand back and recoat whenever the varnish begins to dull.

The heartwood of redwood, cedar and some hardwoods is naturally resistant to rotting. Some softwoods are pressure treated with chemicals to make them resistant to rotting. These woods have the familiar dull green or dull brown coloring. Sapwood and non-pressure-treated pine and fir are not resistant to rotting.

There are five different types of coatings you can use to protect against the problems caused by sunlight and rain: paint, stain, clear finish, water repellant and preserva-

The combination of sunlight and rain causes wood to turn silvery gray. If you like the gray color, and you aren't having other problems, you can leave the wood unprotected. The grayed surface is very effective at blocking further degradation below. UV light erodes wood at only about $1/4''$ per century.

Quartersawn wood (right) is much more resistant to splitting than plainsawn wood (left). If you have a choice, always use quartersawn wood in exterior exposures. The two boards shown here are from a cedar tabletop left outside and unfinished for about eight years.

tive. You can buy any of the first four types of coatings with a preservative included to retard mildew, or you can sometimes buy a concentrated preservative separately and add it yourself.

Paint

Paint is the most effective coating for protecting wood. The thick film blocks water penetration and the pigment blocks UV light. You can find wood siding that is in perfect shape after 200 years because it has been protected continuously with well-maintained coats of paint.

There are two large categories of paint: oil-based and water-based (latex). Because oil-based paint wears better than latex paint, it is best for objects that see a lot of abuse such as chairs and picnic tables.

Oil-based primers are also best when you are painting wood that has been exposed to the weather for a month or longer, especially if the wood has grayed. Oil-based primers penetrate deeper than latex primers, so they are better able to penetrate the degraded wood caused by the destruction of the surface lignin and bond to good wood underneath. If the wood is freshly milled or sanded, acryliclatex primers perform well.

Latex paint is best for wood siding, because it is better than oil paint at allowing moisture vapor created inside a building to pass through. If the moisture vapor can't get through the paint layer, it builds up behind the paint and causes it to peel. (A primer coat of oil-based paint applied under latex paint is not thick enough to stop moisture penetration.)

The mildew on the lower part of this board is a dark fungus that develops in moist conditions, especially in sheltered areas away from sunlight. You can prevent mildew by applying a wood preservative or a coating that contains a preservative. You can remove mildew by pressure washing or applying household bleach diluted with two to four parts water. Mildew causes little harm to the wood, but it looks bad.

Paint is great for siding and house trim because they can be caulked to keep water from getting into the wood and causing the paint to peel. Paint is also great for furniture and exterior doors if they don't get a lot of exposure to moisture.

But paint is a poor choice for decks and often for fences because it's rarely possible to seal off all the end grain effectively. The paint peels and requires too much work to effectively keep up.

Pigmented Stain

Pigmented stain is the next most effective coating for exterior wood. Just as with paint,

Rot is very destructive to wood as is obvious in this photo. Pressure-treated wood and the heartwood of redwood, cedar and a number of exotic woods including teak and ipe resist rot. A wood preservative that is not pressureinjected is fairly ineffective at preventing rot on non-rot-resistant woods.

it resists both moisture and UV-light damage because it contains both binder and pigment. But because there is much less of each and little or no film build, pigmented stains are not as resistant as paint.

On the other hand, the lack of film build makes maintenance easier. Usually, all that is required is a fresh application of the stain every year or two, depending on the climate and amount of exposure. There's seldom a reason to scrape, strip or sand.

There are three types of binder and two concentrations of pigment to choose from.

The binders are oil-based, water-based and alkyd-based. The pigment concentrations are semi-transparent and solid color.

Oil-based stains are the most popular and easiest to use. You can brush, spray or roll on a coat and enough of it will either soak into the wood or evaporate so that you end up with very little or no film build. With no film build, there is nothing to peel, so recoating is easy. Simply clean the wood of dirt and mildew and apply another coat.

Water-based acrylic stains are popular because of their lack of odor, ability to be cleaned up easily and reduced amount of polluting solvents. But water-based stains leave a build that somewhat obscures the wood and may peel if water gets underneath. Water-based stains also show traffic patterns more easily than oil-based stains because of the thin build wearing through.

Alkyd-based stains make use of a soft varnish to attach the pigment to the wood. These stains are meant to build on the wood, but they resist peeling because they attach so well to the wood, and they are so flexible. Often, manufacturers recommend as many as three coats and instruct you to clean the surface and apply an additional coat every year or two.

The disadvantages of these stains are that they will peel anyway if the wood isn't nearly perfectly clean during initial application or recoating, and visible wear is common in high traffic areas. It's very difficult to blend these areas back in.

The primary difference between semi-transparent and solid-color stains is the amount of pigment included. Solid-color stains contain more pigment (and also more binder), so they are better at blocking UV light. But the higher pigment concentration causes greater obscuring of the wood.

Stain is usually the best choice for decks and fences, and a good choice for cedar-shingle siding and cedar shingles and shakes. Stain can also be used on furniture and doors. Alkyd, solid-color, and water-based stains tend to build on the wood, which makes them vulnerable to lap marks and peeling. Semi-transparent stain is less resistant to UV light and water, but there is no peeling so recoating is easier.

Clear Finish

Clear film-building finishes, including water-based and all types of varnish, resist water penetration well, but not UV light. Destructive UV light penetrates the film and causes the wood to degrade. The lignin that glues the cellulose cells together loses its strength, and the surface fibers separate from the rest of the wood. When this happens, the finish, which is bonded to these surface fibers, peels.

The trick to getting a clear finish to survive in UV light is to add UV absorbers, and many manufacturers supply finishes with these added. There is, however, a great deal of difference in effectiveness of various products. "Marine" finishes sold at home centers and paint stores contain much less UV absorber than marine varnishes sold at marinas.

Clear finishes sold for exterior use can be divided into three categories: marine varnish, spar varnish and oil. Water-based exterior finishes are also available, but they have not found much acceptance thus far. Marine varnish is a soft, flexible varnish with UV absorbers added. Spar varnish is a soft, flexible varnish without UV absorbers added. Oil may or may not have UV absorbers added, but it is too thin on the surface to provide much resistance to sunlight even with them.

Linseed oil, whether raw or boiled, is also susceptible to mildew growth. In fact, mildew feeds on the fatty acids in linseed oil, so mildew develops faster than if no linseed oil had been applied. Only in very dry climates should linseed oil be considered as a finish for exterior wood.

Marine varnishes from marinas are the best clear finishes to use outdoors. They are always very glossy (for better light reflection), relatively soft (for better flexibility), and require eight or nine coats to reach maximum UV resistance. In addition, because the UV absorbers in these finishes don't prevent the finish itself from deteriorating, you will need to sand off surface deterioration (dullness, chalking and crazing) and apply a couple additional coats whenever the surface begins to deteriorate. This might be as often as once or twice a year if the finish is exposed to bright sunlight in Southern exposures.

Use marine varnish on objects where you want maximum UV resistance with a clear finish and are willing to deal with peeling if water gets underneath the film. Use spar varnish if UV resistance isn't critical. Use oil only if you are willing to reapply it often and don't expect much UV or water resistance.

Water Repellant

Water repellants are usually mineral spirits with low-surface-tension wax or silicone added to repel water. Sometimes, they are simply thinned water-based finish.

Water repellants are fairly effective at reducing water penetration for a short time. If UV absorbers are included, water repellants block UV light for a short time. Both types of resistance wear away within months, so unless you are willing to devote a lot of attention to upkeep, the wood will gray and split almost as fast as if no coating were applied.

Water repellents provide the least protection of any exterior wood coating, but they are easy to apply because they don't leave lap marks and they don't peel.

Use water repellant on decks if you don't mind the wood graying or splitting. Use water repellent with a preservative included to fight mildew if you live in a humid climate.

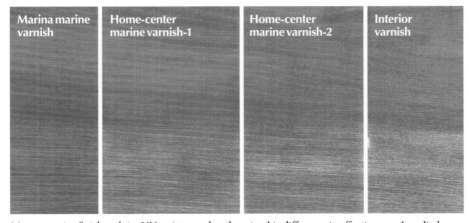

| Marina marine varnish | Home-center marine varnish-1 | Home-center marine varnish-2 | Interior varnish |

Many exterior finishes claim UV resistance, but there is a big difference in effectiveness. I applied a red dye to this panel, followed by five coats of a marine varnish bought at a marina (left), five coats of two common marine varnishes bought at a home center (center) and five coats of an interior varnish (right). Then I exposed the panel to sunlight for six months with the top half protected by newspaper. The fading of the dye shows that the home-center marine varnishes provided little more resistance to UV light than the interior varnish with no UV absorber.

Caring for Furniture

Do furniture care products really 'moisturize' your project or its finish? Learn the truth about furniture cleaners and polishes.

The four types of furniture-care products are (from the two containers at left) simply a petroleum distillate with an added scent, (in the middle) an emulsification of petroleum distillate and water, (aerosols at right) petroleum distillate and silicone oil usually made into an emulsification with water, and paste wax.

Furniture care is a subject you're probably not very interested in, but it's a pretty sure bet that the people to whom you give or sell your projects find it very interesting. In fact, "How do I care for it?" is probably the first question they ask you.

If you give them an intelligent answer, their respect for you grows, but if you fumble around and show you don't really understand the subject, they may lose some confidence in you. There's no reason for this to happen because there are really only two things you need to know: the causes of damage and how to avoid them, and which furniture polish to recommend.

Causes of Damage

The two elements that cause the most damage to furniture, especially to the finish, are light and physical abuse. No one can keep furniture totally away from light, but furniture can be kept away from bright light near windows which causes finishes to deteriorate faster than they would otherwise. To see what light does to finishes, compare the condition of an old finish protected from light under some hardware with the finish around it.

So the first instruction you should give is, "If you want the finish to stay in good shape for as long as possible, keep the furniture away from bright light, especially direct sunlight."

The second is, "Discipline your children and pets so they don't abuse the furniture, and use tablecloths, place mats, and coasters to protect the finish from scratches and water rings."

Furniture-care Products

There's more hype, myth and misinformation about furniture polishes and waxes than about any other product related to furniture.

Most of the problem is created by the suppliers themselves.

Here are the facts.

Furniture-care products do five things more or less well:

> Add shine to a dull surface
> Add scratch resistance
> Aid in dusting
> Aid in cleaning
> Add a pleasant scent to a room

No furniture polish or wax replaces natural oil in the wood (only a few exotic woods ever had it in the first place), feeds or moisturizes the wood, feeds or moisturizes the finish or builds up (unless, of course, the excess isn't wiped off). No furniture polish or wax does any harm to the wood or finish, either. Furniture polishes and waxes are totally inert.

In fact, furniture-care products don't really do much at all, and the United States and, to a lesser extent, Canada are the only countries where these products are used to any great extent. Most people in Europe and Japan just wipe their furniture with a damp cloth when it gets dusty or dirty.

So you could simply advise your family member, friend or customer, "You don't need to do anything at all except keep the furniture clean by wiping now and then with a damp cloth." But this probably won't work because people are conditioned to want to

"use" something, to do something "good" for their furniture.

So, to understand the differences in the furniture-care products they could use, let's look at the ingredients in them and see what each does.

Besides the added scent, which does nothing for the furniture but rewards people for their dusting effort by making their house smell nice, furniture-care products are composed of one or more of four basic ingredients: slow evaporating petroleum-distillate solvent, water, wax and silicone oil.

> Petroleum-distillate solvents used in furniture polishes are essentially slow-evaporating paint thinner. This liquid adds shine and scratch resistance only until it evaporates (usually within a few hours), helps pick up dust and cleans grease and wax. It has no cleaning effect on water-soluble dirt such as sticky fingerprints or soft drink spills.

Most clear polishes on the market, those commonly sold as lemon or some other nice-smelling oil and packaged in clear plastic containers, are composed of this single ingredient.

> Water evaporates too rapidly to be effective at adding shine or scratch resistance, but it helps pick up dust, and it's a great cleaner for most types of dirt. In many liquid and so-called "cream" furniture polishes, and in some liquid and paste waxes, water is added

to improve cleaning ability. You can recognize these products by their milky-white color (they are emulsifications like milk is an emulsification of water and animal fat). Most are packaged in aerosol-spray containers.

❯ Wax is a solid substance at room temperature and is by far the most effective of the four ingredients at adding shine and scratch protection over a long period of time because it doesn't evaporate. But wax is hard to apply (because of the effort necessary to wipe off the excess) and there's no reason to apply it very often, so it's not effective for dusting, cleaning or adding scent.

Sometimes wax is added to liquid polishes, and you can identify these by the settling that occurs over time – polishes containing wax have to be shaken before use. Clearly, these polishes will be more effective at adding long-lasting shine and scratch protection than polishes that don't contain wax, but more effort will be required to remove the excess from the surface.

❯ Silicone oil is a synthetic oil similar to mineral oil in the sense that it is totally inert and doesn't evaporate, but silicone oil is slipperier and bends light better than mineral oil. The first quality makes furniture polishes that contain this oil extremely effective at reducing scratches and the second makes finished wood appear richer and deeper.

Most aerosol-spray polishes contain silicone oil, though rarely is this admitted. Silicone oil has been given a bad reputation by furniture refinishers and museum conservators due to the added difficulty they have refinishing furniture treated with this oil. But consumers love silicone-oil polishes because they keep furniture looking good between polishings better than anything except wax, and they're easy to use.

Most polishes that contain silicone oil also contain petroleum distillates and water, so they're good cleaners.

How to Choose

So how do you make sense of this for the recipients of your projects? Easy.

If they just want something for dusting, choose any liquid furniture polish. I recommend the simple petroleum-distillate polish.

If they want something that will clean in addition to picking up dust, choose any milky-white furniture polish – virtually all polishes in aerosol containers except Scott's Liquid Gold.

If they want maximum scratch resistance and richer depth without the work involved

Light is a prime cause of finish deterioration. Here you can see that the finish protected under the hardware is in near-perfect condition, while the finish exposed to light for about 100 years is badly crazed.

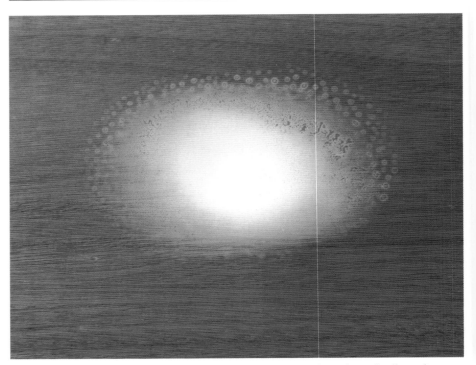

The furniture polishes that clean best are emulsifications of water and petroleum-distillate solvent. These polishes are usually packaged in aerosol spray cans and are always initially milky-white in color.

with using paste wax, choose a polish that contains silicone oil – virtually all polishes in aerosol-spray containers except Endust and Scott's Liquid Gold.

If they want to add shine and protect an old, deteriorated surface from abrasive damage, choose paste wax – because the other possibilities either evaporate too quickly (petroleum distillate) or highlight the cracks in the finish (silicone oil). Dusting and cleaning will have to be done separately with a damp cloth because petroleum-distillate solvents remove wax.

Finishing Wood Floors

With the right tools and equipment, you can finish (and refinish) your own hardwood floors.

Floors used to be finished with shellac, a coating that dries rapidly, brings out a lot of depth in the wood and adds a warm amber coloring.

But shellac doesn't wear well, so it was almost always waxed to reduce scuffing and extend longevity. Keeping wax on floors in good shape was a lot of work, however, so with the introduction in the 1960s of more durable, "no-wax" polyurethane finishes, shellac fell out of favor.

Today, there are a number of durable finishes that can be used successfully on wood floors, including oil-based polyurethane, water-based polyurethane, moisture-cured polyurethane and water-based finish with a catalyst (or "hardener") added. Of these finishes, oil- and water-based polyurethanes are the most popular with do-it-yourselfers because these finishes are considerably less toxic and much easier to use.

Though both of these finishes are based in large part on polyurethane resin, they differ in several significant ways. Oil-based polyurethane is more durable (meaning more wear-resistant), has a slight amber coloring and dries more slowly than water-based polyurethane, so application is easier.

Water-based polyurethane, on the other hand, has a much less irritating smell, is easier to clean up (with just soap and water), is non-flammable and doesn't add color at all. Because of its lack of color, water-based polyurethane generally looks better on "white" woods such as maple and woods that are whitewashed or "pickled."

Clearly, there are legitimate reasons for choosing each of these finishes. But unless the non-yellowing characteristic of water-based polyurethane is very important to you, oil-based polyurethane is your best bet for a floor because of its better durability.

Once you've chosen the finish to use, you need to prepare the surface and apply the

Rob McClanahan from Bethel, Ohio-based Tri-State Hardwood Floors, uses a stand-up sander to start the refinishing process. This type of sander can be rented at rental stores and some flooring-materials suppliers. Look under "rental" in your phone book or on the Internet under "floor sander rental."

product. Finishing floors is like finishing any wood surface – with two rather significant differences. First, the surfaces to be covered are usually very large, so different tools are commonly used to increase speed. Second, there is a reduced need for perfection because flaws in the wood or in the finish aren't easily noticed.

Preparing the Surface

Just as with newly made furniture, newly laid floors are always sanded before finishing. But

Varathane's ezV sander can be rented at many home centers and hardware stores. This consumer-friendly sander has on-board dust collection.

already finished floors are rarely stripped. Instead, they are also sanded and the procedure is the same as with new floors.

Special, 100- to 200-pound, stand-up sanders are used, and sandpaper grits are kept fairly coarse, ranging from #36-grit to #120-grit. (Sanding no finer than #80-grit is a good idea, for example, when whitewashing floors so that more of the white pigment becomes lodged in the deeper sanding scratches.)

Smaller "cut-in" sanders are used to sand right up to baseboards, and inside corners often are scraped and sanded by hand.

All of these tools, including the floor buffers mentioned below, can be rented at rental stores and some flooring-materials suppliers. These stores also stock the needed sandpaper, steel-wool pads and screens, and they can provide more detailed sanding instructions if you should need them.

Applying Stains & Finishes

Methods for applying stains and finishes are similar to those used on furniture or cabinets, with the major difference being the tools used for the job.

You can use a brush, of course, and this is often the best tool for cutting-in near the baseboards. But for covering large expanses, a sponge mop or a similarly shaped tool with a lamb's-wool pad attached is much faster.

The lamb's wool will produce better results. For water-based polyurethane, a paint pad attached to a pole also is a good application tool. Each of these tools is available at hardware and paint stores.

To stain a floor, follow these steps:

Vacuum the floor to remove dust.

Pour some stain into a paint tray and apply the stain using a large brush, sponge mop, lamb's wool applicator, paint pad or simply a large cloth or sponge held in your hand.

Apply the stain rapidly, especially if it's a water-based stain, and wipe up the excess with a large, clean cloth, your last strokes going lengthwise with the wood. It will be helpful to have two people performing this task, one applying the stain and the other wiping up. (To avoid smearing baseboards, tape them off before applying the stain, or cut in a few inches first using a brush.)

Allow the stain to dry overnight if it is oil-based and for at least a couple hours if it is a water-based product.

To apply finish to a floor, follow these steps:

Be sure the room you're working in is warm and there is some ventilation – but not so much that it stirs up dust.

Vacuum the floor to remove dust and walk around in just your socks.

Pour some finish into a paint tray and apply the finish using a large brush, sponge mop, lamb's wool applicator or paint pad. There's no reason to thin the first coat, but you can if you want. The coat will dry faster, but you'll get less build.

Begin at one side of the room and coat a foot-wide strip up to the room's baseboard, working lengthwise with the boards. It's best if you tape off your baseboards or cut in first using a brush.

With one strip coated, begin the next, overlapping a little onto the first strip and working fast enough to keep a "wet edge." That is, the first strip is still wet when you are overlapping with the next so you don't get a double thickness.

Work across the room in this manner, finally exiting through a door.

If you miss any small areas of the floor and the finish is beginning to set, it's best to leave them until the next coat.

Let the finish dry overnight if it's oil-based and a few hours if it's water-based. Be sure that no areas, even in corners, are tacky or soft before going to the next step.

Buff the finish using a floor buffer and a #2 steel-wool pad or a #120-grit screen to remove raised grain and dust nibs. (Don't use steel wool, however, with water-based finishes.) You can also sand by hand using #120- or #150-grit sandpaper.

Vacuum the floor and apply a second coat of finish in the same way you did the first.

Buff or sand again, vacuum up the dust and apply a third coat.

Recoating Floors

There's no need to sand a floor to bare wood every time it gets a little worn. As long as you haven't let the finish wear all the way through, you can screen it using a floor buffer and apply one or two coats of finish in the same manner as described above.

You don't need to use the same brand of finish, but it's best to use the same type to avoid color differences in worn areas. Be aware, though, that you may have bonding problems using water-based polyurethane if the floor has been waxed.

You can purchase oil-based polyurethane and a lamb's wool applicator at your local home center. The lamb's wool applicator shown here requires a handle, which you also can purchase at your home center – or you can disassemble an old broom.

Storing Finishing Materials

A few precautions will keep your finishes ready to use and your shop from burning down.

Storage is probably something you don't think much about until you start to accumulate a lot of finishes and tools, but storing your finishing materials properly will save you money and reduce clutter. And, in the case of flammable materials, proper storage could save your life.

There are three large categories of materials that need to be addressed when it comes to storage: flammable materials, products that can go bad if not stored correctly and finishing equipment that can be expensive to replace if stored improperly.

Flammable Materials

In terms of flammability, the finishing materials you use can be divided into two types: those that burn readily and can feed a fire that has already started in your workshop, and those that burn readily but can also start a fire all by themselves.

Almost all finishing products fit into the first category with the notable exception of water-based stains and finishes. If you have just a few small cans of flammable products sitting on a shelf, there's no particular reason for concern because they won't add significantly to a fire that's already burning so fiercely it engulfs them.

But once you start accumulating a lot of products, you should store them in a metal cabinet, ideally one that is designed for flammables. These are double walled and commonly painted yellow. You want to keep a potential fire from getting to these products for as long as possible.

Oily rags fit into the second category and are probably the most dangerous item you can have in your shop because they can spontaneously combust. It's important to distinguish, though, that it's only oils that cure, such as linseed oil and to a lesser extent tung oil, that are a problem. But because of misleading labeling on finishing materials, you probably

Storing your finish materials properly not only cuts down on clutter, it could also save your life.

should treat all products that thin with petroleum distillate (mineral spirits) as potential hazards. This even includes oil-based stains because manufacturers are now substituting more oil for solvent to comply with regulations on volatile organic compounds.

Drying oils cure by absorbing oxygen, which creates heat as a byproduct. If the heat can't dissipate from a pile of rags, it builds up until the rags reach their combustion temperature and a fire breaks out. The obvious way to prevent fires, therefore, is to spread oily rags out so they are open to the air.

You can, of course, place oily rags in air-tight or water-filled containers, but you should keep in mind that this prevents spontaneous combustion only while the rags remain shielded from oxygen. When they're removed, they are still a hazard.

To allow the oil to cure so the rags are safe to throw in the garbage, hang them separately or spread them out on a table or the floor and let them harden. Unless I have a lot of rags, I usually just drape them over the edge of a trashcan, making sure to avoid overlaps. Throwing rags with cured oil in the trash is no different, environmentally speaking, than throwing a piece of wood with a cured-oil finish in the trash.

Materials with a Shelf Life

All finishing materials will eventually go bad, but the time it takes varies considerably depending on the product.

The most obvious problem in most shops is water-based products that can freeze. Though they may survive a couple of mild freezes, it's unquestionably best if you store these products in a location that never freezes, even in your house if necessary.

Varnishes (including polyurethane varnishes) and oils exposed to oxygen go bad by developing a skin on the surface, or by turning into a gel, then eventually hardening all the way through. Varnishes are much more susceptible to this than oils. (If varnish is still liquid under a skin, you can remove the skin and strain the varnish, and it should be fine to use.)

There are a number of methods to extend the shelf life of varnish, including:

❯ Close containers securely.

❯ Transfer varnish to smaller containers to minimize air spaces.

❯ Displace oxygen in a container with an inert gas (by using Bloxygen, for example).

❯ Turn the can upside down and let the skin form. Then when you open the can, the varnish will be at the top and fully liquid.

❯ Fill the can with marbles or clean rocks (silly in my opinion, but I needed to mention it because others suggest doing this).

Shellac begins losing its water resistance and ability to cure hard from the moment it's dissolved in alcohol. The deterioration rate of this finish is slow, so you can use shellac on furniture or cabinets with good results for up to a year or so from when the finish was dissolved, but you risk poor performance after that. Shelf life is extended if you store the shellac in a refrigerator or other cool place because this slows the deterioration.

Shellac in flake form also goes bad, especially the bleached or blonde varieties. You'll know that the shellac is bad if it doesn't dissolve properly. Again, the process is slowed if the shellac is stored in cool conditions and it is accelerated in hot conditions.

Lacquers and two-part catalyzed finishes have a very long shelf life without any special care.

Dyes fade in bright light, so you should store these colorants in a dark cabinet if you keep them in glass jars.

Drying oils create heat as a byproduct. Wadded up oily rags can cause a disastrous fire. When drying out your rags, drape them over the edge of your garbage can or a bucket and don't overlap them.

Finishing Equipment

Finishing equipment includes brushes and spray guns.

Here's how I recommend you clean and store your brushes:

If you intend to use the brush again in a day or so, you can wrap it in plastic wrap or hang it in its cleaning solvent: water for water-based products; mineral spirits (paint thinner) for varnish and oil; alcohol for shellac; and lacquer thinner for lacquer.

If you want to store the brush for several days or longer, use the following cleaning steps for each finishing material:

❯ For water-based products, wash the brush in soap and water.

❯ For varnish and oil, rinse several times in mineral spirits, then rinse in lacquer thinner or brush cleaner (a similar product) to remove the oiliness of the mineral spirits, then wash with soap and water.

❯ For shellac, wash in half-and-half household ammonia and water or rinse several times in denatured alcohol and then wash with soap and water.

❯ For brushing lacquer, first rinse the brush several times in lacquer thinner, then wash it with soap and water.

Shake the excess water out of the brush and return it to its holder or wrap it in paper to hold the bristles straight while they dry. Secure the paper with a rubber band or masking tape, and store the brush in a drawer or cabinet, or hang it on a wall.

To clean a spray gun, replace the finishing material in the cup with the cleaning solvent for the product, and spray the solvent through the gun. Do this right after you fin-ish spraying so there's not time for the finish to harden in the gun. Including soap with your water will be more effective for water-based finishes, and lacquer thinner is the most effective solvent for all finishes.

Remove the air cap, fluid nozzle and fluid needle from the spray gun and soak them in the proper cleaning solvent or in lacquer thinner. If necessary, scrub them with a brush, such as a toothbrush. When everything is clean, replace the parts and hang or store the gun in a place where it won't get dirty.

The final step in cleaning any stain or finish out of a brush is to wash it in soap and water until suds form easily. That's when you know your brush is clean.

15

Furniture Repair

The Best Way to Reglue Furniture

Quick fixes never last. Here's how to make sure the joints in your antiques stay tight.

Of all the steps involved in restoring old furniture, regluing is by far the most important. Here's why: Poorly done refinish jobs can be redone; badly made replacement parts can be remade and reinserted; sloppy touch-ups can be removed and done over – all without permanent damage to the furniture. But shoddy regluing can, and often does, lead to the complete destruction of the furniture.

Despite the importance of the regluing step, only a small percentage of professional and amateur restorers do it well. As a result, much of our old furniture is becoming unusable.

Five Methods

There are five ways to reglue or "tighten up" old furniture. In order, from worst to best, these methods are as follows.

❯ Use nails, screws, brackets and other metal fasteners to reinforce the joint.

❯ Insert white or yellow glue, cyanoacrylate (super glue), or epoxy into the joints without totally disassembling the furniture.

❯ Disassemble the furniture and apply fresh glue, usually white, yellow or epoxy, on top of the existing glue and clamp back together.

❯ Apply hot animal hide glue over the old hide glue that remains in the joints (after removing any loose or deteriorated glue) then clamp the joints back together.

❯ Clean all the old glue out of the joints, apply fresh glue (usually hot animal hide, white or yellow) and clamp the joints back together. In furniture with dowels, remove all the dowels that are loose and either reuse them after cleaning both them and the holes, or replace them with new dowels after cleaning the holes. Even better, replace all the dowels by drilling out those that are still tight but likely to come loose relatively soon. Then

Old furniture joints were glued with animal hide glue, which must be removed before regluing with any glue other than hot hide glue, so the new glue can bond to the wood. You can easily dissolve and wash off old hide glue with hot water or vinegar. If the glue is stubborn, scrub it with a stainless-steel kitchen scrubber or coarse Scotch-Brite pad and hot water.

clean the holes and reglue the joints with new dowels as if everything were new.

Metal Fasteners

Inserting nails or screws and attaching metal fasteners is the worst thing that can be done to furniture. Any stress put on the joints can cause the wood to split, and sometimes cause tenons or dowels to completely break off. At best, the fasteners just hold the joints together. They don't, however, make the joints tight.

"Wooden nails" (dowels) inserted perpendicularly through a wobbly mortise-and-tenon joint are just as destructive and difficult to deal with as metal nails. Unfortunately, many people find wooden nails somehow romantic, as if these "nails" are evidence of great craftsmanship, so they are sometimes added to old furniture.

Inserting Glue Into Joints

The practice of inserting glue into joints without disassembling the furniture is very widespread. Three methods are used: drip glue at the edges of the joints and hope the glue runs into them; drill holes into the joints and insert the glue through a syringe; and pull the joints open just enough to expose small parts of the tenons or dowels and apply glue to those parts.

The glues most often used with this technique are cyanoacrylate and epoxy, though white and yellow glues are also used. Cyanoacrylate and epoxy are more expensive and difficult to use, but it's usually reasoned that they are stronger.

Though this method produces joints that usually remain tight for a year or so, long-term soundness rarely occurs because only a part of the surface area is "reglued," and it is still sealed with old glue, so the new glue doesn't get to the wood.

Disassembling & Applying Glue

A better practice is to completely disassemble the joints before applying the new glue – usually white, yellow, epoxy or polyurethane glue. This method exposes more surface area to these glues, so there's a better chance that the joints will remain tight for at least a few years.

But the wood is still sealed with the old glue, so just as with the previous method, whatever bond is achieved is made to the old glue, not to the wood. The bond achieved is thus no stronger than that of the remaining old glue to the wood, and that glue has already given way once. Moreover, when the joints break down again, as they surely will, proper regluing will be much more difficult because all the newly applied glue will have to be removed in addition to the original glue.

Using Hide Glue

All furniture made or repaired before the 1950s was glued with animal hide glue. This glue is made from the broth of animal skins, usually cattle, and has to be heated to about 140 Fahrenheit to be made liquid. (When heated, it has a rather unpleasant odor.) Ani-mal hide glue has the unique characteristic of dissolving quickly in hot water.

Because hot hide glue is both hot and wet, it dissolves old hide glue when applied over it, and a strong bond to the wood is usually achieved without the old glue having to be removed first.

The great advantage of continuing to use hide glue in joints glued originally with hide glue is that regluing is fast and very effective. When hide glue was the only glue available, everyone used it, and this is surely a primary reason that so much very old furniture has survived so long. Most of the old-furniture joint problems you see today are the result of one of the three lesser-quality regluing methods (discussed above) having been used.

The product called "Liquid Hide Glue" is the same as hot hide glue, except for added preservatives (to keep the glue from rotting for about a year) and gel depressants (to keep the glue liquid at room temperature). It can be used fairly effectively in place of hot hide glue as long as it is first heated to about 140 F.

Cleaning Joints

An even better practice than using hot hide glue over old hide glue is to clean all the old glue out of the joints before applying new glue. The strongest bonds are achieved when the wood is totally clean. This was the condi-tion that existed when the joints were first glued.

Once the wood is clean, any glue can be applied, and the result will be strong, long-lasting bonds. The only rationale for using hide glue at this point rather than another glue is that the joints will be easier to reglue next time.

There are two ways to clean old glue off of wood: dissolve it off, or scrape or sand it off. Dissolving is the better method by far, because it's totally effective and doesn't change the dimensions of the parts. Because the old glue has penetrated somewhat into the wood, it's not possible to scrape or sand off all the glue without also removing some of the wood, and this creates air spaces in the joints. Tight wood-to-wood contact, which is necessary for a strong bond, is lost when wood is removed.

Hide glue is the easiest glue to dissolve and wash off. White and yellow glues are next. Each of these glues dissolve or break down in hot water or vinegar. Epoxy, urea-formaldehyde (plastic-resin), cyanoacrylate and polyurethane glues have to be scraped or sanded off because they can't be dissolved.

Not all furniture is deserving of the time it takes to reglue with one of the better methods, but all better quality furniture is.

How to Remove Stubborn Dowels

1 *To remove an old dowel that won't budge even with a pair of pliers, first saw off the dowel just above flush.*

2 *Then drill out the center of the dowel using a brad-point drill bit 1/16" smaller in diameter than the diameter of the dowel. The brad point helps maintain center as you're drilling; the smaller bit reduces the risk of changing the location of the hole.*

3 *Use a 1/8" chisel or other narrow tool to pick away the remaining cylindrical part of the dowel. Then clean any remaining dowel or glue from the hole with the correct-size twist drill bit or a needle-nose rasp.*

Animal Hide Glue

Reversibility and quick tack make this traditional glue worth the trouble — sometimes.

Most hide glue is available as Grape-Nuts-sized granules (above), which soak up water and become ready to heat and use quickly. Some hide glue is available in slightly larger "pearl" form (below). This glue has a strong aroma, which indicates it is either "bone" glue or contains a lot of bacteria. In the old days, hide glue came in "brick" form (left). You had to break it into small pieces and soak them for a long time before heating. All three forms have an infinite shelf life when kept dry.

Because hot animal hide glue is more difficult to use than modern adhesives, it's not likely you use it for your projects. I'm not advocating you switch to hide glue, at least for new woodworking. The glue takes getting used to, which means using it regularly for a while. Hot hide glue is very useful in restoration, however.

Even if you don't use hide glue, you may still be interested in it, just as you are probably interested in old methods of woodworking. Following is an introduction to hide glue.

What is Hide Glue?

Animal hide glue is made by decomposing the protein, or collagen, from animal hides. Almost any hide can be used, including horsehides ("take the horse to the glue factory"). In modern times, however, cowhides are universally used. In fact, hide glue factories are commonly located near tanneries.

The hides are washed and soaked in lime for up to a month to break down the collagen. After being neutralized with an acid, the hides are heated in water to extract the glue. The glue is then dried and ground into Grape-Nuts-sized granules, which is the form in which it is usually sold.

The heating process is done a number of times to extract all the glue. Each subsequent extraction produces a lower grade of glue. The grades are measured by how much weight, in grams, it takes to make a dent of a given amount in a 12.5 percent solution of gelled glue.

Standard grades range from a high of 512 grams, called "512 gram-strength glue," to a low of 85 grams. The most common glue used in woodworking and furniture restoration is 192-gram strength. The most common used by musical instrument makers is 251-gram strength. Higher gram strengths gel too quickly to be useful in woodworking.

Animal bones, or at least the sinew in the joints, can also be used to make glue. But "bone" glue is greasy, more odorous, and has less tacking strength than hide glue, so it is not a good choice. Contrary to what you often read, horns and hoofs are never used because they don't contain collagen.

Bad Reputation

Hide glue has an unfortunate reputation of being weak and not water resistant.

As just explained, the strength of hide glue varies depending on the extraction, and also on what additives may be included (for example, to make liquid hide glue). But all hide glues sold for woodworking create a bond stronger than the wood itself as long as the wood is clean and the parts fit snugly. No more strength than this is needed.

It's true that hide glue isn't very water resistant, but this is more an advantage than

a disadvantage because it allows repairs to be done more easily. Poor water resistance is rarely a problem with wooden objects intended for indoor use, anyway.

Proof that less strength and water resistance compared to most modern adhesives aren't serious problems is the survival of so much furniture made before the 1950s.

(Actually, I think the bad reputation began in the 1950s when manufacturers claimed superior strength and water resistance for their white and yellow glues to get craftsmen to switch. These non-issue claims are still used today by suppliers of even stronger and more water-resistant adhesives.)

Disadvantages & Advantages

Nevertheless, hide glue still has a number of disadvantages compared to modern adhesives. Hot hide glue has to be prepared in advance and applied hot. It sets up too fast for relaxed assembly and has a relatively short pot life (several weeks at room temperature) before it begins rotting and losing strength. So there is usually a lot of waste. In addition, and not least important, hot animal hide glue has an aroma many find unpleasant.

But the glue has two unique advantages over all other adhesives: reversibility and quick tack. Both are far more useful for repairing old furniture glued originally with

or softwood blocks so you don't put dents in the wood.)

Corner blocks will usually have separated from one of the rails, so you can also wait until the chair is disassembled to remove them.

Removing nails is a problem. I don't like damaging the wood and finish, but I've given up with nails. The only efficient method of removing them is to dig them out. I first cut away some of the wood on two sides of the nail using a 1/8" chisel, which I don't keep sharp and which I dedicate to this operation. Then I pry out the nail with some sort of tool. My favorite is a pair of electrician's pliers.

Sometimes you can knock the joints apart with just the right amount of force to cause the nails to bend. But you always risk breaking or splitting something. In most cases, I remove the nails first. It's easy enough to fill the damage with a colored wax crayon after the chair has been reassembled. (I don't put the nails back in unless I can see a purpose for doing so.)

With all devices removed, it's usually easy to disassemble a loose chair with a few whacks of a deadblow hammer. To reduce the risk of breaking something, lift the part you are hitting a fraction of an inch above the table or workbench surface and hit the wood as close to the joint as possible. You should place blankets or other soft materials on the surface to avoid causing damage when the part bangs against it.

If you hit the part far from the joint, leverage increases the risk of breaking something. If you hold the parts well above a surface, something may break when they separate out of control.

If the joints resist and they are glued with hide glue (almost all furniture made or restored before the 1950s), you can cause the glue to crystallize, making it easier to separate, by wicking in some denatured alcohol. A syringe is a handy tool to use because it concentrates the alcohol where you want it.

Alcohol may cause the finish to turn white. If you aren't refinishing, you can easily remove this "blushing" by rubbing with #0000 steel wool. In almost all cases, it's best to do the regluing before stripping and refinishing, not after. You don't want to get glue on bare wood or damage a newly applied finish.

As you disassemble the parts, keep track of them so you don't reassemble them incorrectly. There are two easy methods. Number or letter them either directly on the part or on a piece of tape attached to each part. Or lay the parts out on a table in the order they will be reassembled.

I prefer the second method because it's faster. But I have done this many times, so I have a system I can trust. You should probably do both to begin with. Eventually, you will gain trust that your system for laying out is foolproof.

Preparing the Joints

With the parts separated, you can prepare each joint for regluing. To achieve success gluing wood parts together, each part must be clean and you must achieve tight wood-to-wood contact. When gluing new wood, cleanliness is not an issue because the parts are newly machined or cut. To reglue, you must remove the old glue first.

With all restraining devices removed, knock the chair apart. The most efficient tool to use is a deadblow hammer. Hold the parts a fraction of an inch above a soft surface and strike them as close to the joint as possible to avoid breaking or splitting something.

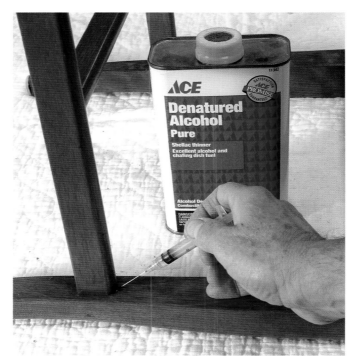

If a joint resists separating, try wicking denatured alcohol into the joint using a syringe. If the glue is animal hide glue, the alcohol will cause it to crystallize making separation easy. If alcohol doesn't work, try white vinegar (white so as not to cause staining). It will soften white and yellow glue, if it can get to the glue.

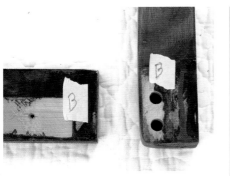

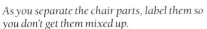

As you separate the chair parts, label them so you don't get them mixed up.

If any dowels separate from rails with their theoretically stronger side-grain-to-side-grain bonds, it's best to replace all the dowels because you can't trust any of the bonds to hold. If the dowels separate only from the perpendicular legs, you can choose to clean the dowels and the holes and avoid having to replace them.

Along with, or instead of, labeling the parts, you can lay them out in an order you understand to keep track of how they will go back together.

The exception is when using hot animal hide glue over old hide glue. Because of the heat and wetness, the new glue dissolves the old and the two become one. I love using hot hide glue because of this time-saving advantage; in most situations, I don't have to clean off the old glue.

But hot hide glue requires effort to prepare and takes practice to learn to use, so for the purpose of this article I'm assuming you will use white or yellow glue. Therefore, you will need to remove the old glue. (White glue provides more working time and still creates a bond stronger than the wood itself; I've never understood the rationale for exterior adhesives on indoor projects.)

You may also have to replace some or all of the dowels.

A basic rule of joinery is that wood bonds well side-grain-to-side-grain and poorly end-grain-to-end-grain or side-grain-to-end-grain. (One reason corner blocks can't be counted on to strengthen joints is that the blocks are cut on a 45° angle.)

Notice that dowels inserted parallel in rails are 100 percent side-grain-to-side-grain while dowels inserted perpendicularly into legs are in contact with end grain on two sides, top and bottom. The leg side of the dowel is therefore weaker than the rail side, and dowels usually separate from the leg long before the rail.

Assuming this happens with a chair you're regluing, you can choose to leave the dowels attached to the rails and hope they remain strong for as long as they do in the reglued legs. Or you can avoid taking chances and replace them. I usually remove all dowels and replace them. But I'm an exception in the professional restoration trade.

Sometimes, as with the chair I'm using for illustration, the chair will tell you which path is best. Notice (above) that some of the

The first step in replacing dowels is to remove them. If you can't knock or twist them loose and pull them out, saw them off about ¹⁄₁₆" above the rail or leg and drill down through the center of each dowel (it's not necessary to be exactly centered) using a brad-point drill bit ¹⁄₁₆" smaller in diameter than the thickness of the dowel. Drill to the bottom of the dowel where you will feel a slight give when you hit the air pocket.

With a hole drilled through the center of the dowel, pick the remainder away from the sides using a ¹⁄₈" chisel.

When you have separated the remaining dowel from the sides of the holes, pick out the pieces.

To clean the glue and any remaining small parts of the dowel out of the hole and get it ready for regluing, first drill it using the correct size twist drill bit, usually ³⁄₈" or ⁷⁄₁₆". Then scrape the sides of the hole using a needle-nose rasp. You can feel and hear the difference between scraping glue and scraping wood.

Be aware that dowel holes are often drilled at an angle. You can set up a guide using a sliding T-bevel. Set the angle using the dowel itself before cutting it off, or set it 90° to the angle of the end of the rail.

dowels separated from the rail rather than the leg. This indicates the bond on the rail side can't be trusted. I always choose to replace all dowels in this situation.

Whatever you decide, the one thing you can't compromise on is cleaning off the old glue, including from the holes, before regluing the chair. There are two ways to do this: Scrape the glue off or dissolve and wash it off.

If the old glue is hide glue, it's easy to wash off using hot water. This is the best method because scraping removes some of the wood, which may reduce wood-to-wood contact.

You can also break down white and yellow glue by soaking in hot water. You can add vinegar to the water to accelerate the process a little. Other adhesives will have to be scraped. Do the best you can to remove as much of the glue and as little of the wood as possible.

Replacing Dowels: First, Out With the Old

Replacing dowels requires removing the old dowels from the joints first. Sometimes you can strike the ends of the dowels with a metal hammer or twist them with pliers to break glue bonds. With the dowels loose, twist and pull them out using pliers.

If the dowels won't break loose and you still want to remove them, follow this procedure.

With the part clamped in a vise, saw off the dowel about ¹⁄₁₆" above the surface. Then,

using a brad-point drill bit ¹⁄₁₆" smaller in diameter than that of the dowel, drill down the center of the dowel until you reach the air pocket at the bottom. You will feel a slight give when you hit it.

It's usually easy to separate the remaining part of the dowel from the original drilled hole using a ¹⁄₈" chisel with a relatively dull edge; you don't want to cut into the sides. (I use the same dedicated chisel I use to remove nails.)

Remove the dowel pieces and clean the hole by drilling out any remaining dowel parts using a twist drill bit the diameter of the hole. You can then scrub the hole with hot water or scrape using a needle-nose rasp. I almost always use the rasp because rasping is faster and new spiral-grooved dowels

are usually a little thicker than necessary anyway.

Assembling

With the joints cleaned, you're ready to reglue. This is the easy step; it's the same process as gluing up a new chair.

In many cases, this one included, the backs of chairs are tight and don't need regluing (they're rarely racked). The order for regluing most doweled chair designs is as follows: First the back (if necessary), then the front legs and rail, and finally join these together simultaneously with the side rails and stretchers.

When replacing dowels, it's critical that the new dowels not be too long. You can use calipers or simply a matchstick or other thin object to determine the depth of the holes. Add the lengths of the two corresponding holes and either trim the dowels to size or drill the holes in the rail deeper to accommodate the length.

The best dowels are spiral-grooved, available from most woodworking suppliers. Straight-grooved dowels have very little wood surface actually contacting the wood in the hole, so they don't hold as well.

Dowels cut from longer rods have two problems. First, the rods most commonly available are no longer cut from maple and don't fill out their listed dimensions. They are too thin, so they don't succeed in producing tight wood-to-wood contact. Second, even when cut from maple they aren't grooved, so they don't allow excess glue to escape during clamping. If you put excess glue into the hole, the dowel won't penetrate as deep as you expected and the joint may not pull fully together.

To add grooves to a maple rod of the proper dimension, scrape with the 90° corner of a chisel or make a jig to add them. Drill a hole slightly larger than the diameter of the dowel (I use metric bits) through a small block of wood and insert a screw from the side so it protrudes about $1/32$" into the hole. Then drive the ungrooved dowels through the hole several times each so several grooves are scraped into them by the screw.

In all cases, the dowels should be chamfered on the ends so they line up quickly in the holes as you are inserting them. You can chamfer cut dowels using a rasp, chisel, large pencil sharpener or sandpaper, ideally attached to some type of sanding machine.

It's usually best to insert new dowels into the rails first. In other words, into the parallel part before the perpendicular. It won't matter if the dowel taps out at the bottom of the parallel hole, but you want to leave at least $1/32$" at the bottom of the perpendicular hole to allow for cross-grain shrinkage. If you don't, the leg might split.

You may need to trim dowels to the proper length before inserting them into the legs.

All surfaces should be coated with glue. This means the sides of both the holes and the dowels. It's easiest to do this with a narrow brush, working out of a glass or plastic container.

When clamping the chair back and chair front, it's important that the parts be square. You can check this by measuring the diagonals – that is, from the top of one leg to the bottom of the other. The two diagonals should be the same. If they aren't, adjust your clamps at angles to make them so. Look at the photo on the first page of this chapter to see an example. I'm lowering the front leg by raising the clamp on it and lowering the clamp on the back leg. I've done the opposite on the far side. I have exaggerated the angles so you can see them better.

When clamping the front to the back, it's important that all four legs touch a flat surface so the chair doesn't rock. With the clamps on

From the left are a spiral-grooved dowel, a straight-grooved dowel, a dowel pin cut from a maple dowel rod and a smooth surface maple dowel rod. Spiral-grooved dowels are the best because they provide plenty of glue surface together with grooves that allow excess glue to escape from the hole. Straight-grooved dowels are weak because they don't provide enough glue surface. To groove dowel pins cut from a dowel rod, drive the pins through a hole drilled in a hardwood block with a screw inserted so it protrudes about $1/32$" into the hole. Be aware that machined dowels and holes often differ slightly in dimension so you may need to make some adjustments.

the chair, place it on a flat surface such as a table, floor or table saw. Adjust the clamps if necessary by raising and lowering opposite sides until the chair doesn't rock.

Hide glue is easy to clean from joints. Simply wash or scrub it off with hot water. For hot water in my shop, I use a commercial coffee maker I bought used at a yard sale. To clean white or yellow glue, you may need to scrub using hot water and a stainless-steel scrubbing pad from the supermarket. For adhesives that don't soften in water, you will need to scrape or rasp them off the wood.

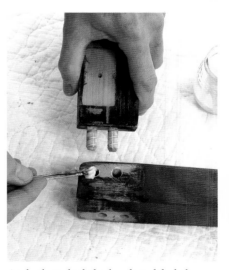

Apply glue to both the dowels and the holes before putting them together. The only way to do this efficiently is with a brush.

The Thick & Thin of Veneer Repair

Veneer is just thin wood – so don't be afraid of it.

I love repairing old furniture – the older the better. I find repairing more challenging and satisfying than making new because someone else, or time and age, has set the parameters within which I have to work. This is surely the case with veneer.

Veneer is used on most old furniture, and lots of things can go wrong with it. For some reason many woodworkers, and even professional furniture restorers, have a fear of working with veneer (some shops even refuse to do it). I find this fear difficult to understand because veneer is just thin wood, subject to the same rules as thick wood.

Recently, I had the opportunity (joy, really) of replacing some missing veneer on one of the oldest pieces of furniture I've ever worked on – an early 18th-century George II bachelor's chest with a hinged top that opens to a desk. The challenges were a little greater than usual, so I thought I'd show you how I dealt with them.

With the hinged top folded closed, the piece serves as a chest of drawers. Notice my veneer repair in the lower left-hand corner of the top.

With the top opened to rest on pull-out lid supports, the chest becomes a bachelor's chest. Notice that the veneer on the back half may have been at some point replaced. The two halves should be bookmatched – but they're not.

One aside before starting. After you've worked on a lot of old furniture, you become adept at spotting anomalies that indicate fakery or a "marriage" of two or more pieces of furniture. On this writing table I saw nothing to make me question its authenticity.

Here's the damage the owner wanted me to repair.

1 *It's far easier to shape a patch when you're dealing with straight rather than curved edges. So, if possible, I always try to straighten the edges before fitting my patch.*

2 It's often possible to pop off the waste veneer as I'm doing here. When I meet resistance, I can usually overcome it if the glue is hide glue by using a syringe to insert a little denatured alcohol under the veneer. The alcohol crystallizes the glue, making it easier to separate.

3 Though it's possible to reglue right over old hide glue using hot hide glue, it's best to clean off the old crumbly glue (and whatever contaminants, such as wax, that might be on the surface) before gluing the patch. Here I'm washing off the old glue with hot water. All contaminants come off with the glue.

4 Above the hinge you can see damage to the substrate that must be repaired so the veneer has something to bond to. Also, you can see that the veneer is considerably thicker than modern 1/32"-thick veneer. Thick veneer is common on furniture made before the machine age. Veneer seems to get thicker the older the furniture.

5 Again, it's always easiest to work with straight edges. So I'm cutting one using a chisel.

6 One of the reasons I love hot hide glue is that I can create a strong bond simply by rubbing two pieces of wood together with the glue in between. Work proceeds very rapidly using rub joints. Arranging a clamping setup for this patch would clearly be difficult.

7 After leveling the repair to the substrate using a chisel, I cut the veneer patch and trim it to fit snugly. The veneer is European walnut, which is considerably lighter in color (closer to tan) than American black walnut. If I didn't have any solid European walnut, I could use American walnut, but I would have to bleach the color out of the wood, then stain it to match, which could be difficult. I could also glue several layers of thinner European walnut veneer on top of one another to create the thickness, but cutting the veneer from solid, as I'm doing here, is always best.

8 Because of its thickness, I can glue the veneer patch, which I cut thicker than needed (called "leaving proud"), quickly and simply using a rub joint. But clamps wouldn't be difficult to arrange here.

9 I use a block plane, scraper and sandpaper to level the veneer patch to the surrounding wood. It's important to avoid cutting into the surrounding old veneer. If you cut off some of the aged surface wood, you may expose wood that is lighter or darker and create difficult color-matching problems. Applying masking tape around the patch can be helpful. Working slowly and carefully is essential.

10 With the top surface of the patch leveled, I trim the end using a chisel because of the difficulty of getting a handplane into the narrow area above the hinge. Notice the missing veneer to the left of the hinge. I popped it off (by inserting denatured alcohol) to make the shaping and trimming of the patch easier. With the patch trimmed flush I will reattach the veneer so it covers the edge as it originally did.

11 Here's the completed repair with a wax finish applied. Wax was the common finish used in the early 18th century and it continues to be the finish on this piece. The repair stands out a little in this close-up, but it disappears in the larger shot shown at the beginning of this article. Only someone who knows it's there would find it, which is all that you can ask for in a repair.

ACKNOWLEDGEMENTS

For more than a decade I've enjoyed working with the staff at *Popular Woodworking Magazine*. The editors have given me the freedom to write what I wanted to write – including the freedom to explore topics I wanted to explore, criticize whomever I wanted to criticize and even name names. You may be surprised, but this license is rare in woodworking magazines.

So when Steve Shanesy called to ask if I'd be interested in assembling the column articles I had written into a book, I jumped at the opportunity because I knew I'd be well taken care of.

Megan Fitzpatrick, managing editor, and Linda Watts, art director, did most of the work on the book, and I especially want to thank them. We put the book together in record time, and this couldn't have been done without their dedication, good cheer and willingness to work long hours.

The entire staff at *Popular Woodworking Magazine*, however, had contributed previously to this book because the articles were written previously. So I also want to thank Steve Shanesy, Christopher Schwarz, David Thiel, Robert Lang, Glen Huey, Kara Gebhart Uhl, Michael Rabkin and Al Parrish, who helped with photography.

And last, but not least, I want to thank my wife, Birthe, who has always supported me, especially during those times when I take on so much work that she has to cover for some of my chores.

Ideas. Instruction. Inspiration.

These and other great Popular Woodworking products are available at your local bookstore, woodworking store or online supplier.

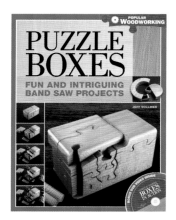

PUZZLE BOXES
BY JEFF VOLLMER
These amazing band-sawn puzzle boxes are intriguing to look at – and a lot of fun to make (and they're a lot easier than they look, too!). Included with the book is a DVD with 90 minutes of video instruction.

ISBN 13: 978-1-5587-0847-1
hardcover • 144 pages • Z2116

POPULAR WOODWORKING MAGAZINE
Whether learning a new hobby or perfecting your craft, Popular Woodworking Magazine has expert information to teach the skill, not just the project. Find the latest issue on newsstands, or order online at www.popularwoodworking.com.

THE PERFECT EDGE
BY RON HOCK
As a woodworker, you know that sharp tools are a must – but what constitutes sharp? And how do you get there? Hock shows you how to sharpen any tool efficiently and effectively.

ISBN 13: 978-1-5587-0858-7
paperback • 224 pages • Z2676

THE BEST OF SHOPS & WORKBENCHES
On this easy-to-use CD, you'll find the 62 best articles from 10 years of Popular Woodworking and Woodworking Magazine on workbenches, shop furniture, shop organization and the essential jigs & fixtures you must have.

ISBN 13: 978-1-5587-0893-8
CD-ROM • Z4247

Visit www.WoodworkersBookShop.com/FonF for a FREE digital back issue of Popular Woodworking Magazine.

Visit the URL below and choose from among 6 digital back issues of Popular Woodworking Magazine. Click on the cover, and your FREE digital download will open as a PDF on your computer. Plus, sign up for the e-newsletter while you're there, and you'll get a coupon code good for 15 percent off your next purchase at WoodworkersBookShop.com.

Choose Your FREE issue today at www.WoodworkersBookShop.com/FonF